CHARACTERISTICALLY AMERICAN

Characteristically American

Memorial Architecture, National Identity, and the Egyptian Revival

JOY M. GIGUERE

THE UNIVERSITY OF TENNESSEE PRESS / KNOXVILLE

Copyright © 2014 by The University of Tennessee Press / Knoxville.
All Rights Reserved. Manufactured in the United States of America.
Cloth: 1st printing, 2014.
Paper: 1st printing, 2023.

Chapter 4 appeared in a different form in *Journal of the Civil War Era*.
Volume 3, no. 1. Copyright © 2013 by the University of North Carolina Press.
Used by permission of the publisher. www.uncpress.unc.edu

Library of Congress Cataloging-in-Publication Data

Giguere, Joy M., 1980–
Characteristically American: memorial architecture, national identity,
and the Egyptian revival / Joy M. Giguere. — First edition.
    pages cm
Includes bibliographical references and index.
ISBN 978-1-62190-818-0 (paperback)
1. Monuments—United States.
2. Egyptian revival (Architecture)—United States.
3. Nationalism and architecture—United States.
4. Architecture and society—United States.
I. Title.

NA9347.G54 2014
725'.940973—dc23
                    2013039690

FOR MY HUSBAND, BEN PROUD, MY CONSTANT SUPPORT
and
FOR MY UNCLE, RICHARD SIEMBAB, MY SOULMATE IN CEMETERIES

CONTENTS

PREFACE TO THE PAPERBACK EDITION   XI
PREFACE   XVII
ACKNOWLEDGMENTS   XXI

INTRODUCTION   1

CHAPTER 1   The Dream of Egypt   17

CHAPTER 2   "The Dead Shall Be Raised":
Egyptianizing in the Rural Cemetery Movement   49

CHAPTER 3   Revolutionary Monuments:
The Obelisks of Bunker Hill and Groton Heights   91

CHAPTER 4   America *Conservata*, Africa *Liberata*:
The American Sphinx at Mount Auburn Cemetery   127

CHAPTER 5   American Obelisk:
The Washington National Monument   163

CHAPTER 6   From Egyptian Revival to American Style   195

CODA   The *Broken Obelisk*   225

NOTES   229
BIBLIOGRAPHY   249
INDEX   265

ILLUSTRATIONS

FIGURE 1   Christopher Columbus Monument, Baltimore, Maryland, 1792   61
FIGURE 2   Henry Griffiths, Baltimore Battle Monument, Engraving, 1838   62
FIGURE 3   Bust of Jacob Bigelow   64
FIGURE 4   Principal Entrance to Mount Auburn Cemetery, Lithograph, c. 1849   66
FIGURE 5   Portal at Karnak Temple, Egypt   67
FIGURE 6   Detail of entrance to Mount Auburn Cemetery   69
FIGURE 7   Medical College of Virginia, Richmond, Virginia, 1845   69
FIGURE 8   Main Entrance to Forest Hills Cemetery, Roxbury, Massachusetts, 1866   75
FIGURE 9   Kirk Boott Tomb, Mount Auburn Cemetery, c. 1830s   78
FIGURE 10   Joseph P. Bradlee Tomb, Mount Auburn Cemetery, c. 1830s   78
FIGURE 11   Nabby Joy Tomb, Mount Auburn Cemetery, c. 1830s   79
FIGURE 12   Lowell Tomb, Mount Auburn Cemetery, c. 1830s   79
FIGURE 13   Hicks-Endicott Tomb, Mount Auburn Cemetery, 1833   80
FIGURE 14   Stephen P. Fuller Tomb, Mount Auburn Cemetery, c. 1830s–40s   80
FIGURE 15   Henry Austin, Entrance to Grove Street Cemetery, New Haven, Connecticut, 1845–48   82
FIGURE 16   Isaiah Rogers, Old Granary Burying Ground Pylon with Winged Hourglass, Boston, 1840   83
FIGURE 17   "Memento Mori" Gate, Old Burying Ground, Farmington, Connecticut, 1850   84
FIGURE 18   Isaiah Rogers, Entrance to the Jewish Touro Cemetery, Newport, Rhode Island, 1843   85
FIGURE 19   Obelisks in the Jewish Touro Cemetery, Newport, Rhode Island   86
FIGURE 20   Entrance to Valley Cemetery, Manchester, New Hampshire, 1907   88
FIGURE 21   Entrance to Dorchester North Burying Ground, Boston, 1912   89
FIGURE 22   Groton Monument, Groton Heights, Connecticut, 1826–1830   93
FIGURE 23   Bunker Hill Monument, Charlestown, Massachusetts, 1825–1843   94
FIGURE 24   Chalmette Battle Monument, New Orleans, 1840–1908   95
FIGURE 25   Saratoga Battle Monument, Saratoga Springs, New York, 1877–1882   96
FIGURE 26   Bennington Battle Monument, Bennington, Vermont, 1889–1891   97
FIGURE 27   Richard Montgomery Monument, St. Paul's Chapel, New York City, 1776   99
FIGURE 28   Lexington Battle Monument, Lexington, Massachusetts, 1799   101
FIGURE 29   *Daniel Webster*, Chromolithograph, c. 1863   107

x ILLUSTRATIONS

FIGURE 30   Henry Wright Smith, *Edward Everett*, Engraving, c. 1860   111
FIGURE 31   *View of Bunker Hill & Monument, June 17, 1843*, Lithograph, c.1835–1856   113
FIGURE 32   Bunker Hill Monument, c.1860–1910   125
FIGURE 33   Memorial Pyramid to the Confederate Dead, Hollywood Cemetery, Richmond, Virginia, 1869   136
FIGURE 34   Soldiers' Monument, Greenfield, Massachusetts, 1870   138
FIGURE 35   Visitors around the Sphinx at Mount Auburn Cemetery, c. 1870   141
FIGURE 36   The Sphinx at Mount Auburn Cemetery, 1872   142
FIGURE 37   Lucerne, Thorwaldsen's Lion, c. 1860–1890   144
FIGURE 38   Edwin Gilbert Monument, Forest Lawn Cemetery, Buffalo, New York, 1888   157
FIGURE 39   Winter Mausoleum Sphinx, Allegheny Cemetery, Pittsburgh, Pennsylvania, 1931   157
FIGURE 40   Harper Mausoleum Sphinx, Cedarville North Cemetery, Cedarville, Ohio, c. 1908–16   159
FIGURE 41   Daniel Chester French, Death and the Sculptor/Milmore Memorial, 1892   160
FIGURE 42   Peter Force, Architectural Drawing for the Washington Monument, 1837   169
FIGURE 43   Robert Mills, Design for the Washington National Monument, Lithograph, c. 1846   171
FIGURE 44   Joseph Goldsborough Bruff, Design for a Grand National Monumental Sphinx, Guarding our Liberties, 1873   180
FIGURE 45   Henry Robinson Searle, Proposed Design for the Completion of the Washington National Monument, c. 1877   181
FIGURE 46   Sid H. Nealy, Setting the Capstone, *Harper's Weekly*, Dec. 20, 1884   184
FIGURE 47   Detail of Elevator Door Surround, Washington National Monument   185
FIGURE 48   Aerial View of Washington Monument and White House, Washington, DC   187
FIGURE 49   Grant's Monument, New York, 1892–1897   201
FIGURE 50   Cleopatra's Needle, Central Park, New York   203
FIGURE 51   Tourists in Front of the Sphinx and Great Pyramid, Giza, c. 1860–1900   205
FIGURE 52   Thomas Nast, *The Little Corporal*, Lithograph, c. 1898   207
FIGURE 53   Fine Arts Building, Midwinter Fair, *The Magic City*, 1894   209
FIGURE 54   Peery's Egyptian Theater, Ogden, Utah, 1923   210
FIGURE 55   Egbert Viele Mausoleum, U.S. Military Academy Cemetery, West Point, New York, c. 1902   212
FIGURE 56   Brown Mausoleum, Homewood Cemetery, Pittsburgh, Pennsylvania, c. 1908   213
FIGURE 57   Winslow Monument, Crown Hill Cemetery, Indianapolis, Indiana, c. 1900–1915   214
FIGURE 58   Cook & Watkins Letterhead, 1902   215
FIGURE 59   McKinley Monument, Buffalo, New York, 1901–1907   219
FIGURE 60   Two men in Front of San Jacinto Monument, c. 1937   223

PREFACE TO THE PAPERBACK EDITION

IF THE EGYPTIAN REVIVAL'S APPEARANCE in memorial and sepulchral architecture appeared to me to be widespread when I first approached the subject for my work on *Characteristically American* during graduate school, it has, in the years since publication of the book in 2014, become even more ubiquitous. I had chosen to address only the most well-known cemeteries and public monuments when writing my dissertation, which then became the book manuscript, but in cemeteries large and small, urban and rural, in monuments and memorials dedicated to soldiers and public figures, Egyptian forms may be found. Not only do I (and seemingly everyone I know) encounter examples everywhere I go, but the Egyptian Revival continues to serve as an attractive form of architectural expression for monuments and memorials.

For instance, across the street from my house, a brick Victorian built in 1905, in the center of a borough with only about 4,500 residents, there is a small (no more than a couple of acres) burying ground called Home Cemetery, owned and operated by the local Bethlehem United Methodist Church. Dallastown Borough, the community where I live, was once a local hub for the cigar manufacturing industry. Those who accrued their wealth from cigars – including the family who built my house, the Spatz's – whose names are known to all Dallastown residents, rest within the cemetery's boundaries. Despite its diminutive size, when I look out my front window, there are six marble Egyptian Revival obelisks and five other monuments with Egyptianizing elements dating to the late-nineteenth century that appear to stare back at me. By contrast, consistent with the trend established among the industrial elite from the 1880s to the 1930s to build lavish mausoleums, eccentric Hollywood actor Nicholas Cage purchased a burial plot at New Orleans' famous St. Louis No. 1 Cemetery in 2010 and built his own pyramid mausoleum bearing the inscription Omnia Ab Uno ("Everything from One") above the door. Albeit an object of controversy among locals, Cage's pyramid, like many earlier mausoleums, has become a key feature of the cemetery and a destination for tourists.¹ In the realm of public memorialization stands a modern obelisk on the grounds of the Pennsylvania Military Museum in Boalsburg, Pennsylvania. Fashioned from steel atop a granite base honoring the 82 marines, soldiers, and sailors from the 2nd Brigade Combat Team, 28th Infantry Division, who died in combat during Operation Iraqi Freedom in 2005-2006, the monument was dedicated in 2012 and in its design, reconceptualizes the obelisk while retaining its fundamental monolithic form. Hollow, with holes punctured in the steel, dog tags from the fallen soldiers are suspended above a wind chime, so that the monument—similar to the famed Colossi of Memnon in Thebes—speaks to passersby.²

Arguably the most striking and culturally significant modern reconceptualization of Egyptian Revival is a work that only existed for a few months before it was dismantled. Prior to the demolition of the Domino Sugar Refinery in Brooklyn, New York, the public-art fund Creative Time commissioned noted Black artist Kara Walker, known for her elaborate paper cutout artworks, to install a large-scale project inside the building. The result, which opened to the public shortly before *Characteristically American* first went into print in 2014, was the monumental "Marvelous Sugar Baby," a 35-foot-tall, 75-foot-long Sphinx "with the kerchiefed head of a mammy figure, her breasts naked, her vulva prominent . . . a chimera of unvarnished American desires, protected by an infantry of black-boy figurines carrying agricultural bounty."³ Constructed using 40 tons of sugar, Walker's Sphinx was the largest single piece of public art ever on display in New York City. The installation attracted over 130,000 visitors and received national media coverage as well as saturation on social media sites Twitter and Instagram. Presented to the public without any textual interpretation beyond the lengthy title of the work—*"A Subtlety": or the Marvelous Sugar Baby, an Homage to the unpaid and overworked Artisans who have refined our Sweet tastes from the cane fields to the Kitchens of the New World on the Occasion of the demolition of the Domino Sugar Refining Plant*—the Sphinx was at once a memorial to the enslaved Africans and African Americans who labored for the sugar industry as well as a harbinger of the factory's destruction.

Albeit made of perishable materials and with the intent that the Sphinx as well as the factory would eventually be destroyed, *A Subtlety* was no less a memorial than the countless others made of stone and bronze located in cemeteries and public spaces across the country. It was also an extraordinary example of the Egyptian Revival, fashioned anew for a twenty-first century audience. The Sphinx, created with the visage of an enslaved Black woman, represented a modern reclamation by a Black artist of the universally recognized figure from antiquity that bound together the African origins of the protective creature with its enslaved African American descendants and *their* modern descendants. Staring straight ahead, with jaw set and the fingers of the right front paw making the *figa* gesture (considered to be simultaneously a lewd gesture as well as one of power and resistance), Walker's figure is simultaneously powerful and defiant even as the display of the Sphinx's genitalia highlights the historical vulnerability of Black women subjected to generations of sexual exploitation and abuse by white enslavers.

While sphinxes dot the American memorial landscape, primarily in cemeteries, *A Subtlety* upended the pattern first established during the nineteenth century and repeated well into the twentieth; that was, to recast the figure as a symbol of white intellect, power, and protection, the muscular body of the lion bearing the face of an Anglo-American man or woman. Rather than creating a sphinx that was purely Egyptian/African in origin, however, Walker, in essence, did much the same as nineteenth century elite whites, except she recast the ancient creature as one that represented a major facet of the historical Black American experience. In this respect, then, Walker's work was consistent with the ways in which Americans have, for over two centuries, claimed and refashioned Egyptian monuments and architecture as indelibly their own.

Whether it was building hollow monumental obelisks hundreds of feet high with internal staircases rather than from a single block of stone, placing biblical verses on portals mimicking those from Luxor and Karnak, carving doves, flowers, or other sentimental memorial images on the sides of Egyptian-inspired private monuments, or recasting the figure of the sphinx with an Anglo-American face, elite and middle class white Americans sought to adopt and adapt Egyptian monuments and architecture in ways that reflected their own values and how they regarded themselves and their own society. Gaining popularity at a time when Americans sought to fashion a historical lineage and usable past for their nation that stretched back to antiquity, Egyptian Revival architecture called to mind images of stability and permanence, qualities that many hoped would define the new nation's institutions and especially its monuments and landscapes dedicated to the dead.

Regarded by many as the progenitor of western civilization, ancient Egypt held a special status in the minds of educated Americans as the most ancient society with qualities to which the most modern of nations might aspire. Embedded in this interpretation, however, was the desire by public intellectuals—those who, during the 1840s and 1850s, were responsible for creating scientific racism, which was used to justify the perpetuation of race-based slavery—to prove the non-blackness (if not whiteness) of the ancient Egyptians. In thus arguing that the people who built the pyramids and taught the Greeks how to build were definitely *not* Black Africans, white Americans could embrace Egyptian-derived architectural and monumental forms and recast them for their own use. Thus, during an era when white Americans created new vast burying grounds known as rural cemeteries and built imposing monuments dedicated to the memory of the nation's wars and its heroes, the Egyptian Revival became inextricably linked to the fashioning of an inherently white national identity whose monuments and memorial landscapes were created by and for white consumers, mourners, and audiences.

In *Characteristically American*, matters concerning race, Egyptomania, and the Egyptian Revival only figure into Chapters 1 (on the public enthusiasm for ancient Egypt) and 4 (on the *Sphinx* at Mount Auburn Cemetery). It is with Walker's 2014 installation in mind, however, that the reconfiguration of Egyptian architectural forms for the commemoration of white achievement and the fashioning of a white supremacist national identity becomes more self-evident. While I have not changed the text of the manuscript for the paperback edition, I believe the modern example of the Marvelous Sugar Baby reframes the discussions in the following chapters of how ancient Egypt and its monumental and architectural forms became embedded within the public sphere of cultural expression and shared identity. In the Coda following Chapter 6, I offer a brief meditation on artist Barnett Newman's *Broken Obelisk*, a permanent art installation with three copies made in 1967—one of which, in Houston, Texas, was dedicated in 1971 as a memorial to Dr. Martin Luther King, Jr. At the time of the book's publication in 2014, there was the uneasy sense that I had shoe-horned this Coda in, as the sculpture of an inverted broken obelisk atop a pyramid and dedicated to the memory of a civil rights leader seemed out of keeping with the rest of the examples of Egyptian Revival discussed throughout the book. If the Egyptian Revival during the nineteenth and early twentieth centuries was a reinvention of Egyptian forms for an American context, however, Newman's

Broken Obelisk, like Walker's *A Subtlety*, was a reinvention of a reinvention. The Egyptian Revival became a "characteristically American" architectural idiom because in its myriad manifestations across the American memorial landscape, it was never reproduced as purely Egyptian. Albeit recreated in nearly infinite varieties of portals, pyramids, obelisks, mastaba tombs, and sphinxes, the Egyptian Revival appeared with such regularity that it became germane to the built environment and thus a subject that has lent itself to perpetual reinvention lasting to the present day.

Even as the Egyptian Revival has retained relevance into the twenty-first century as an engaging form of memorial expression, and Egyptomania remains alive and well in modern popular culture with books, movies, and television shows featuring the land of the pharaohs and reanimated mummies, so, too, has there been expanded attention paid over the last decade to what was once regarded as a minor offshoot of architectural revivalism or indicative of the confused eclecticism of American architecture during the nineteenth century. Especially within the fields of architectural history, archaeology, and public history, scholars have increasingly incorporated discussions of the Egyptian Revival and its significance to the built environment and matters of public memory and identity in American history. Notable works published in recent years that have paid close attention to architectural revivalism and eclecticism generally, and the Egyptian Revival in particular, include *Housing the New Romans: Architectural Reception and Classical Style in the Modern World* (Oxford University Press, 2017), edited by Katharine T. von Stackelberg and Elizabeth Macaulay-Lewis; Civil War historian Thomas J. Brown's *Civil War Monuments and the Militarization of America* (University of North Carolina Press, 2019); archaeologist Elizabeth Macaulay-Lewis's *Antiquity in Gotham: The Ancient Architecture of New York City* (Fordham University Press, 2021); and art historian Kerry Dean Carso's *Follies in America: A History of Garden and Park Architecture* (Cornell University Press, 2021). What had once been generally regarded as a minor architectural oddity favored by wealthy eccentrics is now recognized as an integral part of the United States' commemorative landscapes and memorial sites. No longer regarded as indicative of cultural confusion or the haphazard application of architectural styles without rhyme or reason, the Egyptian Revival is now better understood as having been adopted, refashioned, and utilized within an American context as part of a broader nineteenth century strategy to generate a visual rhetoric and national identity explicitly tied to antiquity.

PREFACE

IN AN OBSCURE PART OF DOWNTOWN CAIRO, EGYPT, that tourists seldom visit stands the imposing mausoleum to Wafd party leader, Saad Zaghloul (1859–1927). A man whose name is hardly recognized by most westerners, Zaghloul was an instrumental figure during the Egyptian Revolution of 1919, as the nation struggled to achieve its independence from Great Britain. Serving as prime minister for only one year, 1924, Zaghloul died in 1927, and the mausoleum that would eventually hold his mortal remains and those of his wife did not adhere to traditional design patterns for Islamic burials. Rather, architect Moustapha Fahmy Bey completed the structure in 1931 in a style that had appeared in countries around the world since the nineteenth century—that is, the Egyptian Revival.

I had the good fortune of visiting Zaghloul's mausoleum in 2008, at a time when I was first conceptualizing how to grapple with my own research on the Egyptian Revival in the United States. I was impressed by the sheer size of the mausoleum, which resembles a sacred temple more than a place of burial, and was further struck by the manifold details incorporated into the building's exterior and interior. The outside bears all of the traditional ancient Egyptian architectural elements—battered walls, touro molding, cavetto cornice, pylons, and massive red granite lotus capital columns supporting the outer portal. The carved image of the winged orb with *uraei* (serpents), the great symbol of protection engraved and painted on so many tombs and temples along the Nile, appears in deep relief above both the outer portal and the doorway. The heavy bronze doors feature lotus flowers, *uraei* flanking a cartouche, at the center of which is another protective figure, the scarab beetle. Even the door handles are in the shape of the uraeus. The interior of the mausoleum is similarly bedecked with many of the same design elements, and located in the center of the room is an immense granite sarcophagus, the solidity of which would make even the pharaoh Khufu jealous. Taken together, these details of the grand mausoleum convey to all visitors that Saad Zaghloul was, indeed, a great man, a modern pharaoh who, in helping to restore his nation's independence, likewise restored for his people a sense of pride and connection to their ancient heritage.

As an American visitor to Zaghloul's mausoleum, I understood the design and significance of using the Egyptian Revival style to house the remains of one of the nation's most heroic dead. The appearance of Egyptian Revival architecture in Egypt made sense; oddly, however, relatively few major examples of the style exist in its home country compared to its application in other parts of the world. Examples of the Egyptian Revival may be found across the globe, in countries such as England, France, Italy, Germany, Russia, Australia, and Brazil. In the United States, the Egyptian Revival became popular during the early nineteenth century and held lasting appeal until the mid-twentieth century. The commemorative landscape, in particular, is replete with monuments and memorials built in the style. But whereas to a visitor to Egypt, the sight of an Egyptian Revival structure does not seem out of place—and its meaning is self-evident—the reason for its popularity in other parts of the world, and in the United States, in particular, is less readily apparent.

As periods of discovery during the nineteenth and twentieth centuries revealed the treasures, mummies, and untold secrets of the Nile land to the world, the result was subsequent waves of Egyptomania. In the United States, fascination for ancient Egypt manifested in a number of arenas: popular culture, literature, art, museums, and public architecture. As the nineteenth century progressed, Egyptian imagery and themes became increasingly pervasive in these areas. That being said, the Egyptian Revival as part of the American enthusiasm for Egypt found its most widespread and profound expression in commemorative architecture and memorials. Scholars from the fields of art history, architecture, and the decorative arts have thoroughly studied the international phenomenon of Egyptian Revival and Egyptomania, but little research has attended to the cultural and political role the style played in the United States in particular. As an aesthetic that gained popularity at precisely the same time as the middle and upper classes of the United States were seeking a lasting place for their young nation—surrounded as it was by countries of far greater antiquity—the Egyptian Revival served a far more significant role for the population and its sense of national identity than as a mere expression of eclectic taste.

This study therefore presents an effort to close the gap in this scholarship and provide an understanding of the context in which the Egyptian Revival became popular and why so many of our local and national commemorative monuments—many of which are well-known symbols of who Americans are as a people—employed aesthetic motifs of Egyptian obelisks, pyramids, tombs, and temples. The Americans who were originally in charge of the construction and dedication of monuments, memorials, and cemetery gates built all across the country understood the implications of having chosen the Egyptian style. For many twenty-first century Americans, however, the original meaning of such structures has become obscured over time. In short, my hope is that this book will reveal to the modern reader what these monuments once meant to the people who built them, so that they might no longer be misconstrued as anachronisms or oddities amid our modern landscape.

ACKNOWLEDGMENTS

MY CHOSEN FIELD OF RESEARCH, cemeteries and commemorative culture, is certainly not one of the more "typical" branches of historical study. When I first decided that this would be my niche, that I would devote my skills as a researcher to what many view, on the surface, as an intrinsically morbid and unpopular field, many expressed concern as to whether there would ultimately be any broad interest in what I would write. Over the past several years, as I have continued to devote myself to studying cemeteries, gravestones, and public memorials, I have learned that I am, indeed, not alone. Many people have offered immeasurable support as I have pursued my work in commemorative studies in general, and the Egyptian Revival in particular, and I would like to offer my thanks. First, I would like to extend my appreciation to my original mentors, Professors Marli Weiner (posthumously) and Nathan Godfried, neither of whom specialized in commemorative studies, but who nevertheless trusted me to become a specialist. To my editor, Thomas Wells at the University of Tennessee Press, who contacted me because he thought my project sounded interesting and who has maintained an unwavering level of enthusiasm for getting this book into print. To Meg Winslow and the Mount Auburn Cemetery Archives; the Massachusetts Historical Society; the Bill Memorial Library in Groton, Connecticut; and the Allen County Public Library in Fort Wayne, Indiana. To my friends and colleagues in the Association for Gravestone Studies, especially John Martine, David Chabala, Beth Santore, Ta Mara Conde, Melvin Mason, Tom Mason, Albin Lohr-Jones, Andrea Lustig, and Keith Harper. To those who read the many drafts of this manuscript, especially Blanche Linden, Erica Risberg, and my husband, Ben Proud. To my family—my parents, Gerard and Patricia Giguere, my uncle, Richard Siembab, and my grandparents, Raymond and Lillian Siembab—all of whom decided to take a personal interest in my research and who have traveled to countless cemeteries, taken photographs, and, because of the auction and antiques business, found all sorts of useful artifacts for me to use over the years. And of course, to Ben. If you hadn't gone to Egypt, then I might not have landed on this topic the way I did. You've been my constant cheerleader, proofreader, and believer that what I have to write about is important. You really are a good sport.

Introduction

EGYPT IN AMERICA

PRIOR TO THE NINETEENTH CENTURY, most Americans knew little and, by and large, cared less, about Egypt—ancient *or* modern. Most only knew about the ancient land from what could be found in the Bible. The Freemasons, whose lodge architecture and symbolism commonly incorporated Egyptian elements, by the eighteenth century, looked to Egypt, as described by architectural historian James Stevens Curl, as "a source of knowledge of building and of all wisdom enshrouded in the Hermetic mysteries." But even their knowledge was restricted to the biblical account that the Israelites had supposedly learned the masonic craft from the Egyptians while in captivity.[1] The few eighteenth-century Americans who did seek greater understanding of the great Nilotic civilization often met with disappointment. For example, Thomas Jefferson expressed an interest in the potential for great discoveries in Egypt and carried on a correspondence with John Ledyard from Connecticut, who set out in 1788 to explore Egypt and the Niger River. Ledyard's letters to Jefferson indicate disappointment bordering on disgust with Egypt and complained of the "dust, eternal hot fainting winds, lice, bugs, mosquitoes, spiders, flies—pox, itch, leprosy, fevers, and almost universal blindness." In Ledyard's last known letter to Jefferson, from November 1788, he chastised the future president's misguided enthusiasm for historical inquiry: "I know your taste for ancient history I think: it does not comport with what experience teaches me. . . . I should have wrote you the truth. . . . The sublime poetry of Homer has nothing to do with historic *facts*. . . . In some cases it is perhaps difficult to determine which does the most mischief: the self-love of the historian, or the curiosity of the reader: but both together have led us into errors that it is now too late to rectify." Ledyard's disillusionment at having gone to Egypt on a fool's errand to retrieve the mysteries of the past and seek the source of the Nile is practically prescient—he died in Cairo before his scheduled departure for Khartoum.² Those like Jefferson, with a desire to understand the mysteries buried in the land of the pharaohs, would have to wait.

Fortunately, they would not have to wait long. The publication of Vivant Denon's *Voyage dans la Basse et le Haut de l'Égypte* (1802) and the monumental nine-volume *Déscription de l'Égypte* (1809–1825) following the Napoleonic campaigns would present the West with its first real archaeological knowledge and accurate images of the country's ancient monuments. As further evidence of the cultural—if not military—triumph of Napoleon's forces, François Champollion's translation of the hieroglyphics on the Rosetta Stone became the primary breakthrough in the centuries-long effort to demystify the people who built the pyramids. Regarding the significance of Champollion's efforts, *The North American Review* exclaimed in 1829, "The new light thrown upon the antiquities of Egypt by the hieroglyphic discoveries of Champollion and others has revived the interest of scholars in the history of that wonderful land, where the arts of civilized life, and, above all, the most important of them the gift of letters, were cultivated, whilst Greece and Italy were still covered with forests and filled with wild beasts and savage hordes."³

The cultural breakthroughs of the Napoleonic campaigns were fortuitous for Americans. Not only would fascination with Egypt result in an explosion of interest known as "Egyptomania," but also the opening to the West of the land of the pharaohs occurred during an era in which many Americans became deeply concerned about how best to express their national identity. Faced with criticism from abroad by the likes of Charles Dickens and Frances Trollope that America was a nation without culture, refinement—indeed, even a meaningful *past*—the country's educated elite began the process of fashioning a national heritage. In constructing a usable past for the United States, one that was based on the great civilizations of antiquity, Americans had the advantage of being able to adopt all of the best aspects of their predecessors while leaving behind all of their faults. Part of this process involved borrowing various architectural styles from antiquity, and subsequently applying them to realms of the American landscape as deemed appropriate. In this way, using the ancient past helped Americans articulate a long chronology of development, so that in the history of Western civilization, the United States stood firmly at the head of the line, the great beneficiary of its antecedents and superior to all.

By the early nineteenth century, then, the western hemisphere was ablaze with interest in the land of the pharaohs. In the United States, in particular, references to Egypt in newspaper and magazine articles became increasingly common during the first twenty years of the nineteenth century. Travelers to Egypt created a market in the United States for travel books, with at least four such volumes published between 1800 and 1810, twelve in the next decade, and seventeen during the 1820s.[4] For example, *The Bee,* out of New London, Connecticut, advertised the availability for sale in 1800 of M. C. F. Volney's *Travels Through Egypt and Syria in the years 1783–1785,* with the exhortation to readers, "It must certainly be a matter worth the attention of the studious and inquisitive to learn the present and recent state of these countries, so famed in ancient history, sacred and profane, and the scene of the latest achievements of the famous Buonaparte."[5] Americans had become so accustomed to reading about Egypt that by mid-century, a traveler known only to *Harper's* readers as "An American," declared in his "Passages of Eastern Travel," his unwillingness to describe the characteristics of the Nile River. His reasoning was, "Every body [sic] has read of all these a hundred times, and Americans are as familiar with the valley of the Nile as with that of the Mississippi."[6] Indeed, comparisons between the massive rivers that bisected each country were likewise common, and some considered the Mississippi River "the American Nile." As art historian Richard Carrott observes, "By mid-century brashly confident Americans had reversed the process, referring to the Nile as 'the Mississippi of Egypt'."[7]

American interest in Egypt, both ancient and modern, remained tangible and seldom diminished throughout the nineteenth century. There were certainly periods during which Egyptian themes in literature and architecture were less prominent—giving way, as one example, to the popular fascination with the Medieval Gothic during the 1850s and 1860s, but ancient Egypt always remained present in American cultural life, influencing American funerary and commemorative practices in particular. In addition to the popularity of enlisting the Egyptian style for cemetery gateways and public memorials, the influence of Egypt penetrated the realm of private memorialization and even the physical care for the dead. The parallels between ancient Egyptian mummification and sarcophagi and the American acceptance of arterial embalming and the rapid transformation of the traditional pine coffin into the increasingly elaborate—and expensive—casket were not lost on commentators. So evident was the inspiration for such developments that Mary A. Dodge, writing for *The Atlantic Monthly* in 1860, noted "Are we not, in this class of our tastes and feelings, becoming rapidly Egyptianized?"[8]

Outside the realm of commemoration, Champollion's philological breakthroughs in the 1820s fueled scholarly interest in Egypt, the result of which included mummy unwrappings intended for both "scientific" ethnological study as well as popular spectacle. These pursuits reached the peak of their vogue during the 1840s and 1850s. The opening of the Suez Canal in 1869 likewise sparked additional fervor for ancient Egypt in popular culture, especially with the premiere of Giuseppe Verdi's opera, *Aïda*, which the composer wrote to commemorate the event. Further, museums as major cultural institutions began to open throughout the American Northeast and much of their pride and popularity rested upon their collections of Egyptian antiquities. Reports and speeches following the removal of the obelisk known as "Cleopatra's Needle" from Alexandria to Central Park in New York City in 1881 viewed the gift as a symbol of the mutual friendship—rather than imperial domination—between the United States and Egypt. Its presence in New York was an object of national pride. Finally, as the jewel in the crown of American civilization, the Columbian Exposition of 1893 in Chicago featured both ancient and modern Egypt—in the figure of the obelisk located in the White City, the recreated Temple of Luxor in the Midway Plaisance, and the Orientalist fantasy embodied in Cairo Street. The exposition was the nineteenth century's last major cultural expression in which the image of ancient Egypt appeared part of the visual rhetoric, proclaiming, as Julian Ralph asserted in *Harper's*, "the progress of the United States" with "the most palpable monuments of a consummate civilization" on display.[9]

By the 1890s, many Americans had some acquaintance with Egyptian history, art and/or architecture. The idea of Egypt as the most ancient civilization with a population obsessed with its care for the dead was, for the most part, taken for granted. In her 1891 monograph, *Pharaohs, Fellahs and Explorers*, Amelia B. Edwards of the Egypt Exploration Fund expressed a sentiment that had been common in the West since the time of Herodotus: "We are accustomed to think of the days of Plato and Pericles, of Horace and the Caesars, as 'ancient times.' But Egypt was old and outworn when Athens and Rome were founded; the great Assyrian Empire was a creation of yesterday as compared with that of the Pharaohs; the middle point of Egyptian history was long past when Moses received his education at the court of Rameses II; and the Pyramids were already hoary with antiquity when Abraham journeyed into the land of Egypt."[10] Edwards, an Englishwoman and dedicated promoter of the Egypt Exploration Fund, delivered lectures in the United States from 1889 to 1890 to raise money and interest in professional Egyptological excavations.[11] Her lectures were a success, in all likelihood due to the strong popular interest that had spanned nearly a century.

In this last realm—the arena of professional Egyptology—the United States lagged behind Europe. Nonetheless, the period from 1894 to 1914 witnessed the transition in American Egyptology from, as Egyptologist John A. Wilson described it, "The pleasant and leisurely avocation of the wealthy amateur to the serious and dedicated vocation of the professional."[12] At this point, with the professionalization of American Egyptology, the symbolic language of cultural and national identity became dominated by Art Deco and Modernist impulses, which in the aesthetic realm meant a general movement away from the architectural revivalism of the nineteenth century. Further, with nationwide confidence in the sophistication of American industrial and consumer technology, the associations of timelessness and solidity lent by ancient Egyptian forms no longer seemed necessary as a major influence on American national identity. Contrastingly, interest in Egypt in popular culture continued to intensify at the dawn of the twentieth century, with Egyptian themes appearing with greater frequency in the new form of American entertainment—cinema. The opening of the tomb of Tutankhamen in 1922 further transformed and commercialized American "Egyptomania," as popular films and literature increasingly drew upon spectacular themes involving reanimated mummies and ancient curses.

This fascination with ancient Egypt reveals that the use of the Egyptian Revival in commemorative architecture did not occur in a vacuum, nor did Americans employ the Egyptian Revival as a minor appendage to the often more popular neoclassical Greek and Roman Revivals. Rather, the period during which Egyptian Revival commemorative architecture and monuments flourished was a period of excitement and exploration, of mummies and hieroglyphics, of questions concerning human origins and anxieties over racial heritage. As a formative period in the United States, the nineteenth century as a whole was an era in which the new nation struggled to establish a sense of legitimacy and a cultural heritage that would lend it greater force in the age of Manifest Destiny and later, imperial expansion. For centuries, since the ascension of the Roman Empire, the image of Egypt and its monuments had been deliberately co-opted to express national or imperial power, wealth, wisdom, and technological superiority. Considered the parent to all future civilizations, Egypt was the root of all human progress. Even early in the nineteenth century, educated Americans were conscious of this association. Massachusetts Chief Justice Isaac Parker noted in his inaugural address delivered at Harvard University in 1816:

> For Rome sent her wise men to Greece, to study the laws and customs of its renowned republicks [sic], and to import the choicest of them into that proud and aspiring city. Greece sought instruction from the priests and sages of Egypt, and these last, without doubt, borrowed the then accumulated wisdom of the world which had preceded them. Thus, the experience of mankind has been from age to age contributing to a system, which grows more perfect as the world improves, and will probably pass down to innumerable generations as the basis of her civil institutions.[13]

For Parker, the United States would carry forth this tradition, adopting "the recorded wisdom of times which are past, drawn from every civilized country in ancient and modern times, and modified to the circumstances of our country, having the sanction of immemorial usage for its authority."[14] Inspired by antiquity to create a national identity steeped in a usable past, nineteenth-century Americans created for the nation's outward symbols of national superiority a cultural atmosphere saturated with references to the most ancient of all Western civilizations.

WADING THROUGH AN ECLECTIC AESTHETIC

As early as the late 1760s, Thomas Jefferson implemented his designs for his Roman-inspired home, Monticello (1768–1808) and later, the capitol building in Richmond (1785–1792). Architectural designs derived from antiquity reached such heights of popularity in the years between 1820 and 1860, that nineteenth-century landscape designer Andrew Jackson Downing noted, "It would certainly be difficult for a stranger in some of our towns, where the taste for Grecian temples prevails, to distinguish with accuracy between a church, a bank, and a hall of justice."[15] Of all the revival styles, the Greek was certainly the most popular. Due to its widespread application in both public and domestic architecture, many writers in the nineteenth and twentieth centuries felt that Greek Revival architecture was *the* American style—to the extent that architectural historian Talbot Hamlin defined the years from 1820 to 1860 the "Greek Revival" period.[16] Gothic Revival, second only to the Greek in popularity and which had its antecedents in eighteenth-century English medievalism, flourished in the United States in ecclesiastical and domestic architecture from 1830 until the *fin-de-siècle*. Taken together, Greek and Gothic Revival architecture canvassed a large proportion of American towns and cities by the latter decades of the century. Harvard professor Dr. Jacob Bigelow (1787–1879), a central figure in the Rural Cemetery Movement and champion of the legitimization of Egyptian Revival in America, noted in his 1829 lectures entitled *Elements of Technology*, "In edifices erected at the present day, the Grecian and Gothic outlines are commonly employed, to the exclusion of the rest."[17]

Americans at the forefront of efforts to design grand monuments and structures of cultural significance were well aware that what they built represented who they were as a people. As such, architecture during the nineteenth century was neither strictly functional nor merely an act of self-expression. Egyptian obelisks and neoclassical temples were reflections of a people striving to find a national identity with a usable past. The civilizations that directly influenced American political and cultural institutions were not merely referenced in the country's governing documents, they were made manifest on the physical landscape. If American democracy and republicanism came directly to the United States from Greece and Rome, what better way to express that political lineage than through civic architecture? Americans regarded ancient Egyptians as history's greatest caretakers of the dead, not to mention technological geniuses unparalleled by any modern society. Theirs were the tombs and temples that had withstood the ravages of time better than any other civilization's—its buildings and sculptures therefore connoted solidity, stability, and timelessness. In a country striving at once for technological supremacy and to convey to the world the perpetuity of its own monuments and institutions, what civilization offered better inspiration than that which had built the eternal pyramids?

Architectural revivalism and expressions of "Egyptomania" within the broader material and popular culture were widespread in Europe at this time as well, especially in England and France. The excitement for the land of the pharaohs could be seen in the construction of the famed Egyptian Hall

(1811–1812) at Piccadilly, London, which housed the widely viewed collection of Egyptian art and artifacts that the Italian strongman, explorer, (and plunderer), Giovanni Battista Belzoni (1778–1823) brought to England.[18] At the domestic level, Europeans purchased furniture, chinaware, and other decorative arts designed by the leading craftsmen of the eighteenth and nineteenth centuries. None was more influential than Giovanni Battista Piranesi (1720–1778), referred to by Curl as the "inventor of a fashion for Egyptianising forms used in an eclectic manner," and whose "published works often include Egyptian or Egyptianising objects."[19] As widespread as the Egyptian Revival became in European domestic, public, and commemorative architecture, the decorative arts and popular culture, its popularity in England and France in particular should not be conflated with the manner in which it appeared in the United States. The adoption of the Egyptian Revival in these nations had fundamentally different implications. By and large, the French and English application of Egyptian architectural forms was an explicit statement of imperial power. Both nations had fought for control over Egypt and, as such, the public excitement for that country's subjugation was clear. This longing manifested in displays of Egypt's antiquities in the British Museum and the Louvre, the acquisition and re-erection of the great obelisks of Alexandria and Luxor in London and Paris, not to mention the design of numerous fountains and monuments, in France especially, to commemorate the Napoleonic campaigns and the great cultural achievements of Dominique Vivant, Baron de Denon (1747–1825) and Jean-François Champollion (1790–1832).[20]

The United States, by contrast, did not have an imperial presence in Egypt. The appearance of Egyptian Revival architecture was therefore not intended to serve as an expression of American superiority over that nation. Rather, Americans acknowledged Egypt, much like Greece and Rome, as a direct predecessor to their own modern civilization. By fashioning a national lineage that stretched all the way back to ancient Egypt—popularly referred to by various nineteenth-century writers as the "mother" or "parent" of civilization[21]—Americans could offer a riposte to European critics' charges that the United States was a country without a history while implying that the nation itself embodied all of the most superior qualities of the civilizations that preceded it. Having the benefit of geographic separation from the Old World, Americans were at liberty to adopt and adapt whatever foreign or historical influences they found best or most appropriate. By using styles of visual expression from the societies that directly influenced their nation's development, nineteenth-century Americans were able to observe their historical lineage in the physical landscape while developing a sense of modern superiority. In the architectural language of eclecticism, the United States therefore possessed all of the best qualities of past societies—and none of their faults. Whereas the European landscape bore the weight of its own history, Americans of the nineteenth century were able to view their own vast territory as a virtual *tabula rasa*—a wide open and virgin land (even including the populated areas) that served as a canvas upon which to create an aesthetic cultural idiom for a young nation seeking to define itself and its place in the history of the world.

Examples of the Egyptian Revival in the United States may be found in a variety of architectural arenas. The style found expression in prisons, fire houses, railroad depots, suspension bridges, churches, and even synagogues; but it was most commonly employed within the commemorative context, in the form of cemetery gateways, sepulchral monuments and public memorials. The obelisk arguably became one of the most widely used and recognized monumental forms for both private and public memorials. During an era when the effort to create outward appearances of culture and refinement was at its height, the rural cemetery emerged as a new landscape that would be copied not only around the United States, but also in Europe. Visitors to the model for all future rural cemeteries, Mount Auburn Cemetery in Cambridge, Massachusetts, would be greeted by an imposing Egyptian portal that would usher them into the land of the dead. And when the citizenry of the nation, at the local level and nationwide, strove to find appropriate ways to commemorate the battles and heroes of wars past, monument associations commonly turned to Egypt for inspiration.

Although extensively applied throughout the nineteenth century in commemorative architecture, the Egyptian Revival was not without its critics. Many Americans disliked the pagan connotations, especially as its use was so common in places of Christian burial. Its widespread appearance, and the sharp disagreements over the propriety of the style for a Christian setting, made the Egyptian the most controversial of the various manifestations of architectural revivalism. America's political heritage from Greece and Rome were clear, and therefore the meaning of buildings constructed in the neoclassical aesthetic was self-evident. As architectural historian Joseph Downs observed, "As the Greek Revival style unfolded and developed in the United

States it became as indigenous to the soil as our system of law based on the Roman code and our democratic system of government, which was founded on the ancient ideal of individual freedom. It was our first national style of architecture."[22] The appearance of Doric temples or Corinthian columns warranted no explanations as to their use or meaning.

By contrast, because the United States did not derive any of its political or religious institutions from ancient Egypt, and its associations were primarily commemorative, the purpose of the Egyptian Revival and the messages it conveyed were, to many, less readily understood and therefore more open to public deliberation. The very struggles and debates that commonly appeared in periodicals of the era reflect just how difficult the process of finding a national aesthetic could be. In a heterogeneous nation in which no single race or creed prevailed as the definitive "American" type, the very process of creating a national identity was characterized by volatility and eclecticism. With waves of immigration occurring at midcentury and again toward the *fin-de-siècle*, the country's population became increasingly polyglot and multiethnic. The eclecticism of American architectural tastes could also be attributed to the democratic tendencies of the young nation, in which individual freedom of choice—especially within a rapidly industrializing consumer economy—was readily apparent on the physical landscape. Within the cemetery landscape alone, the freedom of personal taste could be clearly seen—simple headstones mingled with statuary of angels and allegorical figures, Egyptian pyramids stood side-by-side with Roman temples, and monuments included all manner of designs carved into their surfaces, including flowers, lambs, hands, portraits of the deceased, fraternal and religious symbols, and much more.

Yet, despite these tendencies, the history of architectural revivalism, and that of the Egyptian Revival more particularly, can also be read as the rise in cultural dominance of the urban middle class. It was largely this class of individuals, which comprised college professors, doctors, lawyers, merchants, and statesmen, that made decisions about designs for public monuments and structures. Civic-minded middle class professionals made up the bulk of monument committees and associations and cemetery boards of trustees in the industrializing Northeast. As leaders in the process to determine the design of structures intended to last the ages, these men effectively established a clear hegemony over American taste. Reflective of the aesthetic preferences of a relatively narrow segment of American society, the cemetery gateways and war memorials whose designs these men controlled were nevertheless intended to reflect the sentiments and values of the entire population. Periodical articles, dedication speeches, and guidebooks all served to reinforce for Americans at large that they could look to antiquity as the model for their nation, thus explicitly stating what the monuments implicitly symbolized. Because the intended meaning of the Egyptian Revival was often opaque to many Americans, this kind of literary and verbal reinforcement was even more critical to legitimizing the stylistic choices of the men in charge of these designs. As people tended not to write privately about their architectural preferences, I have therefore relied primarily on public and popular sources—speeches, newspaper and periodical articles, and cemetery guidebooks—that would have been the principal means of explaining to the American public what their monuments and cemetery landscapes meant.

The following study is thus an effort to situate the American use of the Egyptian Revival in the commemorative context of architectural revivalism more generally, in order to examine the ways in which the stylistic choices made by individuals and committees reflected their conception of themselves and their nation. When compared to Americans' adoption of neoclassical forms or the extraordinary popularity of the Gothic Revival—especially during the second half of the nineteenth century—the Egyptian style at first glance seems insignificant. Because this aesthetic was primarily associated with institutions that housed either criminals or the dead, most scholars during the twentieth century tended to dismiss the Egyptian Revival as an aberration from prevailing stylistic trends. It was, at best, a minor element in the broader environment of architectural eclecticism, intimately tied to romanticism and the prevailing Victorian obsession with death;[23] at worst, it was a style associated with Orientalist fantasy, employed by wealthy eccentrics—those with a "flare for the unusual"—in their homes and for their funerary monuments.[24] Nonetheless, the significance of the Egyptian Revival's place in American cultural history should not be diminished, as many architectural historians have believed, even if its scope was more limited than its popular neoclassical or Gothic counterparts. It is, in all likelihood, due to the prevailing attitude that the Egyptian Revival was simply a minor offshoot within the broader architectural revivalism of the period that much has been written on neoclassicism and Gothic Revival while, by contrast, art historian Richard Carrott's *The Egyptian Revival* has remained the only comprehensive treatment of the subject in the United States.[25]

In approaching such a subject, one must note that both the chronology and the geographical reach of the Egyptian Revival as a "revival" has been subject to debate. Carrott limited the actual revival to six decades, 1808 to 1858, whereas other scholars argue that the Egyptian Revival continues today, as evidenced by such structures as the famously kitschy Luxor Casino in Las Vegas. With regard to its application for commemorative monuments and cemetery gates, the most accurate time frame for the style encompasses the years from about 1790 until the late 1930s, though abstract expressionist artist Barnett Newman's *Broken Obelisk*, dedicated as a memorial to Martin Luther King Jr., dates to 1967.[26] As this study represents an effort to understand how the Egyptian Revival was part of the iconography of national identity at a time when Americans were consciously striving to create both a cultural heritage and a tangible identity for their nation, the temporal parameters will span the period from 1790, with the introduction of Egyptian architectural elements as part of the more broadly defined neoclassical style, to 1939, with the completion of the San Jacinto Battle Monument in Texas. The primary reason for examining such an extensive chronology of development is that whereas the commemorative uses of the Egyptian Revival remained consistent for nearly a century and a half, the inherent meanings and associations of the style underwent significant transformation following the dedication of the Washington National Monument in 1885. By the *fin-de-siècle*, most Americans were looking to the future rather than the past to articulate their identity of themselves and their nation, and commentators writing about monuments erected in the style after the turn of the century—particularly obelisks—described their form in relation to their American, not Egyptian, predecessors. Just as architectural historians have regarded the Greek Revival of the mid-nineteenth century as the "American" style, by the early decades of the twentieth century, the Egyptian had likewise become an inherently American aesthetic.

Because the Egyptian and other architectural revivals began in the immediate post-Revolutionary War years, they were at first geographically limited to the East Coast. The Greek Revival saw widespread popularity in both the North and the South, but the Egyptian remained for several decades restricted to the New England and Mid-Atlantic states. By the 1840s, when the Rural Cemetery Movement stretched beyond the Northeast, the Egyptian Revival found expression in such cities as Chicago, St. Louis, Cincinnati, and Cleveland in the West, and in the South, in New Orleans. By the end of the century, examples of Egyptian Revival could be found from Bangor, Maine, to Portland, Oregon. Given what was eventually the transcontinental reach of the style, this study will focus primarily on its appearance in the locations where it found its initial expression: the New England and Mid-Atlantic states, extending south to Maryland (particularly Baltimore) and Washington, D.C. Nonetheless, discussion of twentieth-century examples will show the geographic variability of the Egyptian Revival outside this region.

In considering the commemorative uses of the Egyptian Revival, the following study has been broken up thematically according to architectural and monument themes. This work is not intended to be comprehensive in scope, but rather seeks to highlight major examples of the broader appearance and significance of the style over time. These are addressed in Chapters 2 through 6. Chapter 1 examines the cultural and intellectual context in which professional middle class Americans found themselves drawn to styles derived from antiquity in the first place. It explores American claims to social and political superiority as well as responses to European aspersions concerning the nation's lack of history, culture, and refinement. This initial chapter also considers the emergence of popular Egyptomania in urban middle class culture, specifically the role of mummies both in popular literature and entertainment as well as in contemporary discussions of human origins and race theory. In this way, the chapter introduces what were common perceptions (and misperceptions) of ancient Egypt and Egyptians and establishes the context in which the Egyptian Revival became a meaningful style in nineteenth-century American commemorative culture.

Chapters 2 through 5 address the application of Egyptian Revival architecture and monuments in the public sphere during the nineteenth century. Each of these chapters considers the Egyptian Revival as it manifested within the physical environment, as well as the ways in which the image of ancient Egypt suffused the rhetoric associated with commemorative activities. The language employed for cemetery and monument dedications was, in fact, crucial to giving these structures meaning, and provide insight into *why* the Egyptian style might have been deemed appropriate in the first place. Chapter 2 explores the history of the Rural Cemetery Movement, which began with the establishment of Mount Auburn Cemetery in 1831 and lasted until the end of the 1860s. In the design of these new landscapes for the dead, the Egyptian Revival played an especially central role in the design of entrance gates. These gateways, the first object visible to visitors approaching from a distance, demarcated the land of the living from the land of the dead and defined the nature of the landscape contained within. Both the gateways and the cemeteries themselves carried with them cultural meaning as they were constructed by the proprietors of such institutions—that is, civic-minded urban professional middle class men. This chapter also considers the extent to which the choices for the outward design of cemetery gates influenced the choices of individual Americans when the time came to select private family memorials. It was also within the context of the Rural Cemetery Movement that some of the most heated debates about the propriety of the Egyptian Revival occurred among architects and critics. Albeit associated with a civilization that excelled in their care for the dead, there were those who could not look past what they saw as the overtly pagan connotations associated with Egyptian architecture and iconography.

Whereas Chapter 2 focuses on the significance of the Egyptian Revival within the context of the cultural institution of the cemetery, Chapters 3 through 5 examine the ramifications of the style in the fashioning of national identity through specific public memorials. Chapter 3 addresses the predominant use of monumental obelisks in memorials constructed in honor of the American Revolution. There are four such monuments in the United States, each measuring over one hundred feet tall, including the Bunker Hill Monument (1825–42) in Charlestown, Massachusetts; the Groton Monument (1826–30) at Groton Heights, Connecticut; the Saratoga Battle Monument (1877–82) in Saratoga, New York; and the Bennington Monument (1877–89) in Bennington, Vermont. The monuments themselves defined the national style for memorializing the Revolution and its participants while the rhetoric employed in the dedicatory orations delivered at their bases helped to fuse the images of ancient and modern society as they were embodied in the obelisks. This chapter specifically considers the earliest of these obelisks, the monuments at Bunker Hill and Groton, as they established a precedent whereby future monument associations would model their commemorative projects.

Chapter 4 considers the cultural politics of Civil War commemoration during the 1860s and 1870s through an analysis of a monument situated at the intersection of the public and private spheres of memorialization. The *Sphinx* (1872) at Mount Auburn Cemetery was crafted as a public monument to honor the Union soldiers of the Civil War, but its existence owes entirely to the efforts of a single individual, rather than, as was normal, an entire monument association. Dr. Jacob Bigelow, one of the founders and longtime president of Mount Auburn Cemetery, designed and funded the construction of the *Sphinx*, and many felt that it was as much a memorial to the man as it was a public monument to the soldiers. Placed within the boundaries of Mount Auburn Cemetery, the *Sphinx* sits in a landscape that is at once open to the public but filled with private memorials. Representative of the ideals and values of an individual, the monument nevertheless functions as a public testimonial of the feelings of the many. As a unique example of the Egyptian Revival in the United States, the *Sphinx* reflects Bigelow's own interpretation of the relationship between ancient Egypt and modern America as well as his perception of the war's legacy, the relationship between the races, and the future of the United States.

Returning to the subject of monumental obelisks, Chapter 5 explores the debates and struggles that defined the making of the Washington National Monument (1848–84). A project that had its origins at the beginning of the nineteenth century, with calls for a monument emerging as soon as George Washington died in 1799, by the time the project was finished it had become for many Americans far more than a memorial to the father of the nation. Remaining an incomplete stump—and as such, a national embarrassment—through the duration of the Civil War and Reconstruction, the unfinished Washington Monument represented the nation itself. Popular opinion varied during these years, but the widely held consensus was that the fate of the obelisk rested on the outcome of the war. The eventual completion of the nation's grandest monument in the two decades following the Civil War represented in many ways the reconstruction and preservation of the Union itself. The sheer size and perceived solidity of the design guaranteed that the monument and nation together would last in perpetuity.

This study concludes with a final chapter that examines how, at the close of the nineteenth century, the Egyptian Revival remained for many a style of contested meaning, especially following the completion and dedication of the Washington Monument. As the nation sought to construct a national monument to the Civil War's hero, Ulysses S. Grant, critics railed against the eclecticism that had long dominated American architecture. At the same time that various architects and architectural writers sought to reconsider the prevailing American aesthetic, the end of the nineteenth century was also a period that witnessed a renewed fervor for Egypt—both ancient and modern—in popular culture and the relatively new field of professional archaeology. Americans entered into the twentieth century with ancient Egypt still firmly in the public eye, the controversies surrounding the Washington National Monument largely forgotten. As a result, communities across the country constructed a new wave of large scale monuments and memorials in the Egyptian style. However, their construction and, in the case of the new public memorials, dedications reveal the transformative nature of the Washington Monument on the Egyptian Revival's significance in twentieth century American culture. The reactions to such monuments as the McKinley Memorial (1901–1907) in Buffalo, the Jefferson Davis Monument (1917–1924) in Fairview, Kentucky, and the San Jacinto Battle Monument (1936–1939) near Houston, Texas, reveal that the age of the Egyptian Revival *as* a revival had passed; the repetition and visibility of such monuments in the style for over a century had made it, quite simply, characteristically American.

CHAPTER 1

The Dream of Egypt

BEGINNING IN THE 1790s, a confluence of trends provided the context in which the Egyptian Revival became a popular form of architectural expression in the United States. First was the century-long effort on the part of educated Americans to defend their nation and culture against the aspersions leveled by European travelers and authors. To this end, American writers, especially those for popular periodicals, sought to defend not only their nation's social and democratic institutions, cultural productions in art and literature, architecture, and the manners of its people, they also strove to establish a tangible heritage for the United States that stretched all the way back to antiquity. In doing so, such writers hoped to prove that the United States and her people were, in fact, the modern beneficiaries of what they considered the most critical past achievements of humankind. By firmly establishing for the reading public the major qualities associated with Egyptian civilization and technology—solidity, stability, massiveness, permanence and so on—authors were likewise able to create an intellectual framework whereby those who saw Egyptian Revival structures on the landscape would understand their inherent meaning as well as why they would be considered appropriate within an American context.

The intellectual and cultural atmosphere that augmented the popularity of the Egyptian Revival was further bolstered by the expansion of popular interest in ancient Egypt, often referred to as "Egyptomania." Spurred by the opening of the land of the pharaohs to the West by the Napoleonic campaigns of 1798–1802, middle and upper class Americans became acquainted with Egypt through museum exhibitions, public lectures, mummy unwrappings, popular literature, and research undertaken in the new field of Ethnology. Such intermingling of popular entertainment and scholarly research meant that as a whole, the nineteenth century provided an environment in which educated Americans applied what they learned about Egypt in novel ways. The decision to adopt Egyptian architectural forms as part of an explicit effort to fashion a national identity steeped in the past reflected what Americans thought they knew about ancient Egypt and its relationship to modern nineteenth century America.

"A LAST EFFORT OF THE DIVINE PROVIDENCE"

No more than a generation had passed since the end of the American Revolution when travelers from Great Britain began to explore the young republic and write about their experiences. Oftentimes, their journals and correspondence contained a mixture of admiration and disgust, with particular vitriol reserved for what they perceived as a lack of manners and culture exhibited by the citizens ensconced in a wilderness that purported to be a nation. Such disdain is evident in the letters written by Irish poet Thomas Moore (1779–1852) to his mother while he toured America in 1803 and 1804. As he traveled along the eastern seaboard, Moore blasted the cities of New York and Baltimore with especial fervor. Of New York, he wrote, "there is more than enough of barrenness in intellect, taste, and all in which *heart* is concerned." Regarding his passage to Baltimore, "I have passed the Potomac, the Rappahannock, the Occoguan, the Potapsio, and many other rivers, with names as barbarous as the inhabitants: every step I take not only *reconciles* but *endears* to me, not only the excellencies but even the errors of Old England." Moore was kinder to Philadelphia as "the only place in America which can boast any literary society," but this opinion was no doubt the result of the enthusiastic reception he received by its inhabitants for his poetry.[1] While these letters express privately his feelings about the United States, Moore also articulated his distaste for the nation and its citizens publicly in the Preface to his *Epistles, Odes and Other Poems* (1806):

> The rude familiarity of the lower orders, and indeed the unpolished state of society in general, would neither surprise nor disgust, if they seemed to flow from that simplicity of character, that honest ignorance of the

gloss of refinement, which may be looked for in a new and inexperienced people. But, when we find them arrived at maturity in most of the vices, and all the pride, of civilization, while they are still so remote from its elegant characteristics, it is impossible not to feel that this youthful decay, this crude anticipation of the natural period of corruption, represses every sanguine hope of the future energy and greatness of America.[2]

Even those who had not taken the time to travel to the United States to form such opinions were keen to chastise the young nation. Sydney Smith excoriated American society in his 1820 review for the *Edinburgh Review* of Philadelphia congressman Adam Seybert's *Statistical Annals of the United States of America* (1818). Finding the young nation a veritable cultural wasteland, Smith asked, "In the four quarters of the globe, who reads an American book? Or goes to an American play? Or looks at an American picture or statue? What does the world yet owe to American physicians or surgeons? What new substances have their chemists discovered?" Continuing on in the same vein, Smith posited further questions that ultimately stressed that the Americans were, without doubt, a people without culture, refinement, science, technology, or even material production, asking whether anyone had ever used American-made glasses, plates, coats, gowns or blankets.[3] Criticisms like these from abroad did not abate as the century progressed and if anything, they became more humiliating for a nation seeking to achieve true greatness.

Two of the more controversial travel accounts of the period included Frances Trollope's *Domestic Manners of the Americans* (1832), which "created a sensation on both sides of the Atlantic," and Charles Dickens' *American Notes* (1842).[4] Trollope, who travelled to the United States in 1827 to establish a shop in Cincinnati, provided her opinion on virtually every aspect of the country and its inhabitants. Regarding American attitudes of themselves, she remarked, "They believe themselves in all sincerity to have surpassed, to be surpassing, and to be about to surpass, the whole earth in the intellectual race." She later reminded her readers that "It is a matter of historical notoriety, that the original stock of the white population now inhabiting the United States, were persons who had banished themselves, or were banished from the mother country."[5] The implication here was how could a people descended from the very dregs of the Old World conceive to aspire to the heights they claimed? As for Dickens, he was somewhat gentler in his criticisms of the United States, but no less direct than Trollope in expressing his opinions. Of the American character, he advised "It would be well, if there were greater encouragement to lightness of heart and gaiety, and a wider cultivation of what is beautiful, without being eminently and directly useful," and this because, "They certainly are not a humorous people, and their temperament always impressed me as being of a dull and gloomy character."[6] In concluding his *American Notes*, Dickens anticipated the reaction to his work once it was published: "I have little reason to believe, from certain warnings I have had since I returned to England, that it will be tenderly or favourably received by the American people."[7]

Dickens was accurate in his foreboding. His and Trollope's accounts gained international notoriety for the aspersions cast on American habits as well as their institutions, and because of their popularity, caused much cultural embarrassment. Writers for such periodicals as *The American Whig Review*, *The Atlantic Monthly* and *The United States Democratic Review* railed against "the increasingly contemptuous and insolent tone which British travelers and British criticism, and the British press generally, have chosen to assume towards this country."[8] Such was the intensity of American chagrin and indignation that *The American Whig Review* eventually chastised the public for its hypersensitivity: "Ours is the only nation that resents criticism of its literature, politics or manners as a crime. The West found an ample occasion of an English war in the witticisms and caricatures of captain Hall and Mrs. Trollope. Charles Dickens' Notes on America excited as much national indignation as a cabinet insult."[9] Even with such efforts to dim the furor of Americans' reactions to foreign accounts, American authors nevertheless regularly defended their nation with claims of its fundamental superiority to all societies, both ancient and modern, and especially sought to establish that the United States was far more than, as Smith had asserted, merely "a recent offset indeed from England."[10]

For some, it was a matter of *telling* Americans that theirs was a great and influential country. To this end, *The American Whig Review* declared in 1847 that most American citizens had not yet fully grasped the true greatness of their own nation. "Not-withstanding the proverbial pride of Americans, few have yet attained any due sense of the magnificence of their country and the splendor of their national destiny."[11] That same year, *The United States Democratic Review* reinforced the American claim of distinction from Europe's people and institutions: "[n]o nobility, established church, laws of primogeniture, or any of the attendances of feudalism ever existed in America; an energetic race of men, composed of all the nations of Europe, were located amidst boundless lands of exceeding fertility, and with all the intelligence of Europe they had no restraints upon their enterprise."[12] In other words, the United States was born from the best of Europe but possessed none of its inherited social or political ills.

Such claims to American exceptionalism became only more vehement after mid-century. In 1858, the *Democratic Review* proclaimed, "the American race, in point of liberty, civilization, and political philosophy, is unapproachable."[13] Even as the Civil War threatened to permanently destroy the nation, *The Atlantic Monthly* expressed in 1862 the sentiment that the United States nevertheless continued to stand at the forefront of western civilization as a country preordained for international pre-eminence: "[w]e live in a new and exceptional age. America is another word for Opportunity. Our whole history appears like a last effort of the Divine Providence in behalf of the human race."[14] From this vantage, then, even as the nation was torn asunder and separated by deep ideological conflicts, it was America's destiny, as a result of Divine Will, to be the last bastion of civilized society, to correct the social and political ills wrought by the countries of the Old World and to serve as a beacon of hope, that other nations might follow its example. Part of what gave the United States such a sense of destiny and authority lay in the heritage it sought to claim. A nation comprised of European immigrants and their descendants could not rightfully claim to be the greatest country on earth if its past stretched only so far back as seventeenth century Europe, the time of colonial expansion. To be considered by the world as a "True civilization," as *The American Whig Review* declared in 1846, implied "a ready sympathy and power of appreciation. It enters with facility into the characters and ideas of other nations, and of more imperfect forms of social culture; and by impartially judging them, includes and makes them its own. In fine, its idea, its mission is to bring into one, the past, the present and the future—all nations and all generations."[15] The legitimacy of the United States and its claims to superiority in all realms—socially, culturally, politically, economically and technologically—therefore rested on the creation of a national heredity that stretched back to the antiquity of mankind. The major question, then, was *which* antiquity to embrace as the nation's own?

In their efforts to create a usable heritage based on precedents set in the ancient past, nineteenth century Americans were perfectly aware of the antiquity of their own continent and of its pre-colonial inhabitants. Large burial and ceremonial mounds piqued the interest of many, and as early as 1784, Thomas Jefferson conducted a partial excavation of a mound located on his grounds in Virginia. Understanding their function as places of burial, Jefferson nevertheless dismissed the mounds as evidence of higher civilization. In his *Notes on the State of Virginia*, Jefferson stated, "I know of no such thing existing as an Indian monument. . . . Of labour on the large scale, I think there is no remain as respectable as would be a common ditch for the draining of lands: unless indeed it be the Barrows [mounds], of which many are to be found all over this country."[16] Whatever respect or admiration Anglo-Americans possessed for the indigenous populations of North America was also tempered by the distinction the former made between *ancient* and *contemporary* native societies: regardless of social or technological complexity, all native North Americans were inferior to the ancient populations of the Old World. In short, the prevailing attitude held by most Anglo-Americans was that the absence of monumental architecture and written records indicated the absence of civilization and, to a certain extent, of anything that would merit serious historical study or modern emulation. Even as eighteenth century artists depicted America allegorically as an Indian maiden, modern Anglo-Americans were disinclined to embrace the antiquity of native North America as their own given the prevailing associations concerning the savagery and lack of complexity of the nation's indigenous inhabitants.

Like Jefferson, however, there were those who recognized the significance of the continent's ancient peoples for scientific inquiry and in 1812, the General Court of the Commonwealth of Massachusetts passed an act of incorporation to create the American Antiquarian Society. Among its founders was Isaiah Thomas, who argued in favor of such an institution to "encourage the collection and preservation of the Antiquities of our country, and of curious and valuable productions in Art and Nature [that] have a tendency to enlarge the sphere of human knowledge."[17] Established at a time when Americans were becoming increasingly interested in exploring their own continent and the opportunities it held, there nevertheless remained a certain degree of skepticism toward the idea of "American Antiquity." Almost a decade after the American Antiquarian Society's incorporation, the *North American Review* reflected this attitude in 1821: "[i]t may at first seem singular, that an association should be formed for exploring the *antiquities* of a country, the discovery of which, in a wilderness state, and inhabited only by savage tribes, is an event so recent, that the appellation of 'the New World,' which was then given it, is still retained as appropriate; and which possesses no architectural ruins, no statues, sculptures, and inscriptions, like those of the Old World." However, the same article went on to explain that such an organization merited establishment since the subject of North American antiquity "has acquired increased interest by the discovery of ancient mounds and works of vast extent on the borders of the rivers west of the Alleghany mountains . . . erected by a people who had made greater advances in the arts and in improvement, than the present race of Indians, or than their ancestors, since the Europeans have been acquainted with them."[18] The presence of vast earthworks within the boundaries of the United States, separate and distinct from the vast stone structures and pictographic writing found in Central America, thus provided Anglo-American scholars with evidence of ancient complex societies worthy of serious study.

And yet, educated Americans never looked to the native inhabitants of North America as their cultural forbears. For why would they? Aboriginal inhabitants of the New World were just that—*of* the New World. Those who comprised the modern population of the United States were the descendants of Old World stock. In the development of their own monumental art and architectural aesthetic, Anglo-Americans sought to convey a heritage based on the developments of the most complex of the societies from antiquity, and while, as the *North American Review* observed, the mound complexes of North America "owe[d] their origin to a people far more civilized than our Indians," such people were still considered "far less so than Europeans."[19] In other words, the mounds of the Mississippi and Ohio River Valleys were testaments to the antiquity and relative complexity of early Native American societies in their own right, and this merited scientific investigation. However, in the trajectory of human development, it was clear to American writers and scholars that the ancient inhabitants of North America played no role in the process that, in time, led to the rise of American civilization. Writers gave the indigenous population of the continent at the time of European exploration even less credit. In the view of *The American Whig Review*, "Columbus is said to have discovered America; though multitudes were on the spot before him. But they knew only of the existence of their own tribes, and of their immediate neighbors, whom they chanced to meet in war or hunting—they had no history, no future, *i.e.*, they were savages: they were not properly *men*; and hence they are said to have been *discovered* as if they were mere *things*."[20] Facing similar aspersions from European authors that modern Americans likewise were lacking in history, it was therefore to the ancient Mediterranean that most writers turned their attentions in their efforts to establish a tangible cultural heritage that stretched from antiquity to nineteenth century America.

"THE MYSTERIES OF THE NILE HAVE JUST BURST UPON US"

By and large, in assessing the various merits and deficiencies of the civilizations from antiquity, most American writers tended to focus on ancient Egypt, Greece and Rome. Part of the excitement for Egypt developed as a result of the archaeological breakthroughs of the first half of the century, particularly those made by Englishman Thomas Young (1773–1829) and Frenchman François Champollion (1790–1832) in breaking the hieroglyphic code and therefore unveiling to the world what had even been mysterious to the Greeks and Romans.[21] Widely considered the great "mother" of civilizations, Egypt gave birth to Greece, and Greece to Rome, the great empire heralded by *The American Whig Review* as the world's "mistress."[22] Egypt also held a special allure given its biblical associations. For many, the landscape itself served as evidence of the truth of the Bible, as reflected in *The International Magazine* in 1851: "All nations turn to Egypt, as to the mother of civility, and the Christian sees there the prison where are detained, until the end of the world, the witnesses of truths which vindicate his religion."[23] From time to time, authors referred to ancient Babylon as well, "filled with enormous but fragile buildings," but only to contrast it with "the enormous stonework of Egypt or the Cyclopean fortress of Mycenae."[24] Often, articles that examined ancient societies did so as a means to extol the virtues of modern civilization by comparison and to assess those elements that merited emulation. More often than not, writers argued that nineteenth century America had perfected the various elements of technology and political philosophy that originated in antiquity, and just as Egypt, Greece and Rome had given birth to modern Europe and America, so would the United States function as the model for future nations.

Noting the differences between ancient and modern civilization, *The United States Democratic Review* remarked in 1849 that what gave "the present epoch its tone, its vigor, its progressiveness, is the vast expansion and liberality of the human mind, resulting from taking possession of the country, from being scattered over God's beautiful creation, instead of being immured within the walls of a fortified city."[25] The benefits of broad expanses of land for continental expansion along with modern technological ingenuity were key elements in the arguments in favor of the United States' inherent superiority. The vastness of the American continent not only liberated the human body, but the mind as well, which allowed modern intellectual power to surpass in the span of three hundred fifty years what took "the ancients" three thousand five hundred years to achieve: "[t]he mariner's compass, gunpowder, fire-arms, printing, the steam engine, and electric telegraphs," continued the *Democratic Review*, "are monuments of modern civilization, of infinitely greater value than pyramids, obelisks, and mausoleums."[26] While not all of these inventions were specifically hallmarks of American civilization, the message of the argument here was clear enough: the learning and technological marvels produced in antiquity were impressive, yet modern society—especially modern *American* society—had already surpassed the rest of mankind. "Who is he that can gaze upon the stately steamer as she moves from the wharf as by magic," asked *Scientific American*, "and not feel that the present age with its wonderful inventions, proclaims more triumphantly the divinity of our descent than all the splendid fabrics or enduring monuments of the past?"[27] Yet claims to American exceptionalism based on its contemporary qualities and differences from the past were not enough to satisfy the need to prove to outsiders that, contrary to popular belief, the United States was a nation with a cultural lineage the rest of the world would envy. The same authors who proclaimed the distinctiveness of American institutions therefore also strove to make tangible connections through which Americans could absorb into their own visual and civic culture a symbolic language linking past with present. At the heart of this process was the examination of each of the major ancient civilizations in their turn and the identification of those defining traits worthy of emulation.

Virtually every assessment of the major civilizations from antiquity contained a set of descriptive principles which helped most educated Americans decide how to make use of the ancient styles in their own architectural and monument-building activities: Egypt was "gigantic and superhuman,"[28] a civilization defined by its genius in masonry, the seemingly arbitrary power exerted by its pharaohs, and an obsessive care for the dead; Greece and Rome represented all that was cerebral and for the living. According to the *Democratic Review*, the Greeks and Romans "raised no pyramids—no obelisks, no mausoleums, to perpetuate the names of kings; but their poets, philosophers, historians, and warriors constructed *intellectual* obelisks, pyramids, and mausoleums of far greater magnitude and durability, inscribed with the characters of a euphonius demotic language."[29] This assessment was not entirely based on reality—the Roman emperors had glorified in erecting triumphal arches, colossal sculptures and monumental architecture as expressions of their own martial power. The Appian Way, in addition to serving as the principal road into Rome, also functioned as a vast cemetery littered with monuments to the dead. Nevertheless, nineteenth century writers' perceptions lay in this distinction between Greece and Rome as for the living and based upon the principles of philosophy, democracy and republicanism, and Egypt as extraordinary in the monumentality of its architecture within a landscape specifically designed for the glorification of the dead.

Thus, an almost literal transposition of this view onto the American cultural landscape witnessed Neoclassicism virtually dominate the construction of domestic and civic architecture. The application of neoclassical elements to public buildings, especially those associated with the political sphere, were virtually self-evident in their meaning. But such styles for home construction also had the capacity to speak symbolically of the republican civitas—that is, the citizenship status of the occupants within. By contrast, the Egyptian style became the hallmark for cemetery gates, public monuments in honor of military battles and war combatants, and private cemetery monuments, tombs and mausoleums erected by the professional middle and upper classes. These divisions were certainly not rigid—the neoclassical and Gothic Revivals became prominent within the cemetery landscape as well, while the Egyptian Revival infiltrated the land of the living in the form of railway stations, prisons, fraternal lodges, synagogues and suspension bridges.[30] As a general rule, however, the separations that many Americans made between Classical and Egyptian, the living and the dead, remained fairly consistent.

In establishing such a division of styles upon the cultural landscape, there was a strong predilection among architects and consumers alike in favor of what many considered the more refined designs derived from Greece and Rome. Added to this preference for Classicism in architecture was the central role given to the Roman Republic in particular in late eighteenth and nineteenth century political and civic culture. As architectural historian Talbot Hamlin explained in the 1940s, "The Roman citizen became the ideal of the perfect republican, the Roman tribune the great leader, the Roman general the ideal of all generals."[31] These associations in nineteenth century thinking have continued to be marked as critical to our understanding of the common appearance of Classicism in America. In more recent scholarship, historian Caroline Winterer has remarked, "Americans found a number of interlocking features in republican Rome congenial: the Senate as guarantor of liberty and stability; the ideal of the cultivated, virtuous Ciceronian orator; and agriculture as safeguard to civic virtue."[32] Without a doubt, in the process of establishing a heritage in which the civilizations from antiquity became the progenitors of American intellectual and political life, Greece and Rome enjoyed the highest degree of emulation.

However, despite such evident preference for transposing classical culture into American civic culture and the expanding urban industrial landscape, Egypt nonetheless possessed a peculiar degree of admiration among the educated elite. It also filled a significant hole in the creation of American national identity that Greece and Rome simply could not. A major component of the respect given to Egypt lay in what *The New Englander and Yale Review* described as its "parental relation to Grecian civilization."[33] Greece and Rome, and later, modern Europe and the United States, achieved heights of greatness, but only because of the precedent set by Egypt. As the *North American Review* argued in 1859, "[p]erhaps the true statement would then be, not that the Egyptians gave to Greece the Doric order, but that they taught the men of the Dorian civilization to build."[34] *Harper's* went even further by reinforcing the procreative role of Egypt to all of the West: "When Europe was a wilderness, when savage tribes roamed over the seven hills and the Acropolis, when perhaps a pigmy race inhabited the caves of Kent or Guienne, and the mammoth lingered in the German forests, twenty thousand cities are said to have adorned the valley of the Nile . . . while all the world was barbarous, sculptors, painters, architects, and engineers were urging on those wonderful works that indicate the grandeur of Egyptian thought."[35] In this reading, then, Egypt not only gave birth to western civilization, but was itself considered the point of genesis for all significant human social and cultural development.

As nineteenth century Americans became increasingly exposed to research and observations of the land of the pharaohs during the early years of the nineteenth century, the greater part of new scholarship and travelers' narratives focused on two aspects of Egyptian civilization: the Nile River, the "father of rivers," which "gave birth to a throng of cities whose enormous ruins still cast gigantic shadows over its swelling stream"[36]; and the preponderance of monumental architecture in such ancient cities as Luxor, Karnak, Thebes and Memphis, all of which exuded defiance to the ravages of time. Perhaps the most commonly invoked images of Egypt, the Nile and the monuments that stood upon its banks, helped to define most westerners' perception of the ancient land. Travel literature, both in serial publications and published as individual volumes, catered to an increasingly enthusiastic

American audience, which reveled in tales of the exotic and mysterious Near East. Those who visited Egypt typically traveled by way of riverboat up the Nile and as such, the river held a central place in their narratives. In an excerpt published in *The Living Age* from Englishwoman Eliza Cook's (1818–1889) travel journal from 1852, Cook commented, "We are on the Nile, floating along that majestic old stream, whose history reaches back into remotest antiquity—to Moses and the Patriarchs, and even beyond them, far beyond the known beginning of civilization . . . [t]he land is all solemn, still, and sad." Noting that much of the history of ancient Egypt still remained veiled in mystery, Cook went on to note the Sphinx upon the edge of the desert, a silent sentinel that "ever fails to unriddle the mysteries of the land, which seems to lie under the shadow of death, it is so solemnly still."[37] Such imagery—of the Nile as "majestic," bisecting a landscape dotted with remains that hearkened to "remotest antiquity" and summoning to the viewer thoughts of mystery and death—was relatively common.

The Great Sphinx and Pyramids at Giza were also among the principal features of the landscape described by travelers to Egypt, and it would seem that no visitor to these structures were immune to the sublime awe they inspired. Herman Melville (1819–1891), who visited Egypt as part of a grand excursion through the Mediterranean and the Holy Land in 1857, kept a detailed journal of his experiences. Of the Pyramids at Giza, he wrote, "Nothing in Nature gives such an idea of vastness. . . . A feeling of awe and terror came over me." Melville also wrote of the mystery and seeming permanence of the structures: "As long as earth endures some vestige will remain of the pyramids . . . [they are] something vast, indefinite, incomprehensible, awful."[38] Melville was not alone in expressing such sentiments. Commenting on his experience at seeing the Sphinx in person, Mark Twain (1835–1910) wrote in *Innocents Abroad* (1869), "The Sphynx [sic] is grand in its loneliness; it is imposing in its magnitude; it is impressive in the mystery that hangs over its story. And there is that in the overshadowing majesty of this eternal figure of stone, with its accusing memory of the deeds of all ages, which reveals to one something of what he shall feel when he shall stand at last in the awful presence of God."[39] Both Melville's and Twain's descriptions were representative of the mid-century romanticism that pervaded American art and literature, a central component of which was attraction to the sublimity and terror of both the natural world and the ancient works of mankind. Melville felt overwhelming awe for the pyramids, structures that he saw as timeless and permanent fixtures of the landscape. "Nought but earthquakes or geological revolution can obliterate them," he wrote.[40] For Twain, the Sphinx was sublime in its grandeur but also terrifying in that it recalled to the viewer the judgment that awaited man upon his death.

Grandeur, eternity, technological brilliance—these were qualities associated with Egypt that found almost inexhaustible repetition in the literature of the period. Some writers even granted anthropomorphic characteristics to Egyptian architecture, giving it a conscious knowledge of its own ability to defy time and as such, a certain degree of smug condescension toward successive civilizations and even nature itself. As *Scientific American* observed:

> The pyramids of Egypt look down in grim and solemn grandeur upon the architectural piles of the present age and seem to laugh at every effort to rival them, either in gloomy grandeur or enduring simplicity. It is indeed true, that the highest trophy of modern architectural genius will have mouldered in the dust, when in proud dignity the pyramids will still rear their lofty heads mocking the burning winds and the drifting sands of the arid desert.[41]

Not even the other great civilizations of antiquity, such as those within Mesopotamia, were safe from comparison. According to *Harper's*, "The banks of the Nile are a picture of the unknown past. Its ruins are the most magnificent of all the remains of antiquity. While Babylon and Nineveh have crumbled into dust, Thebes and Memphis still assert their pre-eminence, and the shores of the father of rivers are lined with a solemn array of gigantic palaces, temples, statues, and porticoes, the oldest of the works of man."[42] Indeed, the allure for Americans to apply the Egyptian architectural styles lay in these characteristics, in the hope that the associations of timelessness and solidity might, by their transference to a new landscape, convey the permanence of the new nation. As art historian Richard Carrott observed, "The civilization that was more ancient than Antiquity produced an architecture that seemed to last forever." This idea made the style attractive for use in the commemorative context, but it also "appealed to builders and engineers seeking a style to garb structures of the new technology [especially railroad stations and suspension bridges], to give a sense of security to the untried and yet-to-be-proven instruments of progress."[43]

There was certainly a desire within the United States to convey the future perpetuity of the young nation, but there was also a cognizance within the literature of the nineteenth century that the new United States existed in a landscape that was just as, if not more, antique than Egypt. Part of what informed writers' comparisons of the two lands lay in the prevailing notion of the importance of great rivers in the development of complex civilizations throughout human history. *Harper's* expressed the view in 1866 that "[o]f all the natural features of the earth none are more beautiful, more beneficent, more necessary, more important, than its navigable rivers." And just as many regarded the Nile as the "father of rivers," so too "our own noble stream [the Mississippi River] is called 'the Father of Waters'."[44] As early as the 1840s, writers noted the similarities in size, in the richness of the alluvial plains, and the roles that both the Nile and Mississippi played in promoting the development of bustling towns and cities.[45] By the 1860s, as *Putnam's Monthly* declared, "[n]o other rivers in the world are so frequently compared as the Nile and the Mississippi."[46] Such geographic comparisons were made even more explicit in the naming of cities along the Mississippi—for example, Memphis, Tennessee (founded 1819); Thebes, Illinois (founded 1846; incorporated 1899); Cairo, Illinois (founded 1858); and Karnak, Illinois (founded 1905).[47] Such unambiguous connections made between the two lands comprised an important element in establishing a concrete link between the United States and its ancient predecessor. The nations of Europe possessed no equivalent geographic features on the scale of either the Nile or the Mississippi, nor were their ventures in building and technology even remotely close to the scale of those exhibited by Egypt.

Even in such comparisons, however, there was a need to distinguish America from Egypt. The language employed in describing each of these water systems drew upon similar themes, particularly those associated with remotely ancient times. But in the verbal competition that appears to have developed by mid-century as to which river was more impressive, it was the intersection of imagery in reference to the antiquity of the landscape versus the advanced development of its inhabitants that appears to have been most common. For example, whereas a tourist along the Nile "floats dreamily along the river . . . past the pyramids, past the sites of ancient cities," the "gloomy surroundings" along the Mississippi, by contrast, "remind one of the pictures of those old chaotic times, when the earth first began to emerge from the sea."[48] In other words, the Nile and Egypt had the distinction of being old. The Mississippi and the North American continent, now inhabited by the most modern and advanced society, were prehistoric to the point of primordial, and therefore, somehow, more impressive.

Another element that drew writers' attention in distinguishing the two lands was the difference in climate; in particular, its deleterious effects on modern Arab Egyptians. "The climate is too delicious for man," wrote Eliza Cook. "It effeminates and corrupts; it has no bracing health in it, but only softens, enervates and melts." All of Egypt had remained the same for thousands of years, yet according to Cook, its people had "degenerated and decayed." By contrast, the "western man is a man of energy, character, and business capacities."[49] Thus, despite geographic similarities, the differences in climate could account, at least in part, for the vigorous and enterprising character of the westerner. In an environmental sense, Americans and their land possessed all of the natural benefits and none of the deficiencies as exhibited in the Nile region of Egypt.

Given such views on the effects of climate and ecology on societal development, the ancient Egyptians were therefore to be considered all the more impressive due to their achievements *in spite of* such a "delicious" and "luxuriant" climate. Yet, as with all of the civilizations from antiquity, they too eventually fell. Such differences, between the sensuous East and the industrial West, were most explicitly exhibited at the World's Columbian Exposition at Chicago in 1893. At the Fair, the White City represented the heights to which the United States had achieved superiority in virtually every realm of economic, cultural and technological innovation. By contrast, Cairo Street, situated on the Midway Plaisance—by all accounts the most popular attraction at the Exposition—contained within it every prevailing stereotype from the Arab Near East, including "donkey-drivers, Egyptian serving maids, dancing-girls, jugglers, merchants, women and children."[50] Daily processions, described as "distinctively Egyptian," provided "great amusement to visitors, as much by the comicalities of the participants as by their strange costumes."[51] For tourists to Chicago, the contrasts made between sensuous East and vigorous West for over half a century were manifest in the imported performers who made Cairo Street their home for the duration of the Fair. For the better part of the nineteenth century, writers had exalted the achievements wrought by the civilizations from antiquity and the means by which the United States would ascend to future glory. The Columbian Exposition was the physical manifestation of these written comparisons. The precedents from antiquity, displayed in the architectural forms within the White City—the Doric, Ionic and Corinthian orders as well as a great obelisk modeled on the Alexandrian Cleopatra's Needle located in Central Park—contrasted with the picturesque languor and simplicity as embodied in Cairo Street. In many ways, then, this duality represented at the Exposition was the culmination of nearly a century of comparisons that sought, in short, to make the United States not only look legitimate to outsiders as well as make its citizens feel comfortable in the notion of American superiority.

"THE MUMMY'S FOOT"

Despite the power that nineteenth century periodicals no doubt had on influencing the reading public's opinion of ancient Egypt and its relationship to the rise of the United States, the specter of Egypt was far more wide-ranging and extended particularly into the realms of American science and popular culture. Science and popular culture intermingled in many ways during the nineteenth century in various arenas, including museums, popular literature and public lectures. Travel literature and articles that made connections between the achievements of the ancients and the development of modern America combined with nineteenth century popular and consumer culture as well as the burgeoning discipline of Ethnology, regarded as a uniquely *American science.*[52] All of these elements contributed to the creation of a cultural atmosphere in which references to or images of Egypt became increasingly common by mid-century. With the infiltration of Egyptian themes into the daily lives and leisure activities of educated citizens, this process helped to reaffirm popular associations of ancient Egypt as technologically superior and culturally oriented toward caring for and commemoration of the dead. The broad acceptance of such ideas went hand-in-hand with the increasingly widespread use of the Egyptian style in the American funerary and commemorative context. Taken as a whole, the nineteenth century was a period of both popular and scholarly excitement for ancient Egypt, especially as it pertained to the discovery of the origins of civilization, the racial background of the pharaohs, and the fantastic—at times, unusual—physical remains, which tourists and scholars brought home for study or display in curio cabinets and private museums. At the center of this escalation in popular interest in Egypt lay a product that evoked nearly universal fascination—mummies.

From museum exhibitions to public unwrappings and as reanimated harbingers of curses or criticism of modern civilization, mummies became the objects of both scientific spectacle and entertainment. As early as the 1820s, mummies began to appear in American private and museum collections, as well as appearing in popular literature. During the 1840s and 1850s, as ethnology and race theory became familiar topics among American scholars, the mummified remains of ancient Egyptians became paramount to arguments about human origins and the birth of western civilization. Following the Civil War, the art and mummies of ancient Egypt remained critical components in discussions about the status of the newly freed slaves and the issue of universal male suffrage. Spectacle and science would often mingle, as a public lecture or series of lectures on Egypt would, on occasion, include mummy unwrappings, the purpose of which was both to educate and titillate audiences. However, while a popular phenomenon, such exhibitions in the United States were largely an aspect of elite entertainment. Working class Americans may very well have had the opportunity to view mummies on display at Charles Willson Peale's Museum of Natural History in Philadelphia (est. 1786) or in the collections of showman P.T. Barnum's Museum in Manhattan (1841–65), but like the Rural Cemetery Movement (see Chapter 2) and the Egyptian Revival in architecture, popular Egyptomania in nineteenth century America was, by and large, an expression of middle and upper class consumer culture. Access to such entertainments relied on the availability of discretionary income and leisure time.[53] It would not be until the twentieth century, with the advent of cinema and the development of a mass consumer culture, that Egyptomania—and especially Mummymania—would become a more universally enjoyed phenomenon in American popular culture.

Much of the original American interest in mummies may be attributed to the popularity of William Bullock's Egyptian Hall, also known as the London Museum, built in Piccadilly in 1812.[54] The architecture for the building was "the earliest consciously archaeological attempt in England to revive the Egyptian style, for it was specifically modeled on the Denon plates [from Vivant Denon's *Déscription de l'Égypte* (1809–25)]."[55] The design for the building was, at that point, unique, but what gave the Hall international fame was the opening on May 1, 1821 of an exhibition of "wax impressions, 182 life-size drawings, the 800 small ones, and 500 hieroglyphs from Seti I's tomb" that were the result of Italian strongman Giovanni Belzoni's adventures in Egypt from 1815–1819. Part of the exhibition included the public unrolling of one of the mummies Belzoni had uncovered during his explorations. Following the success of the Belzoni exhibit and mummy unwrapping in London, the unrolling or unwrapping of mummies became increasingly fashionable in Europe during the 1820s. These generally occurred as part of "social events—possibly the highlight of an at home, or the culmination of a dinner or supper party."[56]

Mummy parts—mostly appendages such as hands and feet—began to appear in America as early as 1767, when artist Benjamin West presented a mummified hand and arm to the Library Company of Philadelphia. There was a steady trickle of mummies and mummified parts imported to the United States during the first years of the nineteenth century, but these appear to have neither garnered much public interest nor been put on display. It would not be until the early 1820s when mummies began to appear in natural history and curiosity museums; for example, the Western Museum of Cincinnati at its dedication in 1820 claimed possession of a number of "Egyptian oddities" and in 1822, acquired the "head of an Egyptian mummy."[57] In 1823, "the good people of Boston" received an Egyptian mummy and its coffin from a merchant from Smyrna named van Lennep and it subsequently went on display in the operating room of the Massachusetts General Hospital. Then in 1826, two mummies "became part of the curiosities exhibited at Peale's Museum and Gallery of the Fine Arts in New York," later passing into the collections of P.T. Barnum.[58] The Niagara Falls Museum, first founded by Englishman Thomas Barnett in 1827 to display his private collection of curiosities, eventually became the home for five mummies in 1861 and four more acquired during the 1870s after the Great Fire destroyed the Woods Museum in Chicago.[59] Such museums were often the primary medium through which the paying public could see an Egyptian mummy in person. In this way, for a nominal fee, visitors could enjoy vicariously the treasures of Egypt without having to embark on a transatlantic voyage.

As the importation of mummies and mummy parts escalated during the 1820s, so too did the figure of the mummy become an object of increased scientific interest and popular speculation. Even with the hieroglyphic breakthroughs of Young and Champollion, most of ancient Egyptian history remained shrouded in mystery. Those in possession of mummies began unwrapping these antique personages almost as a means of uncovering the layers of history and knowledge that they might possess. The first such unwrapping occurred in New York in 1824—the mummy owned by Captain Larkin Lee was "opened and examined by Dr. [Samuel L.] Mitchell in the presence of a number of the [hospital] trustees, professors and students" and then subsequently put on display to the public for the admission fee of twenty five cents (half price for children).⁶⁰ However, beyond immediate observation of any given mummy's physical features, outer wrappings, embalming techniques, and decorations on the sarcophagus, any significant knowledge that could be gained from the mummies that were unwrapped remained based primarily on speculation. François Champollion did not publish his first work on hieroglyphic translation until 1829, and as the *North American Review* observed in 1831, that work had not yet been published in English, nor was it yet "in common occurrence in this country."⁶¹ It would still take decades for the public to develop a clear understanding of ancient Egyptian history as scholars necessarily had to become acquainted with the hieroglyphic language in order to systematically translate the inscriptions found on monuments, temples, tomb walls and papyrus rolls.

Without an accurate record of Egypt's past, the notion that its ancient dead held the keys to some lost or mystical knowledge made mummies increasingly attractive in the popular imagination of the period. The earliest novel that featured a mummy as the central character was *The Mummy! A Tale of the Twenty-Second Century*, written by twenty-year-old Englishwoman Jane Webb Loudon in 1827. The novel "combined the Gothic tradition with a speculative theme dealing with science, technology, and morality in the future," and like Mary Shelley's *Frankenstein* (1818), could be considered an early example of science fiction. The story involves the resuscitation of the title character, "the Mummy," in the twenty-second century, who finds that while the society of the future is technologically advanced, it has become morally deficient. The Mummy then proceeds to explore how civilization went wrong.⁶² Largely written as a cautionary tale, Loudon's novel differed from most mid-nineteenth century mummy stories, which drew more on humor or romantic sentimentality.

American readers were introduced to comical mummies with French writer Theophile Gautier's short story, "Le Pied de Momie" ("The Mummy's Foot," also known as "Princess Hermonthis"). In this tale from 1840, a young Frenchman purchases the foot of a mummy princess at a Paris antique shop.⁶³ He uses the foot as a paperweight, describing the effect as "charming, bizarre, romantic."⁶⁴ The young man then falls asleep in his chair and awakens to the sound of the footless princess hopping into his room to reclaim her appendage. As a gesture of gratitude for receiving her lost foot, the Princess Hermonthis whisks the young man to the halls of her ancestors, where he asks the pharaoh for her hand in marriage. The pharaoh scoffs at the man for not being nearly old enough and scorns modern society for lacking the skills necessary to achieve the eternal preservation of the body. Judged entirely unsuitable as a candidate for his daughter's hand in marriage, the young man, so chastened by the pharaoh, is sent back home. He awakens the next morning, believing all to be a dream, only to find the Princess's amulet on his desk in place of the foot.

Another such comedic tale was Englishman Albert Smith's "Mr. Grubbe's Night With Memnon," originally published in the London-based *The Illuminated Magazine* in 1843 and again later in *Putnam's New Monthly* in 1857. Similar to Gautier's "The Mummy's Foot," Smith used the same plot device of the main character falling asleep and then confronting the reanimated dead. In "Mr. Grubbe's Night With Memnon," however, Smith referenced the contemporary fad for mummy unwrappings. Attending one such event, Mr. Grubbe, "listened with intense attention to the remarks of the lecturer, and envied him the proud position he was for the time placed in, as the descriptive link between the present and the long-past epochs. But when the ceremony was finished . . . Mr. Grubbe found, upon reviewing the lecture, that our acquaintance with the ancient Egyptians extended just far enough to show that we knew nothing at all about them . . ."

The next day, Mr. Grubbe heads down to the docks with a friend, where he becomes inebriated on wine, and eventually he finds himself in the Egyptian wing of the British Museum. Having fallen asleep, Grubbe awakens just before midnight and witnesses all of the inhabitants of the Egyptian wing come alive and with music and dancing, enact "the orgies of Memnon." The following morning, he awakes again, believing all to have been real, and proceeds to draw upon his experience to write a great tome to enchant modern scholars. Noting such zeal, Grubbe's friends only hope that "he will be spared from Bedlam" and "on no account will he be induced to venture, with a [wine] tasting-order, to the Docks."[65] Drawing upon themes of mummies and antiquities, fiction writers like Gautier and Smith thus invoked the same kinds of themes associated with Egypt as appeared in other kinds of articles of the period—eternity, mystery, obscure knowledge and the monumentality of the architectural remains on the landscape.

American readers were acquainted with such stories by European authors, but Edgar Allan Poe's "Some Words With A Mummy," published in 1845 for *The American Whig Review*, was in all likelihood the most popular mummy story of the era. In considering the popularity of the theme of reanimated mummies, some have speculated that Poe drew inspiration for his short story from an anonymous piece entitled "Letter from a Revived Mummy," which was published in 1832 in the *New York Evening Mirror*.[66] Similar to the comedic trend established by Gautier and Smith, Poe's story functioned as a humorous jab directed toward the fad for mummy unwrappings and the attitude that many Americans had developed concerning the superiority of their own civilization—an attitude, no doubt, fueled by the preponderance of articles in *The American Whig Review*, *The United States Democratic Review* and *Harper's* extolling the social and political virtues of their nation. The story centers on an evening during which a number of scholars, including the famous amateur Egyptologist George Gliddon, gather together to unroll an Egyptian mummy. Upon identification of the hieroglyphics on the sarcophagus, George Gliddon identifies the individual as *Allamistakeo*. For the sake of scientific inquiry, the men decide to apply electric current to the mummy—a reanimational technique taken right out of Shelley's *Frankenstein*—which indeed results in the mummy returning to life. Conveniently, Gliddon is able to speak in ancient Egyptian with *Allamistakeo*, who turns out to be a Count, and he therefore acts as a translator for his colleagues.

Those present proceed to describe the achievements of American civilization, but with each modern marvel, the Count cites an equivalent or superior example from his own lifetime. When one of the gentlemen asks the Count whether Democracy was known to the ancient Egyptians, *Allamistakeo* responds:

> Thirteen Egyptian provinces determined all at once to be free, and so set a magnificent example to the rest of mankind. They assembled their wise men, and concocted the most ingenious constitution it is possible to conceive. For a while they managed remarkably well; only their habit of bragging was prodigious. The thing ended, however, in the consolidation of the thirteen states, with some fifteen or twenty others, into the most odious and insupportable despotism that ever was heard of upon the face of the earth.

Despite the obvious connections between this account and their own nation, the men seem oblivious to the similarities and frustrated in their attempts to prove the superiority of modern knowledge and technology. Following much irritation with the mummy's ability to respond to their inquiries, the host of the evening, a Doctor Ponnonner, asks the Count whether his civilization ever knew of "Ponnonner's lozenges, or Brandreth's pills." To this question, the mummy can only hang his head in shame. With Count *Allamistakeo* thus defeated, the narrator happily returns home to go to bed, secure in the knowledge that he lives in the most socially, intellectually and technologically advanced nation in the history of human civilization.[67]

Published for a largely middle class audience, "Some Words With A Mummy" effectively poked fun of the very people who had become enamored with the study of Egypt as well as the promotion of American society as the best in the world. Poe's tale exposed the haughtiness exhibited by many within the American educated classes and *Allamistakeo* functioned as the medium through which to show the limits of modern knowledge. American society was technologically advanced, to be sure, but snake oils like "Ponnonner's lozenges, or Brandreth's pills" were hardly proof of the kind of predominance over other societies that so many mid-century Americans claimed for the United States. Added to all of this was Poe's use of a real individual, George Gliddon (1809–1857), who by the 1840s was a noted celebrity-scholar in intellectual circles. A United States Consul to Egypt during the 1830s, Gliddon became one of the first Egyptological experts in America, albeit not formally trained. Upon his return to the United States, Gliddon delivered a series of lectures on ancient Egypt in cities around the country, including Portsmouth, Boston, New York, Brooklyn, Philadelphia, Baltimore, Charleston, Savannah, Richmond, Columbia, Augusta, Mobile, New Orleans, St. Louis, Cincinnati, Chilicothe, and Pittsburgh. In the "Introduction" to Gliddon's popular little volume, *Otia Aegyptiaca (Ancient Egypt)*, which he published in 1849 following his first lecture tour, the editor of the *Ethnological Journal* commented: "Had the publicity been confined to the mere audiences, the effect produced would have been partial and evanescent, but the detailed reports in the newspapers, spread a general knowledge of the subject over the whole community, and rendered the acquisition of the moment in a great degree permanent."[68] The popularity of the lectures spurred demand for Gliddon's book, which sold a remarkable twenty-four thousand copies at twenty-five cents apiece (around $7.25 today).[69]

Gliddon claimed an understanding of Egyptian hieroglyphics and of the history of the ancient Egyptians, and by the mid-1840s, his reputation as an authority on the subject was virtually undisputed. American audiences even relied upon his authority in matters related to the early settlement of the

Americas before Columbus. Following one lecture in Philadelphia in 1846, *Scientific American* reported that Gliddon "exhibited to his audience two earthen jars, one of which had been dug up from an ancient mound in our western country, and the other taken from an ancient tomb in Egypt. They were precisely of the same pattern." Such materials furnished by Gliddon thus confirmed to *Scientific American* "the long entertained opinion" that the ancient inhabitants of North America were not indigenous to the land, but rather had come from "the crews of some Roman or other fleet from the Mediterranean, which had been providentially driven on the Western coast of this continent."[70] However, such arguments, that the ancient mound builders were of Mediterranean descent, were not central to Gliddon's primary interests. Rather, Gliddon's principal focus, which in turn drew widespread interest in his lectures and book, was his analysis of mummified human remains as a means of determining the race of the ancient Egyptians. Linking craniological formation to intellectual abilities, Gliddon commented in *Otia Aegyptiaca* on the ruling class of ancient Egyptians: "Could a people gifted with such facial angles, elevation of forehead, smooth hair and aristocratic noses as these, fail to be great men and great women?" He further argued, "Was it in nature, or are anatomical laws so false, that a people with such physiognomical and osteological characteristics—a people whose mighty deeds are still erected in stone, and who are renowned beyond all others in sacred and profane history for their *wisdom*—should not possess a development of head and volume of brain commensurate with the grandeur of their works?"[71]

While published in 1849, Gliddon's prevailing ideas in *Otia Aegyptiaca* were already well known within scientific circles, as ethnological debates on race theory and the development of human civilizations had become highly contested topics by the beginning of the decade. In the works of Gliddon, together with those by Doctors Samuel George Morton (1799–1851) of Philadelphia, Josiah C. Nott (1804–1873) of Mobile and others, the osteological and craniological evidence gathered from the bodies of ancient Egyptian mummies proved critical to the development of their arguments concerning these issues.

Some of the major ethnological scholars of this era, such as Dr. Josiah Nott, a surgeon trained at the University of Pennsylvania but who called Mobile, Alabama home, were pro-slavery advocates. For men like Nott, one of the major goals in disproving the black African origins of the pharaohs was to justify the perpetual enslavement of African Americans in the United States. By the 1830s, there already existed an elaborate pro-slavery ideology that justified enslavement, in part due to the perceived intellectual inferiority of those of African descent. For most ethnologists, then, the significance of whether the pharaohs of Egypt were more African or "Mediterranean" lay in a number of areas; first, to refute the intellectual and physiological equality of those claiming African descent; and second, to justifiably proclaim ancient Egypt as the predecessor to the ascendance of white western civilization. As has already been established, the prevailing view among nineteenth century writers of Egypt's importance lay in its role as the originator of the elements of civilization which would later be developed by Greece and Rome, and finally, perfected by the United States. If the pharaohs had indeed been of Nubian or otherwise "black African" origins, all claims to the superiority of the Caucasian race and the assumed inferiority of African American slaves could crumble.

During the seventeenth and eighteenth centuries, most American slaveholders had looked to the Old Testament of the Bible—specifically the curse upon Ham and his descendants to be bound in perpetual servitude—as a legitimate means to justify the enslavement of Africans. By the mid-nineteenth century, however, many considered intellectual ability as the crucial element in determining man's equality with his fellow man; science increasingly trumped religion as a way to defend slavery, especially as slaveholders faced the escalating vehemence of the abolitionist movement. Therefore, craniological examinations were critical to the development of racial theories. Dr. Samuel George Morton published two of the earliest major works on the subject in the United States. These were *Crania Americana* (1839) and *Crania Aegyptiaca* (1844), in which he drew upon the measurements and features of different skulls to categorize the indigenous races of North America and ancient Egypt, respectively. In both works, Morton drew upon the assumption of ancient Egypt as the earliest western civilization, and commented in the *Crania Aegyptiaca*, "Egypt is justly regarded as the parent of civilization, the cradle of the arts, the land of mystery. Her monuments excite our wonder, and her history confounds chronology; and the very people who thronged her cities would be unknown to us, were it not for those vast sepulchers whence the dead have arisen, as it were, to bear witness for themselves and their country." In this description of ancient Egypt, Morton expressed sentiments that were already common and accepted as truth among the general public. However, where there was as yet no consensus of opinion regarding the ancient Egyptians, was over what race to which the pyramid-builders belonged. To this end, Morton lamented, "Yet even now, the physical characteristics of the ancient Egyptians are regarded with singular diversity of opinion by the learned, who variously refer them to the Jews, Arabs, Hindoos, Nubians, and Negroes."[72]

This general confusion over the racial heritage of the ruling class of ancient Egypt became a common theme for American ethnologists, since the issue at hand was from which race had the rest of western civilization derived its knowledge of the arts and technology. For Morton, as for others, the most critical point was to refute "that hypothesis which classes the ancient Egyptians with the Negro race," arguing, rather, that the upper classes of Egypt were, in fact, Caucasian.[73] The work that Morton published in order to make this argument was facilitated in large part by the efforts of George Gliddon. While visiting the United States sometime during the 1830s, Gliddon met with Morton and quickly became a follower of his ideas. Upon his return to Egypt in 1838, Gliddon conducted research on Morton's behalf, which resulted in the procurement of "one hundred and thirty-seven human crania, of which one hundred pertain to the ancient inhabitants of Egypt." Of these, Gliddon sent seventeen to Morton.[74] Assisted by what may only be presumed to be Gliddon's systematic grave-robbing activities, Morton's *Crania Aegyptiaca* established a precedent that would be followed by further ethnological researches through the 1860s.

Gliddon carried forth the arguments made by Morton in his *Otia Aegyptiaca* to elaborate upon the intellectual superiority possessed by the ruling classes of ancient Egyptian society, and educated Americans virtually took for granted his status as the American Egyptological authority *par excellence*. However, his reputation was nearly ruined in 1850 as the result of a widely advertised mummy unwrapping gone horribly wrong. After the publication of *Otia Aegyptiaca* in 1849, Gliddon continued his lecture activities, which included hieroglyphic translations and craniological examinations. Mohammad Ali-Pasha had placed a prohibition on the removal of antiquities from Egypt in 1835, so there had been far fewer mummy unwrappings, but also an increased demand in the United States for Egyptian artifacts.[75] During the spring of 1850, Gliddon therefore scheduled the public unrolling in Boston of the mummy of a "high priestess" from his personal collection. The advertisement published in *Scientific American* noted that Gliddon placed a value of $1,500 on the mummy and thus would conduct the unwrapping as part of a three-night lecture if he could get 300 subscriptions at five dollars apiece.[76] Each five-dollar subscriber would receive four tickets for each of the three lectures. Due to the exorbitant cost of admission, the lectures were considered one of the major cultural events of the year in Boston, as the article in *Scientific American* went on to say that a "larger number of our wealthy and influential citizens have already given their names to encourage this curious and interesting undertaking, and we cannot doubt that the requisite subscriptions will be obtained."[77] The list of attendees to the event read like a who's-who of the Boston Brahmin set and included poet Henry Wadsworth Longfellow, Harvard president Jared Sparks, anatomist Oliver Wendell Holmes, obstetrician Dr. Walter Channing, botanist, physician and founding member of Mount Auburn Cemetery, Dr. Jacob Bigelow, and naturalist Louis Agassiz, "who came on stage to inspect the linen mummy cloth."[78]

A month later, *Scientific American* published a follow-up article to what had been for Gliddon a disastrous and embarrassing event. In overly dramatic fashion, the article told readers:

> Well, our Boston scientific friends have paid the piper in the $5 ticket, to see Gliddon's mummy unrolled. It was a most wonderful mummy that—the virgin priestess of a great priest who dwelt in Egypt 1900 years before our blessed era. Well, it was worth $5 to see such a character revealed from amid her swaddling bands of linen and what not. How important was the subject, how intricate the wrappers!—more mysterious than a Boston one truly. Three days—yes, three long days were occupied in the unrolling process.

The article made certain to highlight the element of voyeuristic titillation for attendees, and perhaps even for Gliddon himself, as it continued:

> How eloquently Gliddon discoursed on the subject—the age, the glowing virgin beauty of the within, as she long, long ago used to sing by the banks of the Nile. We can imagine the interest that was excited in the countenances of that intelligent and select audience, as Gliddon approached the last wrapper, and exclaimed "Behold the hour is at hand!" There she was, the ancient maiden of the Delta, the long hid, the long desired to be gazed upon; but alas! for the changes of time upon the human race, she was a *man—yes, a man!* Some felt shockingly disappointed; but why should they? Perhaps it was no mistake at all. The sexes may now be misunderstood by

us. The Egyptian women may have been men. There was Semiramis and the old Amazons. That is surely some evidence to prove this assertion. We therefore think that Mr. Gliddon had no right to say, that a mistake happened in the mummy family.[79]

Gliddon, who had touted his knowledge of hieroglyphic translation, had blamed the mix-up of the sexes on the ancient sarcophagus-makers for their sloppy hieroglyphic painting. Faced with such immediate evidence of his failure to accurately characterize the mummy from his collection, this was recognized by both the audience and the press as a weak cover-up. Gliddon's mistake even became a thing of Boston legend, for even two years after the event, *Scientific American* returned once again to the subject when it stated, "Who can forget the mummy maid unrolled by Gliddon . . . who turned out to be a man?"[80] Despite Gliddon's intellectual *faux pas*, however, the incident remarkably did not ruin his career. Rather, he continued to give public lectures and mummy unwrappings around the country, and eventually met with his greatest success when he traveled South and, as historian Ann Fabian described, "into the camp of intellectual racists" led by Dr. Josiah Clark Nott.[81]

It was in 1854, in collaboration with Nott, that the two men published what would be considered the most comprehensive and influential work on human ethnology in the nineteenth century—the monumental *Types of Mankind; or, Ethnological Researches, Based upon the Ancient Monuments, Paintings, Sculptures, and Crania of Races, and upon their Natural, Geographical, Philological, and Biblical History*.[82] Structured largely around a discussion of ancient Egyptian art, monuments, and mummified remains as evidence, *Types of Mankind* explored the origins of the human races around the globe and promoted a polygenist theory for human diversity. This work was followed in 1857 by another joint publication by Nott and Gliddon, *Indigenous Races of the Earth; or, New Chapters of Ethnological Enquiry*. Again, the two men drew from Egyptian examples, specifically from the arts of Egypt to argue that based upon the visages represented in the "many statues and reliefs," the "Fellàh (peasant) of the present day" resembled "his ancestors of fifty centuries ago, viz: the builders of the pyramids, so closely, that his Nilotic pedigree never can be seriously questioned henceforward."[83] In other words, the arts from Egypt proved, according to Nott and Gliddon, that not only the ruling classes of Egypt, but even the laborers who constituted the workforce to build the pyramids, were the same race as the modern inhabitants of the Nile. Had the pyramid builders been black, so too would be the present population of the country. Further, it was the hope of these men that analysis of the arts and skeletal remains from ancient Egypt would prove the innate intellectual and physiological differences among the races of man. Pro-slavery advocates of the 1850s embraced the arguments made by such men as Morton, Gliddon and Nott, as unbiased scientific proof for the natural subjugation of African Americans in the slave South and they continued to embrace such theories until well after emancipation.[84]

Indeed, following the Civil War, ethnologists and race theorists began to focus on the emergence of a new problem—the intellectual abilities of African Americans to participate as free citizens in the postwar nation, more particularly with regard to the issue of universal male suffrage. In the years leading up to the passage of the 15th Amendment to the Constitution, this issue became an increasingly heated topic of public debate. *The Old Guard*, a periodical edited by northern pro-slavery advocate Chauncey Burr, ran an article in 1867 which asked directly, "what is he [the African American] *mentally—intellectually*? Does he stand on the same plane of the average white man, or fall below it?" Again, the art and mummified remains from ancient Egypt appeared as evidence toward determining the place of those of African descent within the social and political hierarchy of the nation. *The Old Guard* concluded that given the evidence from the arts of ancient Egypt and the craniological analyses conducted by Nott and Gliddon in *Types of Mankind*, "He almost totally lacks in executive ability, and has very little inventive genius," and that "he is incapable of education beyond the simplest rudiments."[85] In *The Natural History of the Human Races*, published in 1869, author John P. Jeffries of Ohio also looked to the works of ancient Egypt to prove the antiquity of racial distinctions: "The Red, White, Black, and Yellow races have been in existence, according to the Egyptian records, for at least 3,300 years. They are plainly represented upon the Egyptian monuments thus early in the world's history; and though it has not yet been fully ascertained, it is strongly conjectured that they have so existed for more than 5,000 years."[86] Like Nott and Gliddon, Jeffries promoted a polygenist history of creation, that the races of mankind had remained distinct and separate since antiquity, with the intellectual and physiological status of each having remained constant over time.

Jeffries further claimed that the depictions of the different races in Egyptian paintings "show most clearly that no radical change has taken place in either of them since they were thus represented" and that the "Egyptian mummies are as living witnesses of the types of mankind." The logic used here was that the "physical history of the races is not a work of chance; they advance in proportion to the degree of intellect." In other words, African "negroes" had been slaves to the ruling classes of Egypt just as they had been slaves in the American South, which meant there was an historic precedent for their subjugated status. Similar to *The Old Guard*, which asked "Who and What are the Negroes?," Jeffries also broached the status of the newly emancipated slaves and their capacity to learn. He asserted, "The comparison of skulls makes the Negro the inferior race; not so much in internal capacity as the character of the brain and its development." Whereas Caucasians had emerged "from barbarism" and become "the polished and refined superior," the "inferior races" by contrast, continued in "their degraded and barbarous condition" due to "want of intellect." Considering the right to suffrage in the United States, Jeffries concluded that "however degraded or refined his condition in life," the American system of government guaranteed the "natural right—[of] extending the elective franchise to all classes of American citizens without regard to color."[87] Albeit an advocate of the intellectual hierarchy of the races, Jeffries ultimately approached the new social and political status of African Americans lightly, and made no conclusions as to the potential success or failure of universal male suffrage. By the end of Reconstruction, the appearance and uses of Egyptian mummies and artifacts for scholarship and public entertainment again began to shift. Fewer ethnologists relied on mummified remains to prove the supposed hierarchy of the human races and the mummy once again became the province of museum displays and popular fiction.

The establishment during the 1870s of such major cultural institutions as the Boston Museum of Fine Arts and the Metropolitan Museum of Art in New York City brought collections of Egyptian mummies and antiquities out of the smaller natural history museums and curiosity cabinets and into the cultural and educational arena for citizens and tourists alike. Rather than being exhibited as ethnological oddities, mummies became an integral part of large-scale exhibitions that sought to recreate with some degree of archaeological verisimilitude the tombs and temples of ancient Egypt for throngs of visitors. This development, which began in the 1870s, escalated during the 1890s, a time when the field of Egyptology in the United States moved away from an avocation of amateur scholars and collectors to become a full-fledged professional discipline.[88] To promote the Boston Museum of Fine Art's "Egypt at Home" exhibit for its reopening in 1890, William C. Winslow touted the institution as "the crown jewel of the city's higher educational advantages," citing the superiority of the collections of Egyptian antiquities acquired by the museum since 1872. Winslow described the feeling of walking into the exhibit as akin to seeing the original monuments *in situ* and assured his readers "the mummies will not harm you; the funerary images are innocuous; the broken sarcophagus has no terrors."[89]

For Winslow, a visit to the Boston Museum could be a substitute for a trip to Egypt, but his last assurance was also revealing of another significant cultural transformation; that is, the transformation the Egyptian mummy had undergone in the public's imagination between the 1820s and the end of the century, a transition that had largely taken place in the realm of popular fiction. Whereas Poe's reanimated *Allamistakeo* had served as a humorous character intended to mock its audience, the reanimated mummy by the end of the century had become a figure of terror. The transition had its roots in the late 1860s, when mummy tales shifted from the humorous to the cautionary, in which curses doomed the main characters, but the mummy involved was generally not at fault. Such was the case in Jane G. Austin's "After Three Thousand Years," published in *Putnam's* in 1868. In this story, a young woman dies after wearing a poisoned scarabaeus necklace, which had been the cause of death three thousand years earlier for the mummy from whom the necklace was stolen.[90] This theme of terrible consequences for grave robbers in Egypt surfaced again in a short story by the more well-known author, Louisa May Alcott, entitled "Lost in a Pyramid, or The Mummy's Curse." Again, items are pilfered from the body of a mummy—this time in the form of two seeds—and the result is madness and death.[91] By the end of the century, the theme of the mummy's curse combined with reanimation in Sir Arthur Conan Doyle's "Lot No. 249," first published in 1890 and again in *Harper's* in 1892. This story features a brilliant yet unpopular college student who reanimates a mummy. The student then proceeds to use the creature to exact revenge upon his enemies at the university. Much like what Bram Stoker's *Dracula* (1897) did for the vampire, Conan Doyle's "Lot No. 249" established the image of the ancient mummy as a monstrous figure of terror that would continue to emerge within the horror genre until the present day.[92]

The appearance and use of the mummy therefore underwent massive transformations during the course of the nineteenth century—first exhibited as an object of spectacle and appearing as a figure of amusement in popular literature, it then became a tool through which the field of ethnology and popular race theory developed, and ultimately, by the fin-de-siècle, took on the dual identity of archaeological artifact and horrific monster. Even with such changes, the mummy of ancient Egypt played a persistent role in nineteenth century American cultural and intellectual life. In each realm in which the mummy appeared—the popular, the intellectual and the scientific—ancient Egypt infiltrated the everyday cultural environment and contributed to the shaping of American understanding of both the ancient past as well as contemporary western society.

EGYPTOMANIA TO EGYPTIAN REVIVAL

In the Preface to his book, *The Khedive's Egypt, or The Old House of Bondage Under New Masters*, author Edwin DeLeon conveyed what must have been, by 1878, a common sentiment. He wrote, "What can anybody have to tell us about the Nile-land that has not already been said or sung *ad nauseum?*"[93] Professional Egyptology in the United States had not yet been established, but the discoveries made by European-led expeditions, popular fiction tales, the dozens of travel narratives published as books and articles in magazines, the works published by American ethnologists and intellectuals, and the countless lectures, mummy unwrappings and museum exhibits that occurred throughout much of the nineteenth century made Egypt a significant aspect of American cultural life. More importantly, the insertion of ancient Egyptian themes and imagery into American culture along with comparisons between their respective benefits in geography and technology allowed for the establishment of a national and cultural identity with strong, tangible ties to the progenitor of western civilization. The nineteenth century taken as a whole was thus an era during which the citizens of the United States sought to develop a concrete, usable past with roots stretching back to the ancient world. The great trinity of Egypt, Greece and Rome, provided the necessary point of origin. The publication of articles that compared the various civilizations of antiquity with each other and with modern American society helped to reinforce prevailing attitudes that the United States already possessed the best elements of antiquity, as well as such modern institutions as democratic republicanism, to quickly ascend as the most advanced society in the history of mankind.

Additionally, within a few decades following the Napoleonic campaigns, Egypt itself had become a consumer commodity in the United States for those with time on their hands and money to spend. For those who enjoyed the pleasures of historical study or descriptions of exotic lands, each successive decade of the nineteenth century witnessed the publication of relevant books and articles about the land of the pharaohs with increasing volume. Attendance at a public lecture or museum exhibit could range from twenty-five cents to the exorbitant rate of five dollars in the case of Gliddon's 1850 mummy unwrapping, and it was therefore, as with the purchase of books or periodicals, a leisure activity that required the availability of discretionary income. In this respect, much of popular Egyptomania in America alienated the working classes until the twentieth century, when the development of a mass consumer culture and the advent of the film industry democratized Egypt for public consumption. Finally, Egyptomania in the United States provided a context, a backdrop, for the Egyptian Revival, which manifested in the American cultural landscape at the same time. However, whereas references to Egypt in print culture and the exhibition of mummies at museums and lectures in all likelihood remained hidden from most working class eyes—either due to prohibitive cost or the absence of spare time—the Egyptian Revival, as it appeared in lofty public war memorials, imposing cemetery gates and private family monuments, made available to the public view the physical manifestations of the role of Egypt in American cultural and national life. As such, the presence of such structures on the physical landscape lent a certain universality, or cultural consensus, to the messages they conveyed: specifically, the perpetuity of the nation and its people, the great wealth amassed by so many of its inhabitants, who were already becoming the beneficiaries of the emerging industrial capitalist economy, and the superiority of modern technological genius.

CHAPTER 2

"The Dead Shall Be Raised": Egyptianizing Trends in the Rural Cemetery Movement

ON SATURDAY, SEPTEMBER 26, 1831, the notable Judge Joseph Story (1779–1845) of Boston delivered the consecration address for the newly established Mount Auburn Cemetery in Cambridge, Massachusetts, to an audience of "thousands of sympathizing auditors."[1] In its design and function, the new "rural cemetery," as Mount Auburn and its successors would be called, was a revolutionary new cultural institution in the United States. Responding to a variety of developments in nineteenth century society— specifically, the forces of industrialization, urbanization, and the increasingly decrepit state of older and overcrowded burying grounds—the new rural cemetery reflected the sentiments of a people caught up in the at times chaotic nature of modernization and the pressures to appear like a polished society to the outside world. The older graveyards had become a point of public embarrassment for many of the major cities, and their condition led many among the educated classes to feel as though a people purported to be "civilized" ought to take better care of their dead. In his address at Mount Auburn, Story spoke "of feelings and associations common to all ages, and all generations of men" regarding the care and disposal of the dead. Such feelings, he exhorted, could be found "in the barrows, and cairns, and mounds of olden times, reared by the uninstructed affection of savage tribes; and, everywhere, the spots seem to have been selected with the same tender regard to the living and the dead; that the magnificence of nature might administer comfort to human sorrow, and incite human sympathy." As one example of this practice, Story cited the ancient Egyptians, who "gratified their pride and soothed their grief, by interring them in their Elysian fields, or embalming them in their vast catacombs, or enclosing them in their stupendous pyramids, the wonder of all succeeding ages."[2] In his further examination of the various civilizations from antiquity, each of which engaged in such reverential care for the dead by placing them in localities enhanced by the beauties of nature, Story asked his audience, "[w]hy should not Christians imitate such examples? They have far nobler motives to cultivate moral sentiments and sensibilities." And imitate they would. With these remarks, Story articulated the principles that would define this new cultural institution, the rural cemetery. Mount Auburn would be the model for a movement resulting in the establishment of numerous other cemeteries likewise conceived and based upon the common desire to return to historical precedents, to the reverential care for the dead suffused with "the sublime consolations of religion," all set within a picturesque landscape.[3] These would be the defining features of the cemetery landscape in particular, and commemorative culture more broadly construed, from the 1830s until the end of the century.

Intimately tied to the Rural Cemetery Movement were the parallel Egyptianizing trends that occurred in American funerary and memorialization practices, a process that became reinforced via repetition in three particular areas: 1) the design of the gateways for both new rural cemeteries and older burying grounds, 2) the private monuments erected for individuals and families within the boundaries of the cemetery landscape, and 3) the rhetoric employed in cemetery consecration addresses and cemetery guidebooks. Albeit these landscapes, monuments and texts were principally made and controlled by the professional middle class, the regular appearance of these forms over time and space reinforced the legitimacy of the Egyptian style as *the* primary influence in American commemorative culture; such repetition also effectively established a middle class hegemony over American taste and identity in the commemorative arena. Contemporary periodicals such as *The North American Review* and *The New Englander and Yale Review* also played an influential part in disseminating ideas about cemetery styles and the Egyptian Revival. Not only did they run articles that discussed ancient Egypt and offer parallels between it and the United States, they also served as the forum in which critics of art and architecture discussed the merits and deficiencies of the Egyptian and other revival styles in American architecture. It was in these texts, and even in the cemetery guidebooks, where it became evident that the Egyptian Revival was not without its severe critics. There were those who maintained that the style smacked too much of paganism and idolatry—and yet, even faced with vehement censure against its use, the same readers of these publications flew in the face of dissenters and chose to build monuments or design cemetery gates in that style. Together with changing funerary practices during the second half of the century, in particular the transition from the use of simple pine coffins to elaborate caskets and the post-Civil War acceptance of arterial embalming to preserve the dead, these trends signified the creation of what may be called an "Egypto-American" way of death.

"THE BEAUTIES OF NATURE"

Until the establishment of Mount Auburn Cemetery in 1831, Americans and their colonial ancestors had buried their dead in graveyards and churchyards, marking burials with simple headstone memorials of slate, granite, and sandstone. More elaborate church burials in subterranean family crypts remained the purview of the well-to-do. All of these practices were derived from the European burial traditions from which American colonists and their successors descended. Many families, owing to the relative isolation of many rural homesteads, created private burial plots on the perimeters of their properties and marked graves with a variety of markers, ranging from professionally carved headstones to unmarked fieldstones and wooden crosses. Many graveyards throughout the Northeast contained the remains of inhabitants from as early as the mid-seventeenth century, as well as a mixture of gravestones with iconographic styles marking each epoch of American habitation and religious outlook. These included the Colonial Era's Puritan-derived winged death's head, which symbolized man's mortality and the corporeality of the human body; the cherub or "soul effigy," made popular during the Great Awakening of the mid-eighteenth century, when the influence of evangelical pietism stressed the immortality of the human soul; and the urn and willow motif, which dominated graveyards during the years of the Early Republic, a period marked by an attraction to neoclassical themes in the material culture associated with mourning and commemoration.[4] By the first quarter of the nineteenth century, many of the older burial places had suffered the indignities of vandalism, removal and abandonment over the course of nearly two centuries of neglect and urban expansion. Added to this was the problem in many cities throughout the Northeast, especially Boston, Philadelphia and New York City, of what Boston physician, Dr. Jacob Bigelow, referred to as "gross abuses in the rites of sepulture."[5] Traditional burial sites had become far too crowded to accommodate an increasing population, and the deterioration of graveyards had become, in many peoples' eyes, a health hazard. Further, many considered such locations an eyesore on the landscape, and their lack of maintenance a sign of disrespect to the dead.

For a society trying to assert its credibility as a "civilized" nation, the state of Colonial Era burying grounds was also a point of embarrassment, an issue that needed to be rectified if the nation and its people hoped to be taken seriously by the rest of the world. After listing the manifold ways in which ancient, "savage" and "heathen" societies each treated their dead with the utmost care, Story asked his listeners

> Why should we deposit the remains of our friends in loathsome vaults, or beneath the gloomy crypts and cells of our churches, where the human foot is never heard. . . . Why should we measure out a narrow portion of our earth for our graveyards in the midst of our cities, and heap the dead upon each other with a cold, calculating parsimony, disturbing their ashes, and wounding the sensibilities of the living? [. . .] It is painful to reflect, that the Cemeteries of our cities, crowded on all sides by the overhanging habitations of the living, are walled in only to preserve them from violation. And that in our country towns they are left in a sad, neglected state, exposed to every sort of intrusion, with scarcely a tree to shelter their barrenness, or a shrub to spread a grateful shade over the new-made hillock.[6]

This sense of shame was also duly noted by Unitarian minister William Peabody (1799–1847), who delivered the consecration address a decade later at the opening in 1841 of Springfield Cemetery in Massachusetts: "In such places [older graveyards] every one feels ashamed of his race; every one feels that the living are unjust and unworthy. Why, the very dog, who has been faithful to his master, deserves a more honored grave."[7]

In a similar vein, *The North American Review* charged in that same year, "it is singular circumstance, and one not very creditable to modern times, that this sentiment of reverence towards the dead was most fully and elaborately manifested in the most remote periods, and in the rudest forms of society, while it has almost uniformly decayed with the progress of civilization."[8] Even after nearly two decades of cemetery reform, writers still despaired of how colonial graveyards served as reminders of the living's negligence in their care for the dead. In the guidebook for Green-Wood Cemetery in New York, published in 1847, author Nehemiah Cleaveland (1796–1877) bemoaned the constant, mocking presence of these relics of the American past: "Bear witness a thousand grave-yards, but too emblematic of decay and dissolution! Witness ten thousand tablets, once bearing the names and virtues of the lamented dead, and fondly reared to their "memory," now mossy, mouldering, inclined, or prostrate, puzzling the groping visiter [sic], and sometimes baffling even antiquarian patience!"[9] Reminders of an age not long past, there was no sense of permanence in these antiquated places of burial. The ongoing practice of churchyard or graveyard burial, even as Northeast towns and cities underwent rapid industrialization, signified a certain degree of carelessness toward the sanctity of the dead and, in this arena, a lack of social progress.

Nor were such places considered suitable for the living to visit and properly mourn the dearly departed. In the eyes of Cornelia Walter (1813–1898), editor of the *Boston Transcript* and author of *Mount Auburn Illustrated* (1847), these older burying grounds were places "of gloom, desertion, and sorrow, at the bare idea of which we shudder with horror and dismay."[10] Civic-minded professional middle class men therefore began in earnest by the 1820s, first in Boston and then elsewhere, to reform burial practices. This was done partly out of concern for the general health of urban citizens, but to a larger extent it derived from the impulse to establish within the modern landscape an unalterable and beautiful site that would indicate proper reverence for the dead, be aesthetically pleasing to visitors and, perhaps most critically, reflect well on American society at large.

Partly inspired by the grand Père-Lachaise Cemetery established in 1804 in Paris, similarly conceived to address the longstanding urban burial crisis, the Rural Cemetery Movement began in the United States with the establishment of Mount Auburn Cemetery in 1831 and continued throughout the country until the 1860s.[11] The rural cemetery itself became one of the principal middle class cultural institutions of nineteenth century America, akin to the later establishment of public libraries, museums and antiquarian societies.[12] Not simply created as abodes for the dead, the new cemeteries were also tourist destinations, designed with park-like features that included walking and carriage paths, which enabled visitors to explore the landscape and monuments at their leisure. Arguably the country's earliest public parks, Americans and Europeans alike visited these places just as they would any other cultural institution.[13] On the list of popular attractions for travelers to the United States, rural cemeteries were among the most frequently visited, so much so that Yale University President Theodore D. Woolsey (1801– 1889) observed in the *New Englander and Yale Review* in 1849: "Already not only the larger towns, as Boston, New York, and Philadelphia, but smaller ones, as Springfield and Worcester, and we know not how many others, have large areas in their neighborhood laid out for the mansions of the dead, where beauty of scenery, taste in landscape gardening, elegance and costliness of monuments awaken wide curiosity, so that the stranger who should not visit them would be regarded as having only half finished his sight-seeing."[14] Physically dominating the landscape of towns and cities throughout the Northeast and Midwest, with large architectural gateways and a profusion of monuments—from simple headstones to grandiose mausoleums—these landscapes tangibly reflected, to citizens and tourists alike, the middle class American impulse to establish cultural institutions that would exude both the legitimacy and perpetuity of their own society. In the efforts to establish landscapes that would reflect the ideals and values unique to American society, the rural cemetery likewise became the locus through which to express common middle class attitudes regarding space, religion and artistic taste.

For example, the term used to describe these institutions—"rural"— reflected the design of the landscape rather than their actual location. As higher concentrations of Americans poured into cities to live and work, the concept of the unblemished "natural" setting was one of the hallmarks of the era that also witnessed the blossoming of romanticism in poetry, literature and art. The great triumvirate of civilizations from antiquity—Egypt, Greece and Rome—often appeared in addresses and articles as particularly romantic and ideal models for emulation. Story noted of the Greeks that they "discouraged interments within the limits of their cities; and consigned their relics to shady groves, in the neighborhood of murmuring streams and mossy fountains . . . and called them, with the elegant expressiveness of their own beautiful language, CEMETERIES, or "Places of Repose."[15] The Reverend Pharcellus Church (1801–1886), who delivered the consecration address in 1838 at Mount Hope Cemetery in Rochester, described Egyptian places of burial in even more dramatic terms: "The common burying ground of the ancient Egyptians was situated beyond a beautiful sheet of water, over which the dead were ferried. And the cemetery itself was surrounded by trees and intersected by canals, to render it, as its name imported, a literal Elysium." Significant to Church's further description was the widely-shared belief that the ancient Egyptians were a people obsessed with their care for the dead, and while Americans certainly did not seek to model themselves so closely to that civilization, there was still inspiration to be derived from the results of such commemorative zeal. "Indeed, a provision for their dead occupied more of their attention than that of the living," exhorted Church, "and while every vestige of their abodes in life has yielded to the oblivious wave of time, their mausoleums, catacombs and massive pyramids still peer aloft in their primeval glory, showing the hoary marks of more than forty centuries."[16]

Even though many saw the Egyptians in particular as taking their devotion to the dead to the extreme, those who were involved in the emergence of the Rural Cemetery Movement saw the impulse to care for the dead and the attraction to natural settings as innate to the human spirit. As these authors argued, such natural feelings had been lost with the forces of modernization and urbanization, and the new cemetery proprietors sought to reignite those sentiments in the hearts of their fellow citizens. Jacob Bigelow aptly expressed this love of his country and of nature as having a direct effect on inspiring the creation of a new place of burial in *A History of the Cemetery of Mount Auburn*. For Bigelow, his patriotism "had long led me to desire the institution of a suburban cemetery," one where "the beauties of nature should, as far as possible, relieve from their repulsive features the tenements of the deceased; and in which, at the same time, some consolation to survivors might be sought in gratifying, as far as possible, the last social and kindred instincts of our nature."[17] The rural cemeteries were therefore, an urban—or, in Bigelow's terms, suburban—phenomenon; situated on the outskirts of cities or within the borders of rapidly industrializing towns, the new institution brought the idyllic elements of nature to an ever-expanding urban population—rolling hills, an abundance of plant life, trees, streams and ponds. As Story explained in his address at Mount Auburn, "while the cities of the living are subject to all the desolations and vicissitudes incident to human affairs, the cities of the dead enjoy an undisturbed repose, without even the shadow of change."[18]

This idea of the new cemetery as an escape from the urban environment became a common theme in consecration addresses. At Mount Hope Cemetery, Church opened his address with this very sentiment: "We have come to consecrate a home for the dead, in which they may rest secure from the encroachments of industry and avarice, till the last trumpet calls them to judgment." Not only would the new cemetery be an escape for the living to get away from the city "to enjoy an hour of sombre [sic] thought," but it would also be an escape for the dead as well. "Among these sequestered shades," Church continued, "the living tenants of our bustling city will soon find a repose which has been denied them amid the activities, the changes and conflicts of time's busy theatre."[19] As a refuge from the land of the living, one of the principal goals of the new rural cemeteries was to ensure that these picturesque landscapes would remain unchanging and sacrosanct, even as the outside built environment continued to expand and evolve.

Such attraction to natural settings coincided with a parallel development in middle class attitudes toward death and the fate of the soul. By the 1820s, religious attitudes throughout much of American society had rejected the older Calvinist doctrine of predestination and softened into a more sentimental, romanticized view of death. Of particular importance was the increasingly pervasive belief in the ongoing relationship maintained between friends and kindred even after death; that the living and the dead retained a tangible connection that would ultimately result in a heavenly reunion.[20] These developments necessitated the creation of an accompanying romantic and beautiful landscape that would suit such sentimentalism. The cemeteries would be, as expressed by Cornelia Walter, "an agreeable resting spot, to which we retire at the close of life, still to be visited, and gazed on, and cared for, by those we hold dear."[21] In his consecration address delivered in 1850 at Pittsfield Rural Cemetery in Massachusetts, the Reverend Henry Neill (1815–1879) reinforced this attitude by claiming that the very environment of the new cemetery would open the lines of spiritual communication between the living and the dead: "It is in some carefully adorned and guarded enclosure, or amidst some beautiful and extended landscape, where affection has reared the emblems of a better world, that sorrowing ones may expect to hear voices that others do not hear, strengthening them with might, and see hands that others do not see, pointing them to heaven."[22] No longer a place in which Death haunted the living as the proverbial "King of Terrors," the rural cemetery offered to the living an extension of the domestic sphere of the home, a place in which families torn apart by physical loss could be reunited spiritually. "Children in tender years will follow their parents to this place," wrote William Peabody, the "husband will follow the wife—the light and joy of his desolated home; and the wife the husband, on whose strong arm she had hoped to lean through all her days."[23]

Thus, early in the process of designing these new burial places, the desire to create a "natural" and unchanging landscape coincided with the developing attitudes toward death and the care for the dead. In the case of Mount Auburn, the model for future such ventures, the early plan to establish the cemetery in Cambridge was, in actuality, an effort undertaken by the newly established Massachusetts Horticultural Society (1829), with General Henry A.S. Dearborn (1783–1851) serving as president, aided by statesman Edward Everett (1794–1865) and Dr. Jacob Bigelow (1787–1879), who in addition to his status as a physician, was also a Harvard professor, botanist, and amateur architect. The relationship between the Horticultural Society and the cemetery dissolved in 1835 following a legislative act of incorporation, which gave control of the cemetery over to the proprietors, the new Mount Auburn Cemetery Association.[24] Led by Judge Joseph Story as its first president from 1835 until his death in 1845 and subsequently by Jacob Bigelow for over twenty years, this association nevertheless carried forth with the idea that the new cemetery landscape would be a rural retreat for the living as well as a peaceful and well-maintained respite for the dead.

Bigelow in particular proved to be one of the most influential individuals in the Rural Cemetery Movement and, more broadly, in American commemorative culture. A true renaissance man of the nineteenth century, Bigelow not only proposed the concept for the cemetery and worked with Dearborn to conceive the layout of the grounds, he also designed the Egyptian Revival gateway (1832 in wood; reconstructed in granite, 1843); the Gothic chapel (1846; reconstructed 1853–58); the Norman round tower dedicated to George Washington (1852); and the monumental *Sphinx* (1872) in commemoration of the Union dead of the Civil War (see Chapter 4).[25] Once established, Mount Auburn Cemetery became the template by which cemetery associations throughout the Northeast and Midwest modeled their own new abodes for the dead, often with the intention of outdoing the original in terms of both size and splendor.

CLASS AND THE CEMETERY

In Story's consecration address, he expounded upon the variety of those whose social and economic differences in life would no longer hold sway in the confines of Mount Auburn: "[t]he rich and the poor, the gay and the wretched, the favorites of thousands, and the forsaken of the world, the stranger in his solitary grave, and the patriarch surrounded by the kindred of a long lineage!"[26] Edward Everett, in his address entitled "The Proposed Rural Cemetery," printed in 1832 for the Boston Horticultural Society, reinforced such ideas of egalitarianism among the dead. The new cemetery, being "removed from all the discordant scenes of life," would offer to every person, "at an expense considerably less of that of a common tomb, or a vault beneath a church," the opportunity to "deposit the mortal remains of his friends, and to provide a place of burial for himself, which, while living, he may contemplate without dread or disgust."[27] This kind of rhetoric from Story and Everett reflected the prevailing values of the Jacksonian "Era of the Common Man" within the context of burial reform by making interment inexpensive and thus available to the public at large. Such values manifested quickly after the opening of Mount Auburn, when in addition to members of the professional classes—doctors, lawyers, professors, publishers and merchants—"a number of craftsmen and artisans, including carpenters, engravers, and sailmakers, purchased family lots."[28]

As like-minded groups of citizens continued to establish rural cemeteries through the middle decades of the century, rhetoric concerning a belief in equality among the dead remained strong. In the 1848 consecration address for the establishment of Forest Hills Cemetery in Roxbury, Massachusetts, the Reverend George Putnam (1807–1878) exhorted to his listeners, "[i]t belongs to the dead. We yield it up this day to them . . . [l]et ambition enter here only to be chastened and elevated; and love only to be refined and sanctified; and worldliness only to be rebuked and softened."[29] Such idealistic language about the collective equality of Americans was true to the atmosphere of the "Era of the Common Man," but it also, as historian David Sloane has observed, masked "the erosion of economic equality," which the forces of industrialization and urbanization had wrought.[30] The reality of these new landscapes revealed that the new cities of the dead mirrored the cities of the living and that even death would not obliterate one's economic and social identity.[31] The new cemeteries were certainly established in the egalitarian spirit of the age, but they ultimately reflected the values of their proprietors, members of the cultural elite who sought to wrest control of the canon of symbols that contributed to the development of American national identity. As expressions of emerging middle class hegemony, the architecture, landscape and monuments that defined the rural cemeteries were all designed according to bourgeois notions of taste, refinement and decorum and the hope that such qualities might spread through the lower reaches of society.[32] As noted in the *Guide to Laurel Hill Cemetery* (1847), "In promoting *taste* and *order, security* and *permanency* and rural ornament in our graveyards, we do but follow the impulse transmitted from the wisest and most remote antiquity; an impulse improved and refined by its exercise, and rewarded by *its good influence on the public mind* [emphasis added]."[33]

Despite the relative lack of expense for an individual grave, it was soon the larger family plots with their accompanying grand monuments that would dominate and define the new cemetery landscape.[34] Nineteenth century mourning practices entailed the proliferation of a consumer culture dependent upon a certain degree of wealth, so the cemetery landscape and the monuments contained therein quickly began to reflect the consumption habits of the urban bourgeoisie, whereas the more uniform slate headstones of the colonial era had conveyed a greater uniformity of status among the dead. Part of this trend had to do with the development of gravestone carving technology. Whereas during the eighteenth century, most gravestones were fashioned from slate or sandstone and were restricted in size due to the absence of advanced stone quarrying and cutting technologies, by the mid-nineteenth century, individuals could commission marble and granite monuments incorporating vast height, bulk and/or complexity. During the seventeenth and eighteenth centuries, the difference between a professionally carved headstone and an unmarked fieldstone was overall less dramatic than the differences between the eclectic tombs, mausoleums, obelisks, shafts and statues for the wealthy and the modest headstones for the working classes of subsequent generations.[35]

The proliferation of cemetery guidebooks, which identified for visitors the monuments of the wealthy and the famous, further eroded the democratic inclinations of these institutions in favor of a cultural identity as defined by the aesthetic tastes of the urban Brahmin class. Guidebooks, as well as mass-produced lithographs featuring cemetery gateways and significant monuments, made for a visual inventory of symbols that defined the rural cemetery and its meaning for outsiders. The gateways in particular, as crucial elements to the design of the cemeteries, were often the most reproduced and therefore most recognizable images associated with these landscapes. The stylistic choices therefore reflected the intentions of their designers in how they desired the cemetery's landscape to be interpreted. Rural cemeteries throughout the Northeast established the earliest precedent by incorporating large gateways as the most dominant outward feature of the landscape and these were built primarily in the Egyptian, Greek and Gothic styles. In the early years of the Rural Cemetery Movement, the first and most influential style to emerge was the Egyptian.

"THEN SHALL THE DUST RETURN"

The carriage gateway at Mount Auburn Cemetery was not the first large scale expression of the Egyptian Revival in American architecture, but it was in all likelihood the most influential. The earliest examples of Egyptian forms in American commemorative art, particularly the obelisk, began to appear in the 1790s as part of the French-inspired neoclassical aesthetic. Images of obelisks or small pyramids atop a pedestal appeared in addition to the popular urn and willow motif on slate headstones, at times with the obelisk or pyramid substituting for the urn image. The French consul in Baltimore erected the first obelisk in the United States in 1792 to commemorate Christopher Columbus's voyage to the western hemisphere three centuries earlier (figure 1).[36] The reasons for the consul's choice remain obscure, but were in all likelihood the result of inspiration from contemporary European garden architecture, which had regularly incorporated eclectic styles derived from antiquity since the 1720s and 1730s.[37]

The French architect and émigré to the United States, Maximilian Godefroy (1765–c. 1840), first introduced the Egyptian Revival in America as a distinct architectural style separate from the neoclassical. Exiled from Paris in 1805, Godefroy had witnessed the establishment of Père-Lachaise Cemetery and drew his design inspiration primarily from French architecture and theory, including the Egyptian Revival as it manifested in Paris, a result of the Napoleonic campaigns in Egypt. Between 1812 and 1815, Godefroy planned and executed the Egyptian Revival carriage gate to Baltimore's Westminster Cemetery, at that time the churchyard for the First Presbyterian Church. During approximately the same period of time, Godefroy also designed the five largest and oldest burial vaults in the cemetery: a pyramid on

FIGURE 1   Christopher Columbus Monument, Baltimore, Maryland, 1792.
(Photograph by Melvin Mason)

FIGURE 2   Henry Griffiths, Baltimore Battle Monument, engraving, 1838.
(Library of Congress)

a high square base modeled on that of Caius Cestius in Rome (18–12 BC); a square mausoleum with three columns and two doors along the front; and three rectangular mausoleums with single doors. Godefroy employed the common Egyptian architectural elements of battered, or canted, walls and cavetto cornice on all of the structures with the obvious exception of the pyramid.[38] The architect also ventured into public memorial architecture with the execution of the blended Egyptian-Classical Revival Baltimore Battle Monument (1815–1825). A rounded column rises from the base of the monument, which consists of an Egyptian Revival mastaba, with cavetto cornice and winged orbs on each of the four sides. A marble statue of the allegorical Fame stands atop the column, with griffins at her feet. Griffins also appear at the four corners where the column meets the base (figure 2).

Another major example of Egyptian Revival commemorative architecture completed before the establishment of Mount Auburn Cemetery was the Groton Monument (1826–1830), a monumental obelisk dedicated to the Battle at Groton Heights in 1781 in Groton, Connecticut. The unfinished Bunker Hill Monument (1825–1842) located in Charlestown,

Massachusetts, was also projected to be a towering obelisk (see Chapter 3). These monumental obelisks, as well as the designs executed by Godefroy in Baltimore, achieved both local and national recognition. However, without diminishing the importance of these structures in the history of the Egyptian Revival in the United States, it was nevertheless the gateway at Mount Auburn, which achieved the most toward transforming the Egyptian style from a minor offshoot of Neoclassicism into a major revival in its own right, with its own associations that became meaningful to American commemorative practices.

Designed by Jacob Bigelow, the Mount Auburn gateway functioned as the public face of the commemorative landscape, which at the time of its construction could be seen from a distance since the cemetery was situated on the outskirts of the urban environment. This is not the case today, as the built environment now surrounds the cemetery on all sides. The towering portal, located on the busy Mount Auburn Street, appears cramped in the twenty-first century environment and far more anachronistic and puzzling to visitors than when it was first built. However, at the time of its construction, with its visibility on the landscape, along with the proliferation of mass-produced lithographs, postcards, stereoviews and other reproductions, the gateway became the primary image associated with the cemetery and the Egyptian style became further associated with the place of burial within. The gateway also served as the physical barrier between the lands of the living and of the dead, standing in a liminal zone between the two worlds and conveying to passersby the intended perpetuity of both the "natural" setting as well as the private monuments contained within its borders.

Part of the long-term significance of the Mount Auburn gateway may be attributed to the influence of Bigelow, who stood out among the Boston Brahmin not only as a professor at Harvard University, but also as a civic leader who actively provided his services to various cultural institutions and committees, including the design committee for the Bunker Hill Monument (figure 3). A man of many talents, Bigelow was prominent among the educated elite of Boston society as an authority on subjects ranging from medicine to botany to architecture and the "useful arts" (technology). The *Proceedings of the Bunker Hill Monument Association* (1879) described Bigelow posthumously as "eminent in every branch of his profession, and a man of great scientific attainments outside of his usual sphere of life."[39]

FIGURE 3   Bust of Jacob Bigelow, frontispiece to *Memoir of Jacob Bigelow* by George E. Ellis, 1879.

Widely considered a figure of significant cultural authority, Bigelow's choice of the Egyptian over every other style—particularly the more popular Greek Revival—for the cemetery's gateway therefore indicated a conscious assessment on his part concerning what this style would convey to the public as well as its possible future ramifications for American taste. Bigelow clearly articulated in his Harvard lectures that he held the arts and technology of the ancient Egyptians in especially high esteem. In his published lectures, *Elements of Technology* (1829), Bigelow specifically praised their skill as architects and referred to the Egyptian style of building as "more massive and substantial than any which has succeeded it."[40]

In another set of published lectures entitled *The Useful Arts* (1840), Bigelow explicitly defined the superiority of Egyptian architecture over that of either the Greeks or Romans, arguing "[m]any of the other structures of antiquity now extant owe their preservation to accident; those of Egypt have the principle of their preservation within themselves."[41] In other words, more than any other civilization from antiquity, the Egyptians successfully built their monuments to last. *The North American Review* echoed this sentiment: "The *early* Egyptians built neither for beauty nor for use, but for eternity."[42] Generally speaking, the prevalent associations attributed to ancient Egyptian architecture were those that involved a sense of permanence—timelessness, solidity, and massiveness. Such qualities as beauty and grace were reserved primarily for the Greek style, which found greater expression in the architecture associated with the living. Therefore, in designing a new burial landscape intended to stand the test of time, one that would serve, literally, as an *eternal* resting place for its inhabitants, associations with permanence trumped beauty with Bigelow's adoption of the Egyptian style.

Measuring twenty-five feet in height and sixty feet wide, Bigelow's gateway was unlike any ever conceived for an American burial ground. Describing his design in *A History of the cemetery of Mount Auburn*, Bigelow explained that the gateway was in "the Egyptian style" and that the "piers or posts are four feet square, the entrance ten feet wide, and the greatest length of the cornice twenty-four feet. Two obelisks are connected with the two lodges by a curved, iron fence." Regarding its decorative elements, Bigelow further noted, "The banded cylinder, the foliage of the cornice, and the winged globe, are Egyptian. On the latter a lotus flower is turned over, so as to conceal the head of the fabulous animal [serpent] with which the ancient examples are usually defaced." Originally constructed in 1832 from wood and painted to resemble stone, it was later reconstructed in 1843 in more durable granite (figure 4). As to the direct inspiration for his gateway, Bigelow noted that it was "mostly taken from some of the best examples in Dendereh and Karnac." Similar to the pyramids, the temples located at these ancient sites gained popular distinction from the publication of Denon's *Description de l'Égypte* (1809–1825) for their solidly constructed columns, lofty obelisks, impressive gates and enormous pylons (figure 5).

Part of what set the Mount Auburn gateway apart, then, was that it was not only the first Egyptian-style portal to be built in the United States, it also represented one of the first attempts to achieve archaeological

FIGURE 4   Principal entrance to Mount Auburn Cemetery, lithograph, c. 1849.
(*Courtesy of Mount Auburn Historical Collections*)

verisimilitude in Egyptian Revival architecture. Bigelow hoped that the similarity in design and the quality of construction would "entitle it to a stability of a thousand years."[43] Bigelow's intent was clear: the structure itself, as well as the landscape beyond, would remain unchanging and inviolate. As the partition between the lands of the living and the dead, the Egyptian gateway embodied the same qualities of timelessness often associated with the original structures along the Nile, and it was thus infused with assurances to the public that the bodies of the deceased—particularly those of the modern, urban industrial pharaohs—and *their* monuments would last forever.

Nineteenth century commentators helped to reinforce the associations Bigelow explicitly attributed to Egyptian architecture. Most texts tended to use similar language to describe the monuments of ancient Egypt and this helped to reinforce popular associations between the architecture of the ancient Egyptians and an almost zealous care for the dead, as well as such notions as perpetuity implied by its use. Louisa Caroline Tuthill (1798–1879), whose *History of Architecture* (1848) was one of the first comprehensive works of its kind published in the United States, observed that the "character of Egyptian Architecture is grave and sublime," and that the "straight lines and angles, unbroken by a single curve, give to the outline of all their structures a heavy, massive appearance."[44] In this manner, Tuthill evoked the literary sense of sublimity that romantic era Americans sought to find in their own

FIGURE 5   Portal at Karnak Temple, Egypt. *(Photograph by the author)*

picturesque landscapes of the dead. She also utilized what were perhaps two of the more commonly employed descriptive terms for the style—"heavy" and "massive." In R.A. Smith's *Illustrated Guide to and through Laurel Hill Cemetery* (1852), the author used similarly-conceived descriptive language: "Egypt surpasses all other nations, either ancient or modern, in the magnificence and grandeur of her monuments and tombs" and of Egyptian architecture, "little remains but tombs and temples."[45] For the *North American Review*, the Egyptian stood out as the "earliest known, and yet the best, building in the world."[46]

In these ways, writers helped to popularize the notion that the architecture of the ancient Egyptians was superior in quality, if not in elegance, to all subsequent civilizations. Since most extant examples of Egyptian architecture known to mid-century westerners were associated with tombs and temple complexes, the Egyptian style itself possessed intimate associations with funerary and commemorative practices. It therefore seemed only natural that Americans would employ the style for structures that would suggest to on-lookers that technological progress and perpetual care for the dead could go hand-in-hand. In *Elements of Technology*, Bigelow reinforced this idea and criticized the relative flimsiness of modern architecture. He commented that whereas the edifices of the ancients "have stood for thousands of years," those from the modern era "abound in the means of making their present tenants comfortable, but are often built too cheaply to be durable."[47] However important it may have been to improve building technologies in American homes, it was of even greater concern to ensure that public structures, especially the newly designed cemeteries, would last for ages to come as most of their colonial predecessors had not.

However, as much as Bigelow sought to achieve a sense of archaeological verisimilitude in his emulation of Egyptian architectural genius, he nevertheless catered to the Christian sensibilities of his fellow citizens by making a number of strategic alterations in the design of the cemetery's central portal. First, he altered the sculpture on the top of the gateway, replacing what on the original examples from Egypt were cobra heads—the "fabulous animal" as he described it—on either side of the winged orb with drooping lotus flowers (figure 6).[48] The figure of the winged orb, or sun-disk, was one of the primary stylistic ornaments from ancient Egyptian architecture, and was almost universally incorporated in American reproductions from the 1810s through the twentieth century, including cemetery entrances, private family monuments, prisons and corrections houses, the Medical College of Virginia (1845) in Richmond, synagogues, Odd Fellows halls, and Masonic temples (figure 7). The symbol bore unequivocal associations with Egypt.

The mid-nineteenth century understanding of the winged orb was aptly expressed in George Gliddon's *Otia Aegyptiaca*. As Gliddon explained in a footnote, "it was a species of *heraldic arms*, the universal *symbol* of their *country*: by which, in the literal Hebrew text, the Prophet apostrophizes *Egypt*; (Isaiah, xviii., 1,) in the sentence 'Ho! Land of the *winged* (Globe!)'."[49] The incorporation of the winged globe or orb—with or without the traditional *uraei* (cobra heads)—often thus made Egyptian Revival architecture *explicitly* Egyptian in character if other structural elements of the monument or building were comparatively subtle.

FIGURE 6   Detail of entrance to Mount Auburn Cemetery. *(Library of Congress)*

FIGURE 7   Medical College of Virginia, Richmond, 1845. *(Library of Congress)*

In addition to this stylistic alteration, Bigelow added the following inscription from Ecclesiastes to the top of the gateway:

THEN SHALL THE DUST RETURN

TO THE EARTH AS IT WAS

AND THE SPIRIT SHALL RETURN

UNTO GOD WHO GAVE IT

In this manner, Bigelow sought to reduce whatever associations with paganism that might have been attached to his design. The use of a biblical inscription signaled to visitors that the landscape within was a space specifically devoted to Christian burial. Like so many of his contemporaries, Bigelow considered ancient Egypt a civilization obsessed with its care for the dead, at the same time having possessed the technology to produce the most superior architecture the world had ever witnessed. Albeit a Unitarian in faith, Bigelow nevertheless possessed a strong interest in the symbolic value to the United States of the products of non-Christian societies. Therefore, in his reconfiguration of ancient symbols and the addition of biblical text, he restructured the style for a Protestant American aesthetic—the gate was not purely Egyptian, but rather, "Egypto-American." It was in this manner that following the construction of the gateway at Mount Auburn, many other Americans followed Bigelow's lead and subsequently adopted and remade the style so that it was indelibly their own, suiting their specific symbolic and cultural needs.

"THE DEAD SHALL BE RAISED"

The cultural impact of the gateway at Mount Auburn Cemetery was almost immediate and in the decades that followed its construction, private citizens erected Egyptian-styled monuments of their own—obelisks, pyramids, portals and mastaba-styled side-hill tombs –, while rural cemetery planners and committees for the revitalization of older surviving burial grounds began to execute architectural plans for Egyptian Revival gateways.[50] That committees chose Egyptian designs for colonial era burying grounds seems particularly significant, for while they were no longer considered suitable places for the burial of the dead, the construction of Egyptian Revival stone entrances implied their historical significance as part of America's cultural heritage. Like the new rural cemeteries, these older burying grounds would become, by the construction of new entrances and greater efforts to protect the pre-existing graves and markers, sacrosanct in the centuries to come, preserved as relics of the nation's past.

Reactions to the popular adoption of the Egyptian Revival for cemetery entrances and private memorials varied from admiration to outright disgust, including repudiation of its use in Christian places of burial as evocative of "a monstrous system of idolatry."[51] Critiques of the widespread appearance of the Egyptian Revival, both positive and negative, appeared in architectural texts, major periodicals and cemetery guidebooks. These sources served as repositories of advice on issues concerning taste and propriety, and were purchased and read by the same educated elite who employed the Egyptian and other revival styles for their own family monuments. Yet despite the variability of reactions to the style in print media, the importance of the Egyptian Revival in cemetery planning lay in its continued usage through the middle decades of the nineteenth century. Committees and individuals no doubt read the manifold commentaries that writers enthusiastically offered and, despite what at times was vehement opposition to the Egyptian Revival, they chose for themselves—often, in favor of the Egyptian over other less controversial styles.

While reactions to the use of the Egyptian Revival in American cemeteries varied over time and space, the most immediate responses to Bigelow's gateway at Mount Auburn appear to have been largely positive. The *Picturesque Pocket Companion and Visitor's Guide Through Mount Auburn*, published in 1839, noted that the design had "met with general favor."[52] Two years later, the *North American Review* gave enthusiastic praise for the structure, remarking that "[t]he gate is a chaste and beautiful specimen of Egyptian architecture . . . it is remarkable for its originality of conception, massiveness, simplicity, and boldness of outline; and, derived as it is from a land which is emphatically a monumental one, and one that may be regarded now as little else than one vast cemetery, it cannot be considered as out of keeping with associations of a place of burial."[53] The article noted those qualities most associated with Egyptian architecture—"massiveness, simplicity, and boldness of outline"—albeit in the context of describing Bigelow's gateway. The connection between this structure and those that had already stood for thousands of years was not lost on visitors to Mount Auburn, many of whom would eventually erect their own private temples and obelisks.

Indeed, it was not long after the cemetery began offering lots for sale that the citizens of Boston began erecting monuments that revealed the great variety of memorials then available from monument companies and stonecutters. Nathaniel Dearborn, in his *Concise History of, and Guide Through Mount Auburn* (1843) provided readers with a sense of the eclecticism they would encounter within the cemetery's landscape: "hill and glen salute the eye at almost every stopping point, and the ever varying forms of mausoleums, temples, and obelisks, from the most splendid production of sculpturing art, to the neat and simple pyramid, claim attention in every direction."[54] Egyptian temples and obelisks mingled with Doric and Corinthian columns, Roman sarcophagi, Gothic spires, open Bibles, sculptured angels and other allegorical figures, in addition to a cornucopia of simple marble headstones carved with images of hands, flowers, wreathes, or nothing beyond a simple inscription in remembrance of the deceased. Diverse in size and style, the monuments that filled Mount Auburn and other rural cemeteries of the period represented every socio-economic status, age and gender, not to mention every conceivable aesthetic taste and budget.[55]

Faced with such eclecticism within the new cemeteries, articles written in periodicals such as *The New England Magazine* encouraged proprietors to retain a sense of "the intrinsic dictates of good taste and reason" when choosing a monument design. It went on to explain,

> *Variety* there must be, in these things, and ought to be; for the ornaments set up here, are but types and expressions of the variety in human feeling and affliction, now taking the form of hope and aspiration, now breaking forth in passionate expression, that cannot rise from under the weight of grief, and, sometimes, in fantastic conceits of sorrow, mingling images and thoughts that even verge upon the grotesque. But, in considering this subject, though there are, doubtless, in the sepulchral, as well as all other arts of decoration, certain principles of taste to be violated or to be followed, yet we have need, before we condemn, to cultivate a catholic and tolerant spirit.[56]

While this author, known only as "G.T.C.," encouraged a universal appreciation for the variety of styles—that is, as long as they were executed tastefully—others, such as architect James Gallier, whose essay on American architecture appeared in an 1836 issue of the *North American Review*, praised and encouraged the appropriation of only specific designs. For Gallier, he was an early advocate of "the sublime, the glorious Gothic," and rejected most other forms of architectural revivalism. Unlike many of his contemporaries, Gallier was simply appalled by his countrymen's predilection for architectural diversity and wrote, "[t]he rules of Architecture are probably violated more frequently, in practice, than those of the other fine arts; and in no civilized country are they less regarded, than in the United States." He further noted that nineteenth century architecture was "in a very chaotic state."[57]

While unhappy with the overall trends in architectural taste, Gallier reserved his most venomous excoriation for the Egyptian Revival. Albeit like many others, Gallier concurred with the general assessment that Egyptian building techniques were technologically superior, he felt that its use in American cemeteries, however, was wholly inappropriate: "Egyptian architecture reminds us of the religion which called it into being, the most degraded and revolting paganism which ever existed. It is the architecture of embalmed cats and deified crocodiles; solid, stupendous, and time-defying we allow, but associated in our minds with all that is disgusting and absurd in superstition."[58] Noting that the original wooden gateway to Mount Auburn would need to be reconstructed in a more durable material, Gallier went on to suggest a replacement in the Gothic style. Bigelow and the other cemetery trustees clearly ignored Gallier's suggestion and in 1843, an identical copy in granite replaced the original.

At the time, Gallier felt that he was alone in his distaste for the Egyptian Revival, but there were others who shared his concerns, at least toward the religion for which such structures were originally constructed. The same author who in 1841 had praised the Mount Auburn gateway as a "chaste and beautiful specimen of Egyptian architecture" went on to assert in the same article that the Egyptians, "whose idolatry was so gross, sottish, and bestial, and its outward expression so grotesque, mean, and contemptible . . . render[ed] them the laughing-stock of even the idolatrous Greeks and Romans."[59] In other words, while they were idolatrous, polytheistic pagans, at least the Greeks and Romans had the good sense to worship divinities that resembled mankind. Nehemiah Cleaveland, who observed in *Green-wood Illustrated* that the popular taste in "most of our rural cemeteries . . . has shown a predilection for pyramidic forms," went on to describe the view of Green-Wood Cemetery as "a ground so full of pyramids and obelisks, that one could almost fancy it a gigantic cabinet of minerals, being all crystals set on end." Not content to simply note the popularity of the style, Cleaveland went on to lament, "is Christian architecture so poor and scanty, - is modern genius so sterile, that we must . . . derive the forms of our sepulchral monuments, gateways, and chapels, from calf-adoring Egypt?"[60] And L.C. Tuthill, who had praised the Egyptian architecture as "grave and sublime," nevertheless commented, albeit more gently than either Gallier or Cleaveland, "[i]ts massiveness may have recommended it, as conveying ideas of duration and strength; but what other association can it have, appropriate to a Christian cemetery? The emblems are such as paganism suggested."[61] Both Gallier and Cleaveland, in their denunciations of the style, alluded to the influence exhibited by Bigelow's entrance at Mount Auburn in promoting further adoption of the Egyptian Revival throughout the Northeast. They likewise indicated that people were most apt to simply imitate the technique without any thought as to its religious or symbolic connotations.

In response to such denunciations of the style, there were those who defended the Egyptian Revival's use for commemorative architecture with equal zeal. In *Mount Auburn Illustrated* (1847), Cornelia Walter countered objections to the supposed pagan connotations embodied in Egyptian architecture:

> The now mythologized doctrines of Egypt, seem to have been the original source of others more ennobling; and hieroglyphical discoveries have traced, and are tracing them far beyond the era of the pyramids, to an unknown limit, but to a pure, sacred, and divine source. When the art of writing was unknown, the primeval Egyptians resorted to symbols and emblems to express their faith; and these, as correctly interpreted, certainly present many sublime ideas in connection with those great truths which in an after age constituted the doctrines of *"Christianity."* Some of their sculptures and paintings were undoubtedly symbolical of the resurrection of the soul, a dread of final judgment, and a belief in Omnipotent justice.[62]

Walter thus reinterpreted the religion of ancient Egypt, not as an example of gross paganism, but as compatible with the Christian doctrines of bodily resurrection and the Last Judgment.

The following year, in 1848, a number of Boston citizens established Forest Hills Cemetery in Roxbury, complete with a wooden Egyptian Revival entrance akin to the one at Mount Auburn, this one designed by General Henry A.S. Dearborn. Evidently knowledgeable about the debates

FIGURE 8   Main Entrance to Forest Hills Cemetery, Roxbury, Massachusetts, 1866. *(Library of Congress)*

circulating with concern to the propriety of the style in Christian cemeteries, William A. Crafts defended the choice of Egyptian Revival for Forest Hills' gateway in the cemetery's guidebook published in 1855. In language akin to Walter's, Crafts wrote, "[t]here is a difference of opinion as to the propriety of using, as is much the custom, the Egyptian architecture about our burial places. A relic of paganism, it is by some esteemed out of place in a Christian cemetery. But it is essentially the architecture of the grave." Crafts went on to argue that Egyptian symbols were not antithetical to Christian beliefs. "Nor is it without the symbols of immortality, which the purer faith of the Christian can well appropriate and associate with the more sacred and divine promises of the gospel."[63] What is ironic here is that despite Craft's published defense of the Egyptian style, it was the Forest Hills gate that would ultimately be replaced in 1865 with a permanent stone entrance in the increasingly popular Gothic Revival (figure 8).[64]

Others who sought to defend the Egyptian Revival's application in American cemeteries focused on the perceived durability of the architecture, rather than trying to reconcile the disconnect in religious connotations.

R.A. Smith's *Illustrated Guide to and through Laurel Hill Cemetery* from 1852 praised the sepulchral monuments of Egypt as "the highest efforts of ancient art" and that they "have survived and resisted all efforts for their destruction."[65] The 1867 guidebook to Forest Lawn Cemetery in Buffalo supported the style's use on these principles: "The pyramid, and its more graceful modification, the obelisk, are types of architectural durability, and should be followed so far as to furnish a broad and solid support."[66] Such defenses of the Egyptian Revival—whether they rested on its religious implications or associations with timelessness and stability—reveal a unique aspect to the style's history in the United States. That is, of all the architectural revivals that became popular during the nineteenth century, the Egyptian was the only one that necessitated constant defense and interpretation. Remarkably, despite such conflicted opinions in the prevailing print culture of the period, Americans were persistent in their attraction to the style.

In between those who denounced the Egyptian Revival and those who defended its use, most writers tended to sympathize with the eclectic tastes bourgeois Americans had clearly developed by mid-century, as *The New Englander* acknowledged in 1849: "although the column, the obelisk, the altar, the slab, and the temple may rise side by side in the cemetery; good taste requires that the end proposed in such structures, and the feeling which they ought to excite, should be contemplated in them all."[67] Unlike Gallier, many writers felt it was best to tread lightly where matters of taste were concerned. For even as many had reservations about the appropriateness of the Egyptian Revival in particular, it is not surprising that writers might have thought twice about upbraiding the choices made by some of the most wealthy and influential citizens in the urban Northeast.

For example, consider the case of Mount Auburn's distinguished occupants. Following his death in 1845, *The American Whig Review* published a biographical sketch of Judge Joseph Story, who served as the cemetery's President of the Board of Trustees in its first ten years. "Among the great men of our country," the *Review* proclaimed, "He was great in the extent of his capacity, in the vastness of his attainments, in his devotedness to duty, in his wide and various usefulness, in the elevation, purity and simplicity of his character, and in the moral thoughtfulness which pervaded his whole life." The article went on to outline Story's legal career, but also noted his involvement with Mount Auburn Cemetery, "whose hallowed precincts are now made more sacred as the resting-place of his own remains."[68] A man for whom his contemporaries gave due respect, Story had chosen for his family's burial plot before his death a marble obelisk atop an explicitly Egyptian base, complete with cavetto cornice and winged globe.

Those who chose to construct even more elaborate structures in the form of Egyptian Revival side-hill tombs numbered among the wealthiest of the Boston Brahmin set. These included Kirk Boott (1790–1837), one of the founders of Lowell and the first agent and treasurer of the mills in that town (figure 9); Joseph P. Bradlee (1783–1838), a Boston merchant who was instrumental in the purchase of the land for Mount Auburn Cemetery and died a millionaire (figure 10); Nabby Joy (d.1869), an unwed heiress and philanthropist, who upon her death bequeathed over $280,000 to be distributed among the charitable societies of Massachusetts (figure 11);[69] and Francis Cabot Lowell (1803–1874), son of the entrepreneur who established the Lowell Mills. In the case of the Lowell tomb, it stands on a plot of land measuring 1,620 square feet, which would have cost Lowell $810 when he most likely made the purchase some time during the 1830s (figure 12).[70] Other examples of Egyptian side-hill tombs at Mount Auburn include the Bacon family tomb (1832); the elaborate Hicks-Endicott tomb (1833), which includes lotus capital columns and a winged orb above the doorway (figure 13); the tomb for civil engineer and surveyor Stephen P. Fuller (d.1871) and his family, which incorporates solid-looking pylons in lieu of the canted mastaba form (figure 14); the tomb for Josiah Bradlee (1778–1860), an early active member of the Massachusetts Horticultural Society; and the Gardner Greenleaf family tomb, a mastaba with inset marble panels inscribed with the names of the family members interred within.

Cemetery guidebooks that were written with the object in mind of leading tourists to the most spectacular or interesting burials help to give a sense of the overall popularity and distribution of the Egyptian Revival along with other memorial styles. For example, *Dearborn's Guide Through Mount Auburn Cemetery*, the eleventh edition of which was published in 1857, provided descriptions with accompanying engravings of seventy-four monuments in the cemetery, though by that time, "about 450 Monuments, Shafts, Cenotaphs, Obelisks, and Slabs, have been raised and hallowed to adorn this spot."[71] Of the structures featured in *Dearborn's Guide*, eighteen (24%) were either Egyptian obelisks or Egyptian Revival side-hill tombs, twenty-three (31%) were derived from Greek or Roman architectural influence, eight (10.8%) were in the Gothic style and six (8%) comprised a blend

FIGURE 9   Kirk Boott tomb, Mount Auburn Cemetery, c. 1830s.
(Photograph by the author)

FIGURE 10   Joseph P. Bradlee tomb, Mount Auburn Cemetery, c. 1830s.
(Photograph by the author)

FIGURE 11 Nabby Joy tomb, Mount Auburn Cemetery, c. 1830s.
(Photograph by the author)

FIGURE 12 Lowell tomb, Mount Auburn Cemetery, c. 1830s. *(Photograph by the author)*

FIGURE 13 Hicks-Endicott tomb, Mount Auburn Cemetery, 1833.
(Photograph by the author)

FIGURE 14 Stephen P. Fuller tomb, Mount Auburn Cemetery, c. 1830s–40s.
(Photograph by the author)

of Egyptian and Classical elements (such as an obelisk topped with an urn). The remaining nineteen (25.7%) monuments included primarily sculptural memorials, either allegorical in nature (such as the figure of Hope with an anchor) or in the guise of the deceased. It should be noted that all of the monuments described by Dearborn marked the burials of Boston's Brahmin class. Other contemporary cemetery guidebooks followed a similar pattern. Nehemiah Cleaveland's *Green-wood Illustrated* and Conger Sherman's *Guide to Laurel Hill Cemetery, near Philadelphia* each discusses only twelve monuments in detail, but in both publications, five are Egyptian Revival, three are Classically-derived, two represent a blend of the two styles, one is Gothic and one is sculptural.[72]

In the instances of the Egyptian Revival tombs and monuments found at Mount Auburn, as well as those in other contemporary cemeteries, there is a striking continuity in the adoption of explicitly Egyptian elements, including the occasionally controversial winged orb (with or without *uraei*). By contrast, while architects designed entrance gates with a certain degree of archaeological verisimilitude, these more often than the private monuments incorporated overtly Christian details, such as biblical quotations or colonial mortality symbols, perhaps as a way to strike a middle ground with those who had reservations about the style. African Americanist Scott Trafton and art historian Richard Carrott have both explicitly made this argument that cemetery planners incorporated biblical quotations on gateways, following the lead of Mount Auburn, as a way to allay anxieties about the appropriateness of the style in a Christian landscape.[73] In addition to Mount Auburn's portal, quotations appear on the entrances to Grove Street Cemetery in New Haven, Connecticut and Forest Hills Cemetery in Roxbury, Massachusetts. Atop the imposing brownstone gateway at Grove Street Cemetery (figure 15), designed by noted architect Henry Austin (1804–1891) in 1845 and completed in 1848, is a quotation from Corinthians: "The Dead Shall Be Raised." In the case of the gateway at Forest Hills, visitors to the cemetery are greeted with "I Am The Resurrection And The Life" and upon leaving the cemetery, "Though I Walk Through The Valley Of Death I Shall Fear No Evil."

Carrott's and Trafton's arguments would certainly make sense if all Egyptian Revival cemetery gates incorporated biblical quotes, but this is not the case. The gateways at Mount Auburn, Forest Hills and Grove Street are indeed important examples of the Egyptian Revival but they do not prove, in

FIGURE 15 Henry Austin, entrance to Grove Street Cemetery, New Haven, Connecticut, 1845–1848. *(Photograph by the author)*

their use of biblical quotations, that designers employed such a device to allay anxieties or criticisms of the style. The case of Forest Hills' gate is especially telling, as the same quote appeared on both the wooden Egyptian Revival gate and the stone Gothic Revival gate which replaced it. Further, while Trafton linked the common theme of resurrection on the Grove Street and Forest Hills gates to mid-century reanimational anxieties about the walking dead, an "ambulatory afterlife" as he calls it, it seems more likely that these particular quotations are indicative of prevailing mid-century attitudes toward death and the fate of the soul.[74] If anything, the choice of biblical quotations for use on these entrances signified a more prominent anxiety within urban society about the constantly changing world *outside* the cemetery.

For example, at the dedication of the Grove Street gateway, Yale science professor Denison Olmstead (1791–1859) alluded to this feeling: "let us all come hither to think calmly but wisely on our own inevitable destiny. May we here learn, in the light of Christian hope, to divest the grave of unavailing gloom and terror and to contemplate it as a refuge from the storms—as *the gate of Heaven*, as a covert 'where the wicked cease from troubling and the weary are at rest'" (emphasis added).[75] In the case of Forest Hills, visitors entering the cemetery would read "I Am The Resurrection And The Life," indicating that it is for the dead in the place of repose that resurrection and eternal life is possible. Upon exiting the cemetery, visitors then would face

FIGURE 16 Isaiah Rogers, Old Granary Burying Ground pylon with winged hourglass, Boston, 1840. *(Photograph by the author)*

"Though I Walk Through The Valley Of Death I Shall Fear No Evil," a not-so-subtle allusion to the land of the living from which modern Christians needed saving. It also seems likely that these quotations simply functioned as a literary reminder to visitors that they were entering a modern Christian place of burial, separate from the noise and activity of the urban world of the living. Finally, the absence of any language on most Egyptian Revival gateways built during the same period appears to be the strongest indicator that most architects or cemetery planners did not feel the need to "Christianize" a pre-Christian architectural style.[76]

Several gates, as part of various communities' attempts to revitalize older graveyards established during the seventeenth and eighteenth centuries, blended Egyptian Revival with colonial era iconography, most likely as part of an effort by their designers to signify the local antiquity of the site. One of these includes the 1840 gateway to the Old Granary Burying Ground in Boston, designed by architect Isaiah Rogers (1800–1869). Stocky Egyptian-style pylons mark the corners of the burying ground, and the front of each one bears the colonial mortality symbol of the winged hourglass (figure 16).

FIGURE 17 "Memento Mori" Gate, Old Burying Ground, Farmington, Connecticut, 1850. *(Photograph by Ty Tryon)*

In Farmington, Connecticut, the simple Egyptian gate that was erected around 1850 for the Old Burying Ground bears the inscription "Memento Mori," again hearkening to the colonial heritage of those buried within (figure 17). By and large, while these were gateway projects that were part of various community efforts to rehabilitate and better protect older places of burial, the stylistic choices for these gateways were consistent with the pattern established during the 1830s and 1840s to opt for the Egyptian style as part of a new Anglo-Protestant way of commemoration.

Far more unusual was the appearance of Egyptian Revival for use in Jewish cemeteries. In 1843, Isaiah Rogers again designed an Egyptian Revival gateway, this time for the Jewish Touro Cemetery in Newport, Rhode Island. The structure is almost identical to the one he executed three years earlier in Boston. However, whereas in the case of the Protestant colonial burying ground, Rogers had incorporated the Puritan iconography of the winged hourglass, the gateway to the Touro Cemetery included simple obelisks flanking each side of the portal (figure 18). Both gateways designed by Rogers incorporated the overtly Egyptian symbol of the winged orb in deep sculptural relief. However, unlike the gates at Mount Auburn and Grove Street Cemetery, the figure of the *uraei* remains conspicuously absent. The

FIGURE 18 Isaiah Rogers, entrance to the Jewish Touro Cemetery, Newport, Rhode Island, 1843. *(Photograph by the author)*

popularity and appropriateness of the Egyptian style in Jewish cemeteries and buildings, including the Mikveh Israel Synagogue (1822–25) in Philadelphia, designed by architect William Strickland (1788–1854), the gatehouse to the Mikveh Israel Cemetery (c. 1845), also in Philadelphia, the Touro Cemetery, and a number of other synagogues built throughout the Northeast, may be attributed to nineteenth century interpretations of Old Testament texts. George Gliddon noted in *Otia Aegyptiaca*, "[t]he Israelites themselves seem to have had *two* "winged Globes,"—one *beneficent*, as in Malachi iv.2—and the other, a "fiery-Whirling-Disk," *maleficent*, as in Zechariah v., 1, 2."[77] If understood according to the verse in Malachi, the winged orb on the entrance to a Jewish cemetery was symbolic of benevolence and protection.

Another possible explanation for the Jewish acceptance of Egyptian Revival relates to the issue of the Jewish diaspora and process of assimilation. As noted by Rabbi Joshua Segal in *The Old Jewish Cemetery of Newport*, Jewish populations historically strive to adapt to and even adopt the popular styles or practices of their new communities, and the same occurred in the United States. When the prevailing Anglo-Protestant taste of the mid-nineteenth century shifted toward Egyptian forms, they were likewise adopted for use in

FIGURE 19 Obelisks in the Jewish Touro Cemetery, Newport, Rhode Island.
(Photograph by the author)

Jewish places of worship and burial.[78] The presence of several sizable obelisks marking family burials in the Touro Cemetery indicates that this may be the likeliest explanation, especially since the Egyptian obelisk did not bear the same biblical connotations as did the winged orb (figure 19).

What ultimately unifies all of these older cemeteries, regardless of religious affiliation—Grove Street in New Haven, Old Granary in Boston, Old Burying Ground in Farmington, and the Touro Cemetery in Newport—is the use of the Egyptian Revival entrances executed with the dual purpose of protection and preservation. The Colonial Era burying grounds embodied the dogmas and commemorative practices of a seemingly less civilized period in American history, yet they nevertheless warranted efforts to preserve them as elements of America's collective cultural heritage.

Overall, the period from 1830 until 1850 witnessed the construction of at least nine Egyptian Revival cemetery entrances in the Northeast. The extension of the style outside this region at this time was also evident in the execution of architect Frederick Wilkinson's Egyptian design for the entrance to New Orleans' Cypress Grove Cemetery (also known as the Firemen's Cemetery) in 1840. Unlike many of its New England counterparts, which copied the portals found at Dendereh and Karnak, the dominant features of Wilkinson's entrance were two monumental pylons.[79] As architects were experimenting with a variety of styles reflective of the eclectic revivalism of the period, there was also a number of unexecuted entrance designs, including two for Laurel Hill Cemetery in Philadelphia offered by William Strickland and Thomas Ustick Walter in 1836, and an Egyptian design by Robert Cary Long, Jr. for Baltimore's Green Mount Cemetery in 1845. By the 1850s, the popular application of the Egyptian style had died out in the planning of cemeteries, giving way to the increasingly popular Gothic Revival. This was nowhere more evident than in the case of Forest Hills Cemetery in Roxbury and Mount Hope Cemetery in Rochester, where the original Egyptian structures were torn down and replaced with permanent Gothic entrances.

However, construction of Egyptian Revival entrances experienced a minor second phase between the 1870s and the 1910s. Overall, the cemetery entrances dating to this later period tended to be more subtle than those constructed during the height of the Egyptian Revival proper and generally consisted of either a pair of obelisks or pylons. In New Orleans at the Catholic St. Roch Cemetery/Campo Santo, established in 1872, the entrance incorporates a metal gate flanked by marble angels atop Egyptian pylons.[80] The two entrances for the Riverside Cemetery in Cornish, Maine, established in 1883, are marked with short, roughly-hewn granite obelisks. Similarly, the entrances to Valley Cemetery in Manchester, New Hampshire, established in 1841, consist of large granite pylons dating to 1907 (figure 20). Erected in 1912 at Boston's Dorchester North Burying Ground, the Egyptian Revival gate there represents the most elaborate of these more recently-constructed entrances, replete with winged orb with *uraei* and lotus capital columns. It is possible that the designer took as inspiration for this gate the one at Mount Auburn, which still stands today. The Dorchester gateway is nevertheless unique for this period (figure 21).

What is perhaps most striking about these entrances is that they all pre-date the discovery of the tomb of Tutankhamen by Howard Carter in 1922 and the second major wave of Egyptomania in American culture. The continued, albeit scattered, adoption of the Egyptian Revival for cemetery entrances into the twentieth century therefore indicates that while the nineteenth century penchant for Egyptian forms waned during the height of

FIGURE 20 Entrance to Valley Cemetery, Manchester, New Hampshire, 1907.
(*Photograph by the author*)

Gothic fashion, it never entirely disappeared.[81] They were not part of the mid-nineteenth century enthusiasm for the Egyptian Revival in cemetery design but they do signify a persistent interest among Americans for the style. Lacking the cultural meaning that had been infused into the gateways for the rural cemeteries and colonial burying grounds of mid-century, these later examples nevertheless reflect that Egyptian forms had successfully become ingrained as part of the American architectural aesthetic even as their ideological associations became lost.

A LANDSCAPE FOR THE LIVING AND THE DEAD

The Stranger's Guide in Philadelphia, published in 1852, devotes a lengthy section to the description of Philadelphia's prominent cemeteries. On one page, the illustration features a dapper young man, dressed in top hat and tails, standing among the memorials in a contemporary cemetery. With his head turned toward the reader, he gestures to a landscape in the distance—one that includes the great pyramids at Giza, a small Egyptian temple and palm trees. With his right hand, he points to the text of the page, which includes a description of Woodland Cemetery, one of Philadelphia's many rest-

FIGURE 21 Entrance to Dorchester North Burying Ground, Boston, 1912.
(Photograph by Richard Siembab)

ing places for the dead.[82] The image provided in the *Guide* clearly illustrates that by mid-century, Americans fully understood the connection between ancient Egypt and reverent care for the dead. Many also perceived Egypt's landscape as one that was inherently funereal by nature. These associations, combined with the impulses embodied in the Rural Cemetery Movement to establish a sense of eternity and timelessness amidst the constantly changing urban industrial environment, informed the decisions made by cemetery planning committees and private citizens as they created a new commemorative aesthetic. In an age of architectural eclecticism, as architects, cemetery committees and individual consumers weighed the many options for gateway and monument designs, many chose in favor of the Egyptian Revival—a style that merited both praise and criticism and, as a result, was arguably the most controversial of the choices then available.

Regardless of the criticism leveled by some, however, these gateways and the monuments scattered throughout the landscapes within embodied a set of ideals concerning aesthetic beauty and the social order as defined by the men who founded and controlled such institutions. The rural cemeteries would be retreats for the living from the harsh urban industrial world and they would at the same time be safe, permanent and picturesque repositories for the dead. As landscapes specifically designed to remain unchanging amid the perpetually-evolving urban environment, the new rural cemeteries—and even the outmoded Colonial Era graveyards—necessitated the construction of exterior symbols that would communicate the intentions of their founders. While promoted by men like Story and Edward Everett as places where the highest and lowest of the socio-economic order could receive a dignified burial, they were nevertheless cultural institutions that were founded and controlled by the educated elite. Through their choices to adopt the Egyptian Revival, men such as Jacob Bigelow and General Henry Dearborn articulated for the greater population what manner of symbolism would define the new way in which Americans would care for their dead; and for those wealthy Americans who opted to use the style for their own monuments, visitors to the cemetery would see who had ascended to power as the new urban industrial pharaohs.

CHAPTER 3

Revolutionary Monuments: The Obelisks of Bunker Hill and Groton Heights

THE OBELISK, as it was designed and used by the ancient Egyptians, was a form that necessarily lent itself to commemoration and fostered associations with power and grandeur. Quarried and constructed out of a single block of stone, these original monoliths consisted of a four-sided tapering shaft with a pointed, pyramidal top. As Jacob Bigelow noted in his published lectures, *Elements of Technology* (1829), "obelisks composed of a single stone, often exceeding 70 feet in height, are structures peculiarly Egyptian."[1] The clean lines of the four sides allowed for the carving of extensive inscriptions to hail the great victories and glories of the pharaoh. As Bigelow would detail more thoroughly in his later published lectures entitled *The Useful Arts* (1840), "the obelisks were slender pyramidal shafts made of a single stone, and generally placed in pairs before gates or propylaea of temples or cities. They have generally been considered as peculiarly Egyptian . . . [and] with the design of communicating to posterity the extent of his [Sesostris or Rameses] power, and the number of the nations he had conquered."[2]

Translated into the American commemorative context throughout the nineteenth century, the obelisk retained its earlier associations with powerful leaders or heroes and the martial context of warfare. Appearing in the guise of both public and private memorials, including the grave markers for ten out of the first seventeen presidents, the obelisk increasingly became the principal cultural symbol for memorializing significant men and events and filtered throughout society in the monuments for regular American families and individuals during the Rural Cemetery Movement.[3] The style became so popular in the private sphere of memorialization that, as has already been seen in the previous chapter, critics like Nehemiah Cleaveland remarked on the "cabinet of minerals" quality of the cemetery landscape.

However, the popularity of the obelisk form was not restricted to private memorialization. The obelisk also became one of the most common designs that architects and monument associations turned to for large-scale public memorial projects, especially those intended to articulate for the public their nation's burgeoning identity and anticipated longevity. Whereas during the eighteenth century, Americans had tended not to erect large public memorials to commemorate significant military events or heroes, by the nineteenth century, the impulse among communities along the eastern seaboard became almost overwhelming due to the sense of embarrassment felt by the current generation that they had done nothing to honor the sacrifices of their forefathers for independence. As such, local monument associations began to form by the early years of the century with the goal of constructing lasting memorials to those who fought and became heroes, in life and in death, on the battlefields of the Revolutionary War. The result was the construction of several monumental obelisks, each measuring one hundred feet or more, dedicated to the American Revolution and that conflict often referred to as the Second American Revolution—the War of 1812.

Derived as they were from Egyptian architecture, the massive obelisks carried the same sense of endurance and timelessness as the original ancient monoliths. With the repetitive use of the form over time, the obelisk increasingly became divided from its ancient origins to transform into a particularly "American" monumental style. The earliest of these structures, the monuments at Fort Griswold in Groton, Connecticut and at Bunker Hill in Charlestown, Massachusetts, established the precedent for future commemorative efforts of the Revolution and its participants (figures 22 and 23). The process whereby these obelisks were built is reflective of the impulses that led to their creation, while the dedicatory addresses delivered at their bases reveal the ways in which Americans continually sought to prove the greatness of their own civilization as well as the antiquity of their cultural and political lineage.

FIGURE 22 Groton Monument, Groton Heights, Connecticut, 1826–1830.
(Photograph by the author)

During a period lasting a century, seven memorial obelisks measuring over one hundred feet tall, dedicated to various battles and individuals associated with the American Revolution and the War of 1812, were constructed in the United States. Of these, four commemorate individual battles from the Revolutionary War—these include, in order of completion, the 134-foot

FIGURE 23 Bunker Hill Monument, Charlestown, Massachusetts, 1825–1843.
(Photograph by the author)

tall Groton Monument (1826–30; heightened in 1881) at Fort Griswold in Groton, Connecticut; the 221-foot tall Bunker Hill Monument (1825–43) in Charlestown, Massachusetts; the 155-foot tall Saratoga Battle Monument (1877–82) in Schuylerville, New York; and the 305-foot tall Bennington Battle Monument (1889–91) in Bennington, Vermont. Also associated with

FIGURE 24 Chalmette Battle Monument, New Orleans, Louisiana, 1840–1908.
(*Library of Congress*)

the American Revolution is the 555-foot tall Washington National Monument (1848–84) dedicated to George Washington in Washington, D.C., which, when it was completed was the tallest such structure in the world (see chapter 5). The two obelisks dedicated to the War of 1812 were completed during the twentieth century: the 100-foot tall Chalmette Battle Monument (1840–1908) in New Orleans, Louisiana (figure 24); and the 135-foot tall Macdonough Monument (1914–26) in Plattsburgh, New York.

FIGURE 25 Saratoga Battle Monument, Saratoga Springs, New York, 1877–1882. *(Photograph by the author)*

While these monuments all share the common trait of being freestanding obelisks, they each nevertheless possess unique details which set them apart from other large-scale public memorials. The Saratoga Monument, for example, includes Gothic architectural elements along its exterior as well as statues of Major General Horatio Gates, General Philip Schuyler and General Daniel Morgan each set in front of recessed windows (figure 25). At

FIGURE 26 Bennington Battle Monument, Bennington, Vermont, 1889–1891.
(Photograph by the author)

Bennington, the shaft gradually slopes to create a pointed apex, rather than ending abruptly with a pyramidion cap on top (figure 26). In the case of the Macdonough Monument, an eagle with outstretched wings is perched at the top of the obelisk. Regardless of stylistic variations in the details, however, the choice of the obelisk form bound all of these structures together into a cohesive symbolic rhetoric that emphasized both the enormity of the event being commemorated as well as the martial valor and heroism of those who participated in these wars, values that each obelisk would proclaim for all time. The communities in which these obelisks were erected each had a vested interest in the successful completion of their respective monuments, since each entailed the outlay of thousands of dollars—millions in the case of the Washington Monument—primarily funded from the donations of private citizens. Therefore, these monuments also functioned as focal points for community and, more broadly, national identity.

However, well before the establishment of the Bunker Hill Monument Association (1824) and the Groton Monument Association (1825), the obelisk and pyramidal forms had already appeared on a smaller scale in commemorative monuments associated with the American Revolution. As early as the 1770s, communities began to participate in the kinds of commemorative activities that would effectively mythologize the American Revolution and its heroes in public memory. The creation of a potent public memory of the war, as argued by historical archaeologist Paul Shackel, "can be about forgetting a past, creating and reinforcing patriotism, and developing a sense of nostalgia to legitimize a heritage."[4] It did not take long for Americans to use the medium of the public monument to reinforce patriotic sentiment, nor did it take long for communities to feel nostalgia for the actions of their heroes, especially those who died gloriously in battle against the British. The earliest such memorial was sculpted in Paris in January 1776 by the royal sculptor J. J. Caffieri for installation in New York City's St. Paul Chapel (figure 27). The monument commemorates Major General Richard Montgomery, who perished in the failed attack on Quebec in 1775. Situated below the east window of the chapel, the memorial is akin to those built into cathedral walls for the aristocracy during the sixteenth and seventeenth centuries in Europe. It features an urn on a pedestal in front of a flat-topped pyramid. At the base is a plaque with the following inscription:

This Monument is erected by the order of CONGRESS

25th Jan^{ry} 1776 to transmit to Posterity a grateful remem-

brance of the patriotism conduct enterprize & perseverance

of *Major General* RICHARD MONTGOMERY.

Who after a series of successes amidst the most discou-

raging Difficulties *Fell* in the attack on

QUEBEC. 31st Dec^{br} 1775. Aged 37 years.[5]

FIGURE 27 Richard Montgomery Monument, St. Paul's Chapel, New York City, 1776.
(Photograph by Albin Lohr-Jones)

The words used to describe Montgomery—his patriotism, conduct, enterprise and perseverance—were qualities that would later be repeated in larger commemorative efforts.[6]

Another early example is the Lexington Battle Monument (1799), a squat obelisk situated atop a pedestal base (Figure 28). The lengthy inscription lists the participants who lost their lives, but like the Montgomery memorial, examines the qualities of these men and the ideals of the Revolution. Noting that those who fell in the battle were "the first victims to the Sword of British Tyranny & Opression," the inscription continues:

The Die was cast!!!

The blood of these Martyr's,

In the cause of God and their country,

Was the cement of the Union of these States, then

Colonies; & gave the spring to the spirit, Firmness

And resolution of their Fellow Citizens.

They rose as one man, to revenge their brethren's

Blood and at the point of the sword, to assert &

Defend their native Rights.

They nobly dar'd to be free!!

The contest was long, bloody & affecting.

Righteous Heaven approved the solemn appeal:

Victory crowned their arms; and

The Peace, Liberty & Independence of the United

States of America, was their glorious Reward.

Built in the year 1799.

When it finally came time to build the obelisks at Bunker Hill and Groton, the conduct of the American soldiers in both victory and defeat had become inseparable from notions of patriotism, and the monuments themselves promoted the gratitude of not just the individual community who witnessed their construction, but of the entire nation as well.

While the sentiments expressed by the monuments remained consistent, the process whereby the obelisk became an Americanized form for large-scale monument building did not begin until the 1820s, as monument associations in the Northeast began to pursue more lofty commemorative projects. The obelisk was a form considered in the early years of the nineteenth century as discussions began for a monument to George Washington. For

FIGURE 28 Lexington Battle Monument, Lexington, Massachusetts, 1799.
(*Library of Congress*)

this purpose, Mark Langdon Hill, writing for the *North American Review*, observed in 1816 that the obelisk "is another of the inventions of the Egyptians, and which has never been attempted by any other people." A non-Egyptian-made obelisk would certainly be unique, but in Hill's opinion, "An object so slender as an obelisk would be of no great duration if formed of different pieces, indeed its magnificence mainly consists in its being of one piece. This species of monument, then, is completely out of the question."[7]

Americans at this time lacked the kind of stone quarrying and cutting technology necessary to construct monoliths akin to those from ancient Egypt, so when it came time for the monument committees in Boston and Groton to choose a form from the designs submitted by various architects, they disregarded such reservations about the style. The design of the resulting monumental obelisks ultimately represented a structural compromise. The American obelisks were multi-stone hollow structures that far outstripped in height and breadth of even the largest of the Egyptian monoliths, with interior staircases that led to look-out platforms above. It does not seem, however, that all Americans were convinced of their durability until the time of their completion. In *Elements of Technology*, Jacob Bigelow's own skepticism about using the style on a monumental scale was evident, despite his enthusiasm for adopting Egyptian forms. He wrote of the obelisk that it was an architectural form, "which we attempt to imitate, but dare not dream of equaling."[8] However, once the monument at Groton Heights was completed in 1830 and the Bunker Hill Monument in 1843, and visitors could see the structures in person and ascend their internal staircases, such doubts tended to disappear.

Given visitors' ability to ascend to the top of these structures and view the countryside for miles, there have been some historians, such as John Zukowsky, who have considered the monuments as "tangible expressions of that sense of Manifest Destiny" and American "expansionism."[9] Such a thesis seems possible when viewed in light of Daniel Webster's oration delivered in 1825 at the laying of the cornerstone of the Bunker Hill Monument:

> Two or three millions of people have been augmented to twelve, the great forests of the West prostrated beneath the arm of successful industry, and the dwellers on the banks of the Ohio and the Mississippi become the fellow citizens and neighbors of those who cultivate the hills of New England. We have a commerce that leaves no sea unexplored, navies which take no law from superior force, revenues adequate to all the exigencies of government, almost without taxation, and peace with all nations, founded on equal rights and mutual respect.[10]

In this manner, Webster linked the deeds of those who fought in the American Revolution with the prosperity and expansion of the still-young republic. The fate of the monument itself, intended to last an eternity, became for Webster intimately tied with the success and longevity of the still young nation. Twenty years before columnist John L. O'Sullivan would coin the phrase "Manifest Destiny," Webster thus articulated in this speech an imperial ideology of expansion at the base of what would eventually be a 221-foot tall structure from which visitors could view land and sea in all directions that had come under the domain of Anglo-American settlement and industry.

Far more significant to the building and completion of these monuments, however, was the collective desire to state the official meaning of the war and establish a collective identity for Americans living in the nineteenth century. As the efforts of these later years resulted in truly monumental structures on the landscape—neither hidden away in a church nor small enough to go unobserved from a distance—the combination of size and sentiment went hand-in-hand. The obelisk was not the only style communities opted for in their memorialization activities, but it quickly became the most recognizable commemorative form associated with what many considered to be one of the signal events in the history of modern western civilization. Signifying their belief in the importance of their work, the Bunker Hill Monument Association explicitly linked the magnitude of the Revolution's importance with the size of their proposed monument: "As it will commemorate the greatest event in the history of civil liberty, it should be, and shall be, the grandest monument in the world."[11] Charles Griswold, who delivered the dedication speech at the laying of the cornerstone of the Groton Monument in 1826, also alluded to this popular sentiment. He asserted, "next after the glorious Reformation of the sixteenth century, the American Revolution is the most important event in modern history."[12] As it was for Griswold, many Americans at this time believed the significance of their Revolution was not restricted to their own country, but to the history of the entire western world.

Part of what made the Egyptian obelisk an attractive option for architects and monument design committees was the simple matter that a historically significant event warranted an equally significant memorial. Famed sculptor Horatio Greenough (1805–1852), who submitted an obelisk design for the Bunker Hill Monument, explained his thoughts on the form in straightforward terms. He wrote, "I have made the choice of the obelisk as the most purely *monumental* form of structure."[13] At the same time, the obelisk satisfied the need to glorify the democratic values of the American people as a whole, rather than apotheosize any particular individual, as was the case with many European memorials, which often took the form of statuary.[14] As described by historian Robert Alexander, such European monument types as the equestrian statue were "heroic" or "dynastic" portraits, whereas the obelisk was "dedicated in ideals such as Liberty or to groups of people whose actions have benefited a whole people."[15] Even the Washington National Monument bears no outward sign indicating for whom it was constructed and so presents to the outside observer a monolithic statement of universal American solidarity. Made as it was, like the other monumental obelisks around the country, out of many blocks united into a solid, unified mass of stone, it represents a perfect embodiment of *E Pluribus Unum*.

TWINNED IMPULSES

By the beginning of the 1820s, civic leaders began to despair that there existed no significant monuments in honor of the American Revolution. Massachusetts statesman Daniel Webster, who drafted the Act of Incorporation for the Bunker Hill Monument Association in 1823, lamented: "glorious and beneficent as its [the war's] consequences have proved to this nation, not a single monument worthy of being named has hitherto been elevated to testify public gratitude or do honor to national sentiment in the eyes of our own citizens or of strangers."[16] Therefore, as a reaction against this embarrassing state of affairs, Webster joined with other members of the Boston elite to form the association,—men who participated in the establishment of several major cultural institutions, including Mount Auburn Cemetery, the Boston Athenaeum and the American Antiquarian Society—including William Tudor, founder and early editor of the *North American Review*; orator and statesman Edward Everett; Colonel Thomas Handasyd Perkins, "a leading citizen of the wealthy classes;"[17] and General Henry A.S. Dearborn, who would later be so instrumental in the design and incorporation of the Mount Auburn and Forest Hills Cemeteries. The purpose of the Association was to procure funds sufficient to erect "a permanent memorial, consecrated by the gratitude of the present generation, to the memory of those statesmen and soldiers who led the way in the American Revolution."[18]

Two years later, on September 6, 1825, the Groton Monument Association in Connecticut first convened. One commentator for the *New London Advocate* mirrored Webster's earlier declaration, charging that the absence of a proper memorial in honor of the Battle at Groton Heights had sped cultural forgetfulness and apathy for the events that took place on that date in

1781: "No notice had been taken of the day [of the battle], for many years, and the history of the catastrophe was fast fading from the recollection of the survivors, and present generation." Such a lack of interest in local and national history had, in the *Advocate*'s view, made the battle at Groton Heights "like the fabled days of antiquity, a mere historical epoch." However, the formation of the Groton Monument Association was a sign that the people of Groton no longer "slept in oblivion" with regard to their local history. As the *Advocate* concluded, the prospect of a monument would enroll the names of those who fought at Fort Griswold on Groton Heights "on the same page of history with the patriots of Thermopylae, Marathon, and Plataea!"[19] At their first meeting, the Association members drafted a proposal, which eloquently outlined the people's need to erect a monument "as a witness of their gratitude" for those who fell in what most locals considered the worst massacre of the war enacted by the British, aided by the traitor Benedict Arnold, at Fort Griswold. The members wrote,

> To honor the brave who have devoted their lives in the defence [sic] of their country, is the high and grateful duty of posterity; it warms & animates the heart in the love of country and gives life and energy to the best feelings of our nature. Here we have before us a nobler theme, here we celebrate the memory of Fathers, Sons & Brothers, a united band, who met the enemy at the threshold, and in sight of their burning houses, their wives and children, devoted their lives to the love of country, its rights and liberties.[20]

Thus, in the most animated language, which evoked images of patriotism and sacrifice as well as the ideals for which the men at Fort Griswold fought and died, the committee members proposed to erect an appropriate memorial to their memory.

Given that the monuments at Bunker Hill and Groton Heights were conceived and built at approximately the same time, they share a number of parallels. First, these were both sites of American defeat during the Revolutionary War. The monuments, once completed, would pay homage to the martyrs to the cause of liberty. This signified a major break with European war memorial traditions, which had regularly commemorated only heroism in victory. Second, the orations delivered at various stages of planning, construction, completion and anniversaries established a pattern whereby speakers articulated the meaning of the war as well as the meaning of the monuments in relation to their function and symbolism. The repetitive nature of such practices, which took place at the base of these monuments, reaffirmed the associations made between the obelisks, American patriotism and national identity.

The Bunker Hill Monument

When, on July 9, 1823, Daniel Webster (figure 29) presented his first "address to the public" regarding the need for a monument at Bunker Hill, he urged that "some grand and striking object, often recurring to the sight and impressing the mind with interesting associations, would be one, it is thought, neither useless nor unworthy for the present generation to rear to the memory of the past." He then went on to exhort that while the design for such a memorial would remain to be decided upon, it would nevertheless have to be "distinguished by simplicity and grandeur, rather than by elaborate and elegant ornaments."[21] In presenting the proposal in such language, it is clear that Webster and those involved in the Bunker Hill Monument Association hoped for a structure that would be truly grand in stature.

Once enough start-up capital had been raised and the decision had been made to move forward with the project to build a monument at Bunker Hill, it was followed on June 17, 1825 with an imposing ceremony for the laying of the cornerstone. Those in attendance included about two hundred veterans of the Revolutionary War; the members of the Bunker Hill Monument Association; "thousands in number" from the Masonic fraternity; the esteemed General Lafayette; and numerous other members of the Boston community.[22] Daniel Webster, who delivered the principal oration to commemorate the event, referred to the Revolution as "the wonder and the blessing of the world" and that during the nation's "day of extraordinary prosperity and happiness, of high national honor, distinction, and power, we are brought together in this place by our love of country, by our admiration of exalted character, by our gratitude for signal services and patriotic devotion."[23] In this manner, Webster publicly proclaimed the reasons for the American people to memorialize the war and its heroes. He further declared that the country would "itself become a vast and splendid monument, not of oppression and terror, but of Wisdom, of Peace, and of Liberty, upon which the world may gaze with admiration forever!" According to Webster, then, the monument at Bunker Hill would rise and make "known to all future times" the achievements of those Americans who came before, while the

FIGURE 29 *Daniel Webster,* chromolithograph, c. 1863. *(Library of Congress)*

actions of his prosperous and ever-expanding United States would be as a living monument to be admired by the rest of the world.[24]

Concerning the style of the monument that would ultimately be constructed on Bunker Hill, Webster employed language that unequivocally linked the American memorial to its stylistic precedents in ancient Egypt. Intoning commonly employed descriptions for Egyptian architecture, the nation's great orator proclaimed, "rising high in massive solidity and unadorned grandeur, it may remain as long as Heaven permits the works of man to last." Webster thus inferred that like the great monoliths of ancient Egypt, the structure at Bunker Hill would withstand the test of time. He further referred to what he anticipated would be the vast height of the future monument, the style of which, oddly enough, had not yet been firmly decided upon: "Let it rise! Let it rise till it meet the sun in his coming; let the earliest light of the morning gild it, and parting day linger and play on its summit."[25]

The members of the Second Committee on the Design of the monument—there were ultimately three such committees—had, by the time of Webster's oration, voted eleven to five in favor of an obelisk or pyramidal form as opposed to a column or some other style.[26] Mindful that the decision on the monument's design had gone at least this far, Webster's words reflect his own understanding of the symbolic connections between Pharaonic power, Egyptian architecture and the sun. In July, following the cornerstone ceremony, the Monument Association accepted the final design submitted by Solomon Willard (1783–1861). In a letter written to Association member George Ticknor, Willard provided his own thoughts on the obelisk as an appropriate style for so profound a commemorative project. He wrote,

> It has always seemed to me that any of the three figures [column, pyramid, obelisk] which have been proposed, if well designed, would make a respectable monument. The obelisk I have always preferred for its severe cast and its nearer approach to the simplicity of nature than the others. The column might be more splendid. The character of the obelisk, without a pedestal, seems to me to be strictly appropriate for the occasion and I think would rank first as a specimen of art and be highly creditable to the taste of the age.[27]

From Willard's perspective, then, the future Bunker Hill Monument, in the form of an obelisk, would speak more closely to the sentiments the Association hoped it would express while also representing the prevailing aesthetic and architectural tastes of the period.

Little progress occurred on the monument's construction after the laying of the cornerstone and there were those who, despite Webster's compelling address, questioned the necessity for a grandiose memorial structure dedicated to the war's dead. The *Middlesex Gazette* asked the question in May of 1826, "Why was it necessary to erect a monument on Bunker's Hill? The hill itself will last while the earth endures, and transmit to future ages a record imperishable as time. Why burden it with an edifice, which honours the memory of the dead, but confers no benefit upon the living?" The opposition here had nothing to do with the *style* of the monument, but rather focused on its purported *function*. Expressing the belief that earlier societies that had been dependent upon oral traditions required monuments to "serve as historical records," the editors of the *Gazette* felt it was "a waste of skill and treasure to dedicate a magnificent structure to *no other end* than the perpetuity of some illustrious deed." Rather, such a structure, if completed should "be devoted to the double purpose of commemorating the triumph of valour and virtue, and of instructing the children of the men, whose labours merited so high a tribute of respect." Hoping that the Monument Association would incorporate into the design a means to educate "the indigent descendants of revolutionary officers and soldiers," the *Gazette* felt such a function would make the resulting work "truly national and munificent."[28] These sentiments were, according to Kirk Savage, relatively widespread during the first decades of the nineteenth century, during which time many Americans viewed public monuments "in suspicion" and that they "were mere gestures by a powerful few rather than spontaneous outpourings of popular feeling."[29] Given that the Bunker Hill Monument Association and others like it *were* headed by men of standing in their communities, they did, indeed, bear the task of transforming such monument projects into truly public works. Yet regardless of any lingering public doubt about the value of pursuing the monument project at Bunker Hill, construction finally began in earnest in 1827, two years after the laying of the cornerstone.

By August of that year, area newspapers reported the completion of the monument's base.[30] By November, workers had laid four courses of stone, at which point work was suspended for the winter season. The *Bangor Weekly Register* noted that the "progress already made is not very flattering, but the work looks remarkably neat and substantial."[31] Unfortunately, the "building committee" appointed by the Monument Association reported in March of the following year that after having completed so little work toward the monument's completion, they were nevertheless "*entirely destitute of funds*."[32] Construction resumed at a slowed pace by Summer, however there remained little indication as to whether Willard's original design would ultimately be finished. By Fall, newspapers like the *New Bedford Mercury* began a campaign of chastising New Englanders for their lack of support for the project. "Let not New England rest under the disgrace of wanting sufficient patriotism to complete this memorial of their purest patriots, and of one of the proudest events in her honored annals."[33] By 1829, the Monument Association was making active appeals to the public for additional funds. Part of their strategy was to outline how impressive the obelisk would be once completed. As the Association stated in one circular, "This monument will be the *highest of the kind in the world*, and only below the height of the Egyptian Pyramids," it "will endure until the foundations of the earth itself are shaken" and "[o]ur descendants in the most remote ages will have this perpetual memorial before them."[34] By appealing to such comparisons with the Great Pyramids at Giza and the anticipated endurance of the monument, the Association hoped to appeal not only to the public's patriotism, but to their pride as well in erecting such an impressive and long-lasting structure that would ultimately serve as a symbol of their city and nation.

However, construction on the Bunker Hill Monument remained stagnated at about forty feet in height, even with the formation of an auxiliary Ladies' Bunker Hill Monument Association whose purpose was the raising of funds through voluntary subscriptions. At a point of near desperation, on May 28, 1833, Edward Everett (figure 30) delivered a speech in Faneuil Hall at a meeting called by the Massachusetts Charitable Mechanic Association, "to take measures for its completion." As with earlier calls for money and support, Everett called upon his audience to aid in finishing the monument so that their generation would not be disgraced as unpatriotic. Reflective of the kind of pride and aspirations to grandeur exhibited by many Americans of the period, Everett could not help but praise the quality of the monument, even in its partial state of completion. Turning to a comparison with Egyptian architecture, Everett declared, "What is already done is as substantial as the great pyramid of Egypt. The foundations have been laid with such depth and solidity, that nothing but an earthquake can shake them. The part already constructed will stand to the end of time."[35] And so, even with the extended hiatus in construction, Everett appealed to his audience on the principles that finished or not, the modern obelisk as a representation of American technology and ingenuity already surpassed its predecessors from antiquity.

Following Everett's admonition, it still took nearly another decade for the Monument Association to raise enough funds to complete the obelisk. When construction finally resumed in 1842, the Boston-area newspapers were happy to report on the progress and likelihood of completion. The editors of *The Daily Atlas* wrote in April that "We are glad to perceive that the work on the unfinished Monument is resumed," and they noted the role that modern technology would play to help complete the project. "We expect to see them [the quarried stones] rising from day to day by the magic influence of steam, as regularly and unceasingly as the materials for the walls of Thebes were made to ascend by the dulcet sound of the lyre of Amphion."[36]

FIGURE 30 Henry Wright Smith, *Edward Everett,* engraving, c. 1860. *(Library of Congress)*

While the *Atlas* mixed images of modernity and antiquity to marvel at the anticipated completion of the great shaft, the *Boston Courier* titillated readers by describing the vast size of the structure. Mindful of the delays that had prohibited a more timely completion of the obelisk, the editors wrote, "*The last stair has been laid,* and those whose curiosity may induce them to take a view of the surrounding country, the harbor and its beautiful islands, may take a walk of *two hundred feet* towards the zenith, and find no obstruction of vision but the distant horizon." The *Courier* noted that the laying of the capstone would take place sometime during the summer, but such was then considered "the imposing appearance of the monument, that we imagine the addition of this twenty feet will not perceptibly increase the height."[37]

As significant an affair as had occurred at the laying of the cornerstone in 1825, it paled in comparison to the ceremonies held for the formal dedication of the completed monument, which took place on June 17, 1843, exactly eighteen years after the ceremony for the laying of the cornerstone (figure 31).[38] Again, the country's most beloved orator Daniel Webster delivered the principal address, this time to a crowd of thousands that included President John Tyler and his Cabinet, governors from various states of the union, 108 surviving veterans of the Revolution, and "delegations of the descendants of New England [. . .] from the remotest parts of the Union."[39] The presence of such figures as the President of the United States confirmed the assertions of the Monument Association that the obelisk would become a *national* monument embodying universal American sentiments. Newspapers noted those in attendance as well as the significance of the event as a "double anniversary"—the anniversary of the battle then being commemorated and that of the laying of the cornerstone of the monument. With the lofty shaft completed at last, journalists and the public at large experienced an almost immediate amnesia regarding the delays in its construction. No longer considered a potentially useless folly, the *Charlestown Mercury* reported that the monument at Bunker Hill and other such monuments "serve the purposes of daily remembrances of scenes honorable to the actors in them, and beneficial to us; to mankind now, to the cause of liberty everywhere, and to our posterity in an especial manner; and thus they prevent the possible slumberings of patriotism, stimulate the spirit of emulation, and excite all the feelings necessary for the preservation of our national liberty and independence."[40]

It almost went without saying that Webster, who had been involved with the monument project since 1823, would be the man to mark the occasion of its completion in 1843. However, the thrust of Webster's 1843 oration was markedly different from the one he delivered in 1825. Whereas his cornerstone speech in 1825 had focused on the reasons for erecting a monument in the first place, on the gratitude of the nation and of its status in the world, his oration delivered upon its completion dealt explicitly with the monument itself. In addition to once again invoking the descriptive terms of "simplicity" and "grandeur" to describe the 221-foot tall shaft, Webster's rhetoric drew upon imagery taken from increasingly popular gothic literary

FIGURE 31 J. Fisher and N. Currier, *View of Bunker Hill & Monument, June 17, 1843*, lithograph, c. 1835–1856. *(Library of Congress)*

tropes. Visitors for generations to come would "look up to it with a feeling of awe" and it conveyed a "silent but awful utterance" composed of "deep pathos."⁴¹ Webster's description of what future visitors' reactions would be to the American obelisk paralleled to a striking degree the kinds of descriptions that would later be used by such visitors to the pyramids and the sphinx as Herman Melville and Mark Twain (see chapter 1). And just as Melville and Twain were struck by such sensations as awe and sublime terror when visiting the land of the pharaohs in the 1850s, traveler Constance Fenimore Woolson wrote toward the end of the century, "[t]here is something in the pyramids which overawes our boasted civilization."⁴² For Webster in the 1840s, however, Americans possessed their own vast monument capable of overawing everyone who saw it, years before many of the wealthiest and notable citizens of the nation would make the grand tour to Egypt and see its predecessors firsthand. Like the ancient Egyptians, whose great monoliths had stood through the ravages of time, the Americans had now built their own sublime shaft, "from which the future antiquary shall wipe the dust."⁴³ Albeit constructed from multiple blocks of stone, the new obelisk would last in perpetuity like its ancient predecessors and would, at some future time, become an artifact for scholarly study.

Yet beyond simple acknowledgement that the Egyptian obelisks inspired Willard's design for the monument, Webster's dedication articulated the difference in meaning and therefore of the value of the structure to future generations. Alluding to the famed Colossi at Memnon, seated figures said to "sing" with the rising sun, Webster declared, "the rising sun [does not] cause tones of music to issue from its [the obelisk's] summit," but rather, the obelisk "looks, it speaks, it acts, to the full comprehension of every American mind, and the awakening of glowing enthusiasm in every American heart." He further contrasted the lofty ideals encompassed in the Bunker Hill Monument with the Great Pyramid at Giza. With particular emphasis on the relationship between morality and the monument, Webster felt that the Great Pyramid was silent with regard to any kind of "moral object" or "instruction to mankind." Without a moral force behind its construction, "it excites only conviction of power mixed with strange wonder." By contrast, the "object and purpose" of the modern obelisk at Bunker Hill would be known to everyone until the last hours of man's existence, as it had been raised to the skies by "the civilization of the present race of men—founded as it is in solid science, the true knowledge of nature, and vast discoveries in art, and which is elevated and purified by moral sentiment and by the truths of

Christianity."⁴⁴ Morality, science, progress and Christianity—these were the sentiments that separated the modern obelisk from its ancient predecessors. The pyramids of Egypt had been constructed with no nobler purpose than to glorify the power of the pharaoh and house his remains for eternity; the American people had built a monument that served not only as a war memorial, but also as a monument for the living to ascend and enjoy, and as a statement to the world of those qualities that defined the nation and its people.

Webster's interpretation of the meaning of the monument at Bunker Hill was not his alone. Articulating for citizens the monument's value as a national symbol, others wrote in the years following its dedication similar proclamations. In 1844, a letter to the editor of the *Boston Evening Transcript* compared the Bunker Hill Monument to the Great Pyramid of Cheops. In the view of the author, the Bunker Hill Monument, "being erected to commemorate the physical and intellectual *freedom* of a people, will endure to the end of time to attest the victory of social *liberty* and of *mental emancipation*, whilst the existence of the Pyramid that has outlived the very race of its builders bears witness of the utter futility of human individual vaingloriousness." In the view of the *Transcript*, the Pyramid actually served as a cautionary tale to those in the present generation who seek recognition for posterity but do not hope to do so through deeds devoted to "the social and intellectual benefit of their fellow-men."⁴⁵ Webster's earlier exhortations about the stability of the monument also reappeared in later years. As Edward Everett declared at the base of the Bunker Hill Monument in 1850, "We have indeed erected an enduring monument on the hill before us. No ordinary human violence will shake the solid column. The storms of a thousand winters will beat upon it in vain; the earthquake and the lightning alone can lay it low."⁴⁶ The size and style of the massive obelisk necessarily drew explicit connections between the United States and ancient Egypt, but the public sentiment associated with the shaft had a transformative effect, which ultimately Americanized the form as an appropriate expression of American patriotism.

The Groton Monument

Witnessing the early enthusiasm in the Boston area for a monument at Bunker Hill, the people of Connecticut took notice as they began to consider the need for a monument to the American Revolution in their own state. Thinking of the role Connecticut had played in the war, especially the site of Fort Griswold, where one of the most brutal massacres enacted by British soldiers upon surrendered Americans took place, the citizens of that state began to promote the idea of erecting their own lofty memorial. The editors of the *New London Gazette* were early supporters of such an idea, and promoted a monument project beginning in May of 1825. Noting that such a project could commence through the efforts of "some influential person of property and liberality," the *Gazette* hoped that any monument erected at the fort would instead be a state-sponsored memorial, so that "more perhaps might be done" and the final product would be "worthy of the State, as well as of the occasion."[47] However, while the citizens of Connecticut expressed enthusiasm for the idea, others were more skeptical that such a project would come to fruition. As the *New York Spectator*'s editors wryly noted in August, "The Connecticut editors are laboring to write up a monument to the memory of Col. [William] Ledyard and his brave companions, who were inhumanly slain on Groton heights by the troops of [Benedict] Arnold, in 1781. We hope they will not write, as we editors too often do, in vain."[48]

Whenever such doubts arose from outside sources, writers for local Connecticut newspapers would rush to defend the decision to raise a monument at Groton Heights. The *Connecticut Mirror* acknowledged that outside Connecticut, Groton's hoped-for monument was not taken seriously. Mimicking naysayers, the *Mirror* wrote, "The suggestion may raise a sneer,—it may be said, 'now that the great Mr. [Daniel] Webster has made a great speech to a great man on a great occasion, every little spot where a skirmish may have taken place, must, to follow the Boston fashion, go through in conceited mimickry, the same sort of ceremony'." To such objections—both real and imagined—the *Mirror* offered its justification for a monument; that, "If not on account of the heroes who were there slain in the extremity of bravery and honor—if not for the pride of the state—if not for the glory of the country; at least let some stone be cast there with the name of [Benedict] Arnold upon it." As the greatest traitor of the revolutionary cause, the *Mirror* felt that even if the monument did nothing else, it ought to exist so that future generations would know "the story of his infamy."[49]

The Hartford-based *American Mercury* further reinforced the necessity to erect a monument: "The sacrifices, the virtues, the memories of those who fought at Fort Griswold; the honor and the gratitude of their children, require a memorial . . . posterity will look for a more exalted testimony of our patriotism, than the record of history." The editors of the *Mercury* went further to link the degree of patriotism to those who did, or did not, support the monument project. "That man's heart was noble and patriotic, who proposed to erect a monument on Fort Griswold. His name should be inscribed on it. . . . We should doubt the truth of patriotism, if there was one man, who opposed this design. His motives must indeed be sordid. We ask not of him his reasons or patronage!" And well before any design had yet been settled upon for the future monument, it was nevertheless a point of significance that any future memorial should be built to outlast the ravages of time, even to survive the destruction of American civilization itself, should it occur in some distant future:

> Long after we shall be sleeping in the dust . . . this monument will tour [sic] uninjured and unchanged, and bear on it the endless marks of our freedom and glory. If our country ever falls from its honour and peace; if the spirit of liberty should be obliged to leave its only dwelling place and return to heaven; this will be the monument of our former strength, and beneath its shade may the weeping patriot hide his wounded heart, bleeding for his country. Yes, when some future moralist may wander among the desolate cities, the crumbling domes, the devastated plains, and muse over the ruins of his country, there should be one land mark to guide his way, and if he could find it nowhere else, here should be a refuge.[50]

Such ideas no doubt helped to inform the goals of those who would pursue the monument project and within a matter of weeks, the Groton Monument Association convened for the first time. At their initial meeting, the members formally laid out the Association's purpose to erect an appropriate memorial to the patriot dead. In their formal recommendation to the people of Groton, Chairman of the Association Charles Bulkeley and the Association's clerk, L. Fosdick, wrote, "Assembled here to commemorate their glory and their fate, we your Committee, are impelled upon this occasion, by sentiments which all must approve, to recommend to our fellow citizens, the erecting a monument which shall remain to posterity as a witness of their gratitude & perpetuate the memory of those who here sealed with their blood the liberties of their country."[51]

The raising of funds moved swiftly through the sale of subscriptions and while it took the Bunker Hill Monument Association two years to gather enough money to hold their cornerstone ceremony, Groton was able to do so upon the first anniversary of the Association's initial meeting. At the laying of the cornerstone on September 6, 1826—which, it should be noted, was also the anniversary of the Battle of Groton Heights—speaker Charles Griswold, Esq., went beyond the concept of public gratitude and drew upon the romance entailed in the popular memory of the war. He began his speech by remarking, "[t]he history of this period contains a Revolution, not the Revolution of Hayti [sic]; not a Spanish, nor a French Revolution, but the *American Revolution*—Magical words! What strong emotions do they excite! What images do they call up to the fancy!" Such images, Griswold continued, included "the insolence of pride and power, of oppressive laws and exactions, and of military coercion and tyranny—of the moral energy and physical effort put forth under the most appalling discouragements, to resist this oppression and refuse this yoke of tyranny—of battles and blood stained fields, and at last of the triumphant result!"[52] Griswold's impassioned words, which reminded his listeners of the abuses of power that led to the formation of the United States, summarized what would be for most Americans the popular memory of the war. He further noted that "the character of our Revolutionary contest" involved the noble motive of independence and "freedom from the galling effects of her [Britain's] tyranny and oppression"; with such a righteous cause, unique in the history of warfare, the Revolution "could not and did not fail to fix the attention of the whole civilized world."[53] Albeit a monument dedicated to the fallen of Fort Griswold, by focusing the first half of his oration on the significance of the war overall, Charles Griswold lent a more universal meaning to the structure that would be built.

After exploring the importance of the Revolution, Griswold launched into a brief recollection of the battle that took place at Fort Griswold and addressed the surviving veterans in the audience, "a small remnant of that patriotic band, whose valour and self-devotion to the cause of our common country, was once so signally displayed on this spot."[54] Griswold then concluded by examining the reasons why people "of both enlightened and barbarous nations" erect monuments and why the monument to be constructed at Groton Heights would be important beyond the present generation. In language similar to that employed by Daniel Webster and Edward Everett in Boston, Griswold spoke that the future monument of Groton Heights "will here stand a lasting testimony of the patriotism and heroic valour that was here exhibited in opposing the enemies of our country, and in defending her rights and liberties."[55] And while the notion of large-scale commemorative efforts was a new activity for Americans, Griswold argued that the practice was one handed down from antiquity. The "practice of raising monuments, to perpetuate a remembrance of distinguished persons and events, is coeval with the history of the world."[56] In the eyes of Griswold, then, it was only logical that Americans should carry on such an ancient tradition.

As was the case at Bunker Hill, the monument at Groton reflected that devotion to the memory of those who died in defeat was no less strongly expressed than to those who achieved victory. Bunker Hill had been a major site of American defeat, but in the case of Groton in particular, the battle had become known as the Fort Griswold Massacre. The monument, erected in memory of "a handful of our countrymen, against a very superior British force, and the bravery, heroism, and desperate fighting exhibited here in defence [sic] of this fort," served the added purpose of demonizing the British soldiers, led by Benedict Arnold, who unnecessarily slaughtered the remaining unarmed combatants after taking the fort.[57] The plaque above the doorway to the monument bears the following inscription:

This Monument

Was erected under the patronage of the State of Connecticut, A.D. 1830,

And in the 55th year of the Independence of the U.S.A.

In Memory of the *Brave Patriots*

Who fell in the massacre at Fort Griswold near this spot

On the 6th of September, A.D. 1781,

When the British under the command of

The *traitor Benedict Arnold*,

Burnt the towns of New London & Groton, and spread

Desolation and woe throughout this region.

The meaning of the Groton Monument as a memorial to those who fell at Fort Griswold might have been self-evident to visitors, but in addition to signifying the martyrdom of the American patriots, the inscription articulates the obelisk's second most important function—to remind future generations of Americans of the infamy of Benedict Arnold, traitor to the American cause for independence.

Concerning the style of the monument that would be constructed, Griswold was well aware that more than any speeches, its form and stature would be critical to the public's collective understanding of its purpose as a symbol of patriotism and shared identity. Invoking descriptive language almost identical to Webster's Bunker Hill oration of 1825, Griswold asserted in 1826, "when the work already begun on this Height, shall rise as we trust it will, *in simplicity and unadorned solidity*, it will constitute a common centre [sic] of attraction for the patriotic sentiments of all such as visit this spot [emphasis added]." Acknowledging the variety of social and political ideologies possessed by Americans of every walk of life, Griswold admonished future visitors that they be "impressed with one united sentiment and feeling of love for country, and of respect for the men who fell in defence [sic] of our rights and liberties" upon viewing the Groton Monument. In such an explanation of the monument's meaning, Griswold employed universalizing language to promote the idea that the memorial would be a focal point for patriots, one that would by its very presence unite all Americans regardless of their differences of "opinions and feelings."[58] The obelisk at Groton Heights would therefore be a universal symbol of both remembrance and national pride.

Having already accepted the proposed design of the monument by architects Ithiel Town and A.J. Davis, the Monument Association hired Nathaniel F. Potter of Providence, Rhode Island to execute the construction. Not facing the kinds of funding crises experienced by the Bunker Hill Monument Association, the building of the Groton Monument proceeded swiftly. Upon its completion in 1830, the formal dedication was accompanied by "imposing ceremonies."[59] The following year, the *New-London Gazette* praised the structure as "stately and simple," possessing such well known Egyptian qualities as "height, solidity and durability." Possibly taking a jab at the Bostonians and their as-yet incomplete obelisk, the *Gazette* remarked upon the "plain habits of the economical people of Connecticut" as preventing any attempt to compete "with their more wealthy neighbors in cost and elegance." Rather, using what funding they had on hand—roughly thirteen thousand dollars—the people did not "undertake a work either in style, magnitude, or materials, which they could not finish." Albeit the Groton Monument when it was finished in 1830 stood nearly one hundred feet shorter than the Bunker Hill Monument when it was ultimately completed in 1843, the citizens of Connecticut necessarily took it as a point of pride that they did not try to over-extend themselves with a project to rival their Boston neighbors in size or cost. Expending only about one-eighth the amount of money it would take to complete the Bunker Hill Monument, Connecticut residents admired their "plain Monument" in Groton, constructed out of locally-quarried unfinished gray granite, a material that gave the structure a "rough, massy, and lofty" quality.[60] Capped with an iron "cage-like cupola," the Groton Monument measured 127 feet in height.[61] With its internal stairway, visitors could ascend to the cupola to enjoy, as *The New-London Gazette* described, "one of the most sublime and extensive prospects, that can be imagined, [and] it will amply repay the admirers of nature for the toil of ascending."[62]

While the *Gazette* had, in 1830, confidently asserted that the completed structure would "probably stand when more finished and expensive materials will yield to time," within twenty years local residents feared the monument's collapse.[63] It was noted in local papers in August of 1850 that "there are indications of the falling of this noble monument." According to the New Haven *Columbian Register*, "The south-east corner stones have slipped from their position, and the upper seams are widening on the opposite side. Such is the alarm felt, that the keeper's family have moved from the monument house nearby, lest they be crushed by the anticipated fall of the monument."[64] The Connecticut Legislature eventually approved, in 1852, a motion to appropriate $1,600 in funds for the structure's repair.[65]

Following its completion, Groton held celebrations every year on the anniversary of the Battle of Groton Heights, but in the interim years preceding the battle's centennial, they received little press or publicity. However, as the centennial for the battle approached, there was a renewed fervor to celebrate the fallen of Fort Griswold. At the ninety-ninth anniversary of the battle, held on September 6, 1880, former Connecticut statesman and jurist Lafayette S. Foster invoked language similar to that used by Charles Griswold fifty-four years earlier at the laying of the cornerstone. Drawing upon scenes of heroic defeat from antiquity, Foster exhorted his listeners to think upon similar instances of heroic martyrdom as a way to emphasize the eternal admiration that should be shown to the men who perished at Fort Griswold: "If Miltiades and the ten thousand who fought at Marathon, if Leonidas and the three hundred who fought and perished at Thermopylae have thus made their names immortal, shall not Ledyard and his devoted band who perished here, *in a cause no less sacred*, have their names on the roll of immortality?"[66] Foster's allusion to the heroes of ancient Greece who fought against the Persian Empire to preserve their own manner of government reaffirmed the choice of a monument style taken from antiquity as appropriate, especially given the already well-known associations between Egyptian monuments and sturdy timelessness.

Foster's oration, however, was not solely focused on comparing the deeds of the American fallen to those from antiquity. He also drew upon the monument's function as a universal symbol of American fraternity and national identity as he exhorted the young men in attendance in 1880 to "come up to these heights annually, and at the base of this memorial column, reverently, as at a sacred shrine, pay your vows and honors. Here get inspiration to lead lives worthy of these your illustrious progenitors."[67] For Foster, the monument was at once a memorial to the bravery of the fallen soldiers as well as a reminder to present and future generations to live honorably; its significance lay in its centrality as a symbol embodying universal sentiments of patriotism.

As the centennial anniversary approached, the Groton Monument Association sought to once again raise money for repairs as well as to reconstruct the top of the monument, so as to make it a perfect obelisk like its counterpart in Boston. The *New Haven Evening Register* reported in March of 1881 that a "committee of the Groton Monument Association visited Bunker Hill Monument to-day to obtain ideas as to the best plan for repairing and improving the Groton tower."[68] There is a certain degree of irony here, for local papers had rejected so vehemently in the 1820s claims that the people of Connecticut were copying their Boston counterparts, while now in 1881, the Bunker Hill Monument became the model for the Groton Monument's reconstruction. By May, "diagrams and plans for the alterations" had been completed. As the *Register* reported, "The present top, or dome, is to be removed and the shaft is to be carried up with stone twenty-three feet to an apex, and, when completed the whole structure will be 150 feet high, giving it a fine monumental appearance."[69] Two days before the centennial celebration on September 6th, the *New York Herald* reported on the site and reconstructed monument. Describing the changes the monument had undergone, the editors wrote, "As originally constructed the monument was twelve feet square at its top, but this summer the Monument Committee, who are repairing the structure, have increased the height twenty-three feet, bringing the work to an apex and then making a perfect obelisk of it. The outlooks from the top are about 130 feet from the summit of the height." While reports varied on the height of the completed obelisk, its final measurement was 134 feet tall. As one of the earliest monumental obelisks completed and dedicated to the American Revolution, the Groton Monument had been a precursor to and inspiration for later, similarly-conceived monument projects. With its heightening in 1881, it joined the Bunker Hill Monument as a more pure obelisk in shape. Those who had seen the monument before and after the reconstruction of its top approved of the alteration. As the *New York Herald* noted, "The appearance of the monolith has been greatly improved by the change."[70]

THE PEOPLES' MONUMENTS

Derived as they were from the original Egyptian monoliths, the obelisk form used for the monuments at Bunker Hill and Groton Heights conveyed to visitors that they would last in perpetuity. The obelisks likewise embodied the public memory of the American Revolution, based largely on allusions to bravery and martial valor, and reflected contemporary nineteenth century American qualities such as technological ingenuity, Christian morality and social progressiveness. With the publicity that surrounded the formation of the Bunker Hill and Groton Monument Associations, the laying of their cornerstones and their dedication ceremonies, the choice of the obelisk as the form for both of these monuments established a precedent whereby large scale expressions of public commemoration would likewise appear in the same guise. The eventual construction of the Washington National Monument and the obelisks dedicated to the American victories at Saratoga and Bennington would serve as a testament to the effectiveness with which the Bunker Hill and Groton Monuments laid the groundwork for architectural representations of public sentiment. The repetition of the obelisk form throughout the century also reaffirmed the connection between ancient and modern in the ways that Americans conceived their nation and its legacy.

As memorials to civic virtue, martial valor, courage and heroism in the face of defeat, these monuments had a profound effect in strengthening both local and national efforts to create an American national identity during the nineteenth century. Indeed, despite the loss at Bunker Hill and the gruesome conclusion to the Fort Griswold engagement, the official memory of these events as it was established through the erection of these monuments and the speeches delivered at their bases at various dedications and anniversaries, remained an embodiment of what historian Sarah J. Purcell has referred to as "one vision of the idealized past, which could stand as a perpetual link between generations of American patriots."⁷¹ Through defeat as much as through victory, it was the lasting memory of the heroism exhibited by the American combatants that became one of the focal points in immortalizing the war, and in its repeated use in sites of American defeat, the obelisk became equally associated with American martyrdom as with American greatness through victory. This association between the obelisk and martyrdom would ultimately not be limited to these Revolutionary War battle sites—the form would appear again later in the mausoleum that houses the remains of Abraham Lincoln; the memorial to President William McKinley located in Buffalo, New York, where he was assassinated; and even the 351-foot tall obelisk to the President of the Confederacy, Jefferson Davis in Fairview, Kentucky, may be read as a monument to Davis' heroism in the face of Confederate defeat (see chapter 6).

However, the simple presence of the monuments themselves did not establish the legitimacy of the ancient form as appropriate for the creation of a modern national identity, nor did they guarantee the repetition of the obelisk design later in the century. One of the most important factors to this end was the mythologizing rhetoric employed in the public orations delivered by such men as Daniel Webster, Edward Everett, Charles Griswold and Lafayette Foster, which cemented the associations between the noble heritage of the American Revolution and its heroes, and the appropriateness of the Egyptian obelisk as the symbol through which to memorialize them. Their speeches also helped to justify the expenditure of vast sums of money for the erection of enormous monuments by calling upon all Americans to express their gratitude to those who fought and died for independence. Especially in the case of the dedicatory addresses given at each monument's completion, when the structure was no longer a monument *project* but rather a *fait-accompli*, it lay on the shoulders of the orators to reassure the public that the lofty obelisk before them, which had cost tens of thousands of dollars, had actually been a good idea. The job of any given orator at this time was to not only make the public feel pride in their monument but to also, as historian James M. Mayo has observed, "convert victory into patriotism."⁷² Of course, this sentiment had to be modified slightly in the case of Bunker Hill and Groton—the pattern in these instances was to romanticize the war as a whole and valorize the perseverance of the men who fell to the British. The heroism exhibited in martyrdom and defeat during the war thus converted into patriotism in the nineteenth century.

FIGURE 32 Stereoview from the America Illustrated Series, *Boston & Suburbs,* "Bunker Hill Monument," c. 1860–1910. *(Author's collection)*

Another important factor that helped reinforce the legitimacy of the obelisk design was the sense of collective ownership that resulted during the course of the monuments' construction—they were, after all, primarily funded through subscriptions—and after their completion, when the towering structures became tourist attractions, pilgrimage sites, and identified through popular and consumer culture as symbols of local and national identity. From decade to decade following their completion, visitors to the Bunker Hill and Groton Monuments ascended their staircases so they could view the sprawling landscape from high above. In an age before the availability of easily portable and user-friendly Kodak cameras, mass-produced mementos, such as cartes-de-visites, stereoview cards and postcards could be purchased for a trifle.

For example, in the *America Illustrated* series of stereoviews featuring Boston and its suburbs, images of the monument at Bunker Hill as well as views from its summit offered viewers the opportunity to recreate their experience of not only seeing the monument but also the expanse of land visible from the lookout platform (figure 32). On the back, each card provided information about the history of the monument, including the history of its construction and cost ($156,276), its dimensions and materials, as well as the following comment, "The views from the top of the monument are justly considered among the finest in the world. They embrace Boston, Boston Harbor its Islands, Cambridge, Roxbury, Chelsea, Somerville, Quincy,

Medford, Marblehead, Dorchester, Nahant, Cape Ann, and, in clear weather, the summits of the White Mountains."[73] Through the purchase of such portable reminders of their visit, the monuments, collectively owned by the American people, could be taken home in souvenir form by individual visitors; collective ownership could therefore be translated into private ownership by way of popular consumption. At the more local level, the monuments became common symbols associated with various organizations. In the case of the New London County Historical Society, incorporated in 1870, the organization's official seal features the harbor in the foreground with the Groton Monument next to the rays of the rising sun in the background.

Thus, through their visibility on the physical landscape, the regular appearance of articles about the monuments in newspapers, the easy availability of visual materials for tourists and consumers and the publication of dedicatory orations, Americans throughout the nineteenth century were constantly reminded of both the form and meaning of the Bunker Hill and Groton Monuments. Finally, because the obelisks erected at Bunker Hill and Groton were *both* obelisks, the form itself transcended use in the private realm of the rural cemetery, entered into the public political discourse concerning the legacy and meaning of the Revolutionary War, and became a common symbol associated with such collective American qualities as heroism, independence and sacrifice.

CHAPTER 4

America *Conservata*, Africa *Liberata*: The American Sphinx at Mount Auburn Cemetery

ON FEBRUARY 24, 1871, when Dr. Jacob Bigelow formally presented to the Mount Auburn Cemetery Board of Trustees the plan for a monumental Sphinx to honor the fallen Union soldiers of the Civil War—a monument by then already completed in model and contracted for in granite—be began his presentation with the following remarks, "It has at various times been proposed to erect at Mount Auburn Cemetery some monumental structure commemorative of the great events which have taken place in our country during the last ten years. It is also desired to express, though imperfectly, the gratitude felt to those of our countrymen who have given their lives to achieve the greatest moral and social results of modern times."[1]

Bigelow's desire at this time to erect a memorial to the war's dead was not unusual, but his subject for the monument was. His was an impulse shared by communities throughout the United States in the decades following the war: to erect monuments to honor the fallen; express gratitude for the sacrifices made by the participants on both sides of the conflict; and to memorialize the causes and consequences of the war. By the time Bigelow offered his proposal to the Board, the Egyptian Revival had already long become embedded in the fabric of the commemorative landscape in the form of cemetery gates, family monuments and war memorials. Pyramids, obelisks, portals with cavetto cornice and winged orb, and mastabas with battered walls and touro molding had all become so common that even before the first shots rang out over Fort Sumter, Americans had effectively established an Egypto-American identity in the commemorative sphere. Of all these forms, however, that protective sentinel that signified the height of Egyptian sculptural genius in the public mind—the Sphinx—had remained conspicuously absent in public memorial projects.[2] It would be Jacob Bigelow, one of the most noted physicians of New England and key figure in the establishment of the Rural Cemetery Movement, who would "restore for modern application" the stoic figure from antiquity in his design for the *Sphinx* that would come to rest at Mount Auburn.[3]

Not unlike other memorials erected during the 1860s and 1870s to the Civil War, the *Sphinx* is situated within the cemetery landscape and visited annually by thousands. Surrounded by thousands of private family monuments, the *Sphinx* sits—both physically and metaphorically—at the intersection between the public and private realms of memory. There are no other monuments within the immediate vicinity of the sculpture, and seated as it is directly across from the Gothic Revival chapel, the *Sphinx* exists in a liminal space between the more visible public structures of the cemetery and the more secluded realm dominated by private memorials. Its public versus private meaning is further complicated by the fact that whereas other war memorials were the products of committee decisions, the *Sphinx*'s existence was due entirely to the efforts of Jacob Bigelow. Infused with his own attitudes toward the war's outcome, the future of the nation, and even the country's racial hierarchy, the *Sphinx* purports to express a universal feeling of gratitude for the sacrifices made by the soldiers during the war, but it is also every bit a monument to Bigelow's personal ideologies and achievements as a Boston Brahmin.

Further, albeit the only war memorial appearing in the United States in the form of a sphinx, Bigelow's *Sphinx* at Mount Auburn established a precedent for incorporating such figures into later phases of Egyptian Revival memorial sculpture. More significantly, it provided the necessary inspiration for sculptor Daniel Chester French's (1850–1931) *Milmore Memorial* (1892) in honor of the *Sphinx*'s sculptor, Martin Milmore (1844–1883), a wall-sized tour-de-force in cast bronze that would achieve international fame for both men at the fin-de-siècle. The meaning of Bigelow's *Sphinx*, however, which he had hoped would serve as an appropriate memorial to the soldiers as well as be a symbol for the nation as it looked to a future of "illimitable progress," would fall into obscurity as observers and writers would misinterpret the monument's design and consider it just as puzzling and enigmatic as its predecessor on the Giza plateau.[4]

MAKING A MONUMENT

Whereas most monument projects in memory of the American Revolution did not begin until the beginning of the nineteenth century, the impulse to recognize the sacrifices of the Civil War's combatants and commemorate the conflict's causes and consequences emerged even as the war was still being fought. As early as 1863, communities began to rally funds for the construction of civic monuments to be placed in cemeteries or town squares and artists submitted designs to local monument committees. Among the earliest of these efforts was Randolph Rodger's design for a Soldiers' Monument (c. 1863), which is located in Spring Grove Cemetery in Cincinnati, Ohio.[5] The monuments that were ultimately erected in the North and South reveal stark differences in attitudes toward the war and its outcome, but towns, cities and memorial associations throughout the country shared a common urge to create lasting memorials. As the cost of the war in human lives and suffering was so high, commemoration went beyond the gesture of remembering the dead; for communities across the country, it became a sacred duty, while the process itself was, as historian John Neff has argued, "the quintessential forum for engaging—and, most important, expressing—the war's meaning."[6] Thus, in ways similar to the shaping of the public's memory of the American Revolution, communities engaged in the creation of cultural memory on the local, regional and national scale through the erection of monuments that often involved the manipulation of a variety of styles and symbols to create a visually didactic interpretation of the conflict. When Jacob Bigelow first proposed on April 3, 1865 that the Mount Auburn Cemetery Board of Trustees "contribute towards the erection at Mount Auburn, of a monument to the brave citizens who have fallen in defence [sic] of the Laws, during the Civil War," this process was therefore already well underway across the North and soon would begin across the ravaged South.[7]

By and large, the erection of commemorative monuments in the aftermath of the Civil War was a corporate effort performed by ladies' memorial associations (LMAs) in the South and male-dominated monument associations in the North. Albeit both kinds of organizations operated with the common purpose of commemorating the war and its participants, the differences in organizational makeup highlight just how different the cultural goals were on each side. Whereas the memorialization of the American Revolution had conveyed a sense of national unity, the construction of public memory of the Civil War was far more contested terrain. Not only did the victors seek to attribute purpose and meaning to the war's causes and consequences, but the losing side also sought to write its own history in the stone of its monuments. Monuments to the Union cause declared that the war had been fought to preserve the Union; they noted as a secondary outcome, that slavery had been destroyed. Confederate monuments, by contrast, sought to immortalize the patriotism and valor of the South's soldiers and such monuments aided in fashioning the enduring mythos of the "Lost Cause."[8] The rhetoric used on monument inscriptions and in dedicatory orations played an especially fundamental role in articulating the purpose of these monuments and the intentions of their respective communities or memorial associations involved in their creation. For while the monument designs were drawn from a variety of fairly typical interpretive sculptural or architectural forms—obelisks, columns, standing soldiers, eagles and allegorical figures—the specific use of language tended to dictate how observers should interpret the monuments' meaning.

For example, the inscription on the South Carolina Soldiers' Monument (1879) located in front of the state's capitol building in Columbia exemplifies the Southern trend to perpetuate the idea of the "Lost Cause" through especially lengthy inscriptions. On the front, the inscription notes the heroism and patriotism of the men who "HAVE GLORIFIED A FALLEN CAUSE" and that they were able to endure the sufferings on the battlefield, the army hospital and the army prison camps through the unwavering belief that at home, "THEY WOULD NOT BE FORGOTTEN." The rear of the monument contains the rest of the inscription, which exhorts the observer to recognize the virtues of the soldiers who died and "FOR THE JUST JUDGMENT OF THE CAUSE IN WHICH THEY PERISHED." In this way, the inscription on the South Carolina Soldiers' Monument and others throughout the South glorified what historian Thomas Brown has described as "the purity of the soldiers' motives without explaining what these motives were." Such inscriptions also showed faith that the survivors in the South would neither abandon the soldiers' memory nor would they succumb to the postwar reconstruction of the social order.[9]

By contrast, the predominant memorializing trend in the North was, first and foremost, to celebrate the preservation of the Union and honor the combatants as patriots, heroes and martyrs. A significant number of Union memorials, included among them the *Sphinx* at Mount Auburn, acknowledged the emancipation of the slaves as one of the major consequences of the conflict, but seldom did any give primacy to this outcome. The inscription on the Soldiers' and Sailors' Monument (1877) in Boston signifies this trend:

> TO THE MEN OF BOSTON
> WHO DIED FOR THEIR COUNTRY
> ON LAND AND SEA IN THE WAR
> WHICH KEPT THE UNION WHOLE
> DESTROYED SLAVERY
> AND MAINTAINED THE CONSTITUTION
> THE GRATEFUL CITY
> HAS BUILT THIS MONUMENT
> THAT THEIR EXAMPLE MAY SPEAK
> TO COMING GENERATIONS

However, for as many monuments in the North that acknowledged the end of slavery, there were as many, if not more, that ignored altogether that facet of the war's outcome. The Soldiers' Monument (1870) in Greenfield, Massachusetts, offers a case in point:

> GREENFIELD ERECTS THIS MONUMENT IN GRATEFUL HONOR
> TO HER PATRIOTIC SONS WHO OFFERED THEIR LIVES
> IN SUPPRESSING THE GREAT REBELLION
> AND FOR THE PRESERVATION OF THE NATIONAL UNION, 1861–5.

The inscription on the Soldiers' Monument in Wells, Maine, also shows this rhetorical selectivity:

> SOLDIERS MONUMENT
> ERECTED BY
> JOHN STORER Esqr
> OF SANFORD
> AND THE INHABITANTS OF WELLS
> IN MEMORY
> of the brave and patriotic Soldiers
> of Wells who sacrificed their lives

> during the Great Rebellion in main-
> taining our Government and thus es-
> tablishing on a broader and firmer
> foundation the principle of civil and
> religious liberty.

The emphasis on both monuments therefore concerns the patriotism of the fallen in defense of the union against the "Great Rebellion" and while the inscription on the Wells monument concludes with a reference to "civil and religious liberty," there is no explicit reference to slave emancipation.

Historian John Neff argues that particularly in the North, the prevailing concern among communities was to erect memorials that would foster reconciliation between the former combatants, which provides a compelling explanation why references to slavery and emancipation remained absent in so many monument inscriptions. "So powerful was the need to find reconciliation to such a disruptive war," argues Neff, "even the logical consequences of the Union victory—predicated at least in part on emancipation—could be rather easily relinquished in the name of the reunited nation." For while the cause for black freedom had been a "bitterly fought and hard-won struggle during the war," in the war's aftermath "black citizenship and political participation were sacrificed for the sake of white reconciliation."[10] It did not suffice, however, to simply allow the monuments to speak for themselves when it came to expressing the desire for reconciliation. Halcyon calls for the rekindling of the bonds of white brotherhood were also a common theme at monument dedication ceremonies. In the case of the Soldiers' and Sailors' Monument (1870) in Hingham, Massachusetts, the inscriptions on the 30-foot tall obelisk include only the names of the men who perished in the war with no further words to their memory. What the monument's inscription lacked in prescriptive language, however, was duly made up for by Solomon Lincoln, who delivered the dedication oration:

> While, therefore, we devote this day to commemorate the patriot dead, we will rejoice that our country is free, that the Union is preserved, that our institutions are safe, that time, the great arbiter, will heal all animosities, and conquer all prejudices, that justice will reign, that the rights of every citizen will be secured, and that amid the trials and perplexities consequent upon a state of civil war, the nation will rise above all adverse influences, and animated by a spirit of patriotism, the love of freedom, and a just

regard for the rights of every citizen, will commence a new career of true glory and renown.

The monument itself, exhorted Lincoln, "shall remind the living of their duty to themselves, to their country, and to posterity." Finally, while Lincoln noted that "our country is free," he made no specific reference to the emancipation or citizenship of African Americans in the United States. Rather, his emphasis lay in affirming that despite four years of bloodshed, the country would see a harmonious, united future.[11]

Even in the cases when references to emancipation *did* appear on monument inscriptions, such as in the case of the Boston Soldiers' and Sailors' Monument, calls for reconciliation between the North and South as the most important priority for the postwar years could be found in the accompanying dedication speeches. Frederick O. Prince, speaking at the dedication of Boston's monument, employed language eerily familiar to Daniel Webster's Bunker Hill Monument oration: "Long may this structure stand undisturbed by man and the elements. May centuries outnumbering those that look down from the pyramids roll on and find the statue of America beholding, as now, from yonder shaft, over all our vast domain, a free, happy, prosperous, and united people."[12] However, whereas Webster drew upon such Egyptian-inspired imagery and the idea of timelessness to link the durability of the obelisk at Bunker Hill with the eternal gratitude of the American people, Prince used the same concepts to speak of the nation's future as "free, happy, prosperous, and united." To emphasize the importance of unity and reconciliation, Prince went on to explain that the people of Boston did not erect their monument so as "to perpetuate strife" or "keep alive sectional animosity and acrimony" through sculptured stone and bronze. Nor did they want the monument to recollect to the viewer "fields red with the blood of countrymen" or for its symbolism to rub into the faces of Southern visitors "victories over the descendants of sires who fought side by side under Washington."[13] Even though the monument's inscription articulated slavery's destruction, Prince made it clear to the audience in attendance that the objective was to commemorate, not to gloat or linger over sectional tensions, especially since so many of the white combatants claimed common ancestry stretching back to the American Revolution.

Within such a milieu of diverse commemorative goals, the process whereby memorials came into being followed a remarkably similar pattern across the country; they involved meetings, fundraising, and competitions in which architects and sculptors submitted their designs, which would then be voted on by the monument committees. In his early efforts to erect a Civil War memorial at Mount Auburn, Bigelow followed the traditional course of action; that is, he presented his idea to the Board of Trustees and it would be up to the members to hold meetings, pursue fundraising efforts, hold design competitions, and finally vote upon which design to accept and execute in stone. While the Trustees showed early enthusiasm for Bigelow's initial proposal, further progress stalled toward the end of 1865 and in January 1866, the Board abandoned all efforts to move forward with the project.[14]

Memorial associations across the country underwent a similar process as that which occurred at Mount Auburn Cemetery, albeit with more success. In some instances, even when monument committees encountered few obstructions, it took over a decade to complete such a project. The Boston Soldiers' and Sailors' Monument is illustrative of how lengthy the process could be: the Board of Aldermen first convened and submitted plans to erect a memorial in 1866; after approval of the City Council in 1870, the decision was made to hire the Irish-born Boston sculptor Martin Milmore to execute the work at a cost not to exceed $75,000; Milmore finished a model of the monument in 1874; and the completed memorial was unveiled to the public in 1877.[15] When the dedicatory ceremonies finally occurred on September 17, it was one of the major cultural events in Boston that year and was reflective of how significant a monument unveiling could be. The 15,000 square foot platform erected at the base of the monument accommodated 3,200 seated spectators and beyond the immediate environs of the platform, there were thousands more in attendance. In the Procession alone, the number of men who marched totaled 25,429.[16]

In other instances, the process to erect a monument took less time and involved fewer complexities. Such was the case with the Hollywood Memorial Association in Richmond, Virginia. Reflective of the lack of funding that was a hallmark of the Southern LMAs' efforts to commemorate their dead, the ladies who comprised the group approached the city engineer, Charles H. Dimmock in 1867 to "submit a design for a memorial to be completed for less than $15,000." The purpose of the monument was to serve as a collective memorial for the 18,000 Confederate dead who had been exhumed from battlefield graves and reinterred in Hollywood Cemetery, another key activity of the Southern LMAs. In order to remain within the fiscal guidelines outlined by the Association, Dimmock "suggested erecting a ninety-foot pyramidal structure of large blocks cut from James River granite," which could be quarried locally and would therefore be less expensive than the cut-stone monument or memorial chapel the Association originally had in mind (figure 33). A small ceremony attended the laying of the cornerstone in 1868 and according to historian Caroline E. Janney, the women in attendance "placed a variety of Confederate relics and symbols in the stone." These included the first Confederate flag made in Richmond; Confederate insignia; Confederate money and postage stamps; a fragment of the coat worn by Stonewall Jackson the day he was wounded; photographs of Jefferson Davis and Confederate generals; along with many other similar objects. Finally, the women placed a copy of the Bible, the Virginia Masonic textbook, the *Richmond Daily Dispatch*, the *State Journal*, and records of the HMA into the cornerstone.

As Janney has further noted, upon its completion in 1869, the pyramid became the symbol of the Hollywood Memorial Association and appeared on their stationary as well as on the frontispiece of the "Register of the Confederate Dead."[17] The pyramid at Hollywood Cemetery and the Boston Soldiers' and Sailors' Monument are both illustrative examples for how Civil War memorial activities typically involved a collective effort with the end result reflecting the shared values and needs of the entire community. However, as is evident in the case of the Confederate pyramid, the decision to choose one monument style over another was at times dictated by cost of materials and construction rather than by an adherence to a particular aesthetic.

In this vein, the stylistic palette from which Civil War memorial associations and monument designers chose their subjects was broad. Monument styles included the widely popular citizen soldier statue; allegorical figures such as Liberty, Columbia and Victory; and statuary and reliefs taken from life, such as the Robert E. Lee Monument (1890) in Richmond and the *Shaw Memorial* (1884–1897) dedicated to Colonel Robert Gould Shaw and the 54th Massachusetts Regiment in Boston.[18] Memorials found throughout the country often incorporate a variety of these elements, such as a citizen soldier statue or figure of Liberty standing atop a column or obelisk, with other sculptural figures or reliefs mounted at the base. Examples of these kinds of composite sculptural/architectural memorials may be found in Providence, Rhode Island (1871); Detroit, Michigan (1872); Worcester (1874) and Boston, Massachusetts (1877); and Indianapolis, Indiana (1888). In the case of some monuments such as the Soldiers' and Sailors' Monument on Exchange

FIGURE 33 Memorial pyramid to the Confederate dead, Hollywood Cemetery, Richmond, Virginia, 1869. *(Library of Congress)*

Plaza in Providence, it was necessary for memorial committees to hire both an architect (J.G. Batterson) and a sculptor (Randolph Rogers), since the finished structure included sculptures and bas-reliefs arrayed on an architectural base.[19]

Throughout the entire period during which communities commemorated the war with local monuments, the popularity of the Egyptian

Revival in Civil War commemoration was readily apparent, especially in the widespread appearance of obelisks, which offered the only significant rival in popularity over the citizen-soldier statue. Memorial obelisks to the war's participants appeared regularly in cemeteries and town squares throughout the North, South and West from the 1860s through the 1910s and included, among others, a memorial obelisk dedicated to the country's "defenders in the war of the rebellion" in Brimfield, Massachusetts (1866); the memorial obelisk in Key West, Florida (1866) erected by the Navy Club in honor of the Union soldiers, sailors and marines who fell at the station located there; "The First Civil War Monument" (1867) in Lancaster, Wisconsin, which bears quotations from Abraham Lincoln's Gettysburg Address and the Emancipation Proclamation; the Mount View Cemetery Civil War Memorial (1867) in Pekin, New York; the Oakland Cemetery Confederate Memorial Obelisk (1874) erected in Atlanta by the Atlanta Ladies' Memorial Association; the Civil War Soldiers' Monument (1885) in Kent, Connecticut; and the Confederate Memorial (1910) at Finn's Point National Cemetery in Pennsville, New Jersey, dedicated to the Confederate prisoners who died at Fort Delaware. In addition to this popular form, other Egyptian designs emerged for the same purpose, including the 90-foot Confederate pyramid in Hollywood Cemetery and a 33-foot tall granite lotus column surmounted by an American eagle, located on the village common in Greenfield, Massachusetts (1870) (figure 34).

It did not take long after the war's end for writers to observe that communities systematically drew from the same stylistic patterns for their Civil War memorials, thus creating a sense of repetitious copycatting across the country. As early as 1866, William Dean Howells, writing for *The Atlantic Monthly*, urged Americans to think upon how to interpret the war and encouraged his readers to develop innovative memorial styles, rather than rely upon "the dreary means of conventional allegory." Howells went on to criticize the use of "bas-reliefs of battles, and statues of captains, and groups of privates, or many scantily-draped, improper figures, happily called Liberties," and further exhorted that memorials to the war should not be funereal in nature and placed in the cemeteries. Rather, they should appear in public areas, such as town squares and commons, since their intended purpose should be to honor the living as well as the dead.[20] In Howells's view, then, commemorative monuments need not incorporate any of the popular expressive forms—such as the Liberties and the citizen soldier statue—nor

FIGURE 34 Soldiers' Monument, Greenfield, Massachusetts, 1870.
(Photograph by Andrea Lustig)

should they call to mind images of death. Yet despite Howells's appeals that communities focus on the moral imperatives of the war and exercise ingenuity and imagination in the erection of monuments to the soldiers and their cause, the landscape reveals that his advice went largely unheeded. In the cemeteries, obelisks erected in honor of the war's dead became arguably the most common form, while in public town squares and parks, memorial associations adhered faithfully to the sculptural forms so discouraged by Howells.

As communities around the nation proceeded with erecting their monuments, Bigelow once again brought forth the subject in December 1870, four years after the Trustees abandoned the project. However, this time, Bigelow proposed to donate a "Memorial Work of Art" to the cemetery and thus bypassed the kinds of funding restrictions and conflicts over aesthetic taste that could occur when a committee was involved.[21] It is clear that Bigelow was of a similar opinion with Howells about avoiding what had by that time become overly familiar sculptural forms. At the board meeting of August 9, 1871, the plan to donate a granite statue of a "Sphynx" was formally unveiled to the Trustees, and in September, the *Sphinx*, executed by Martin Milmore in granite quarried from Hallowell, Maine, had been successfully placed upon its pedestal facing the cemetery chapel.[22] Bigelow conveyed to the Board his intentions, that the monument would commemorate the "great events" that had taken place and express gratitude to the soldiers who died "to achieve the greatest moral and social results of modern times."[23] Regarding the common theme of reconciliation, Bigelow remained silent.

After the *Sphinx*'s formal unveiling in August of 1872 but shortly before Bigelow proceeded with the official donation of the monument to the cemetery, a minor dispute broke out that lasted until November between Bigelow and the Board that was indicative of how the monument's creation strayed from normal practice. Since Bigelow designed, commissioned and paid for the monument, the Board felt that it would be appropriate to have his name placed conspicuously on the front of the pedestal in large letters. Bigelow vehemently objected to the Board's desire to have his name prominently displayed on the base and in a letter to the Board's president, John T. Bradlee, he argued "this would be a departure from the object and intentions of the Monument which are already expressed on both sides." He went on to "respectfully request that if my name is to appear at all on the Stone it may be made in small and unostentatious letters on one side of the base as I have fully explained to the Superintendent."[24]

Bigelow's wishes were not granted as quickly as he had hoped and so, in another letter dated November 1, he expressed more strenuously that "I am unalterably opposed to the display of my name on the front of the Sphinx," stating that only after his name was carved inconspicuously on the side of the pedestal would he "be ready to sign a transfer of the whole Monument to the Proprietors of Mnt [sic] Auburn."[25] After having effectively held the transfer of ownership to the Board of Trustees hostage, the members of the Board conceded to the aged doctor's request and had JACOB BIGELOW STATUIT ET DEDICAVIT carved on one side of the pedestal and MARTIN MILMORE SCULPTOR BOSTON 1872 on the other side.[26] Although not prominently displayed as the Trustees had originally intended, the presence of Bigelow's name on the monument nevertheless weakened his original intention, that it should merely express "the gratitude of the donor."[27] It remains unclear whether or not the board wanted to inscribe Bigelow's name prominently due to the unprecedented process whereby the *Sphinx* came into being, but it did set a precedent for future misinterpretations of the monument's origin and symbolism.

"THE BENIGNITY OF WOMAN"

Measuring fifteen feet in length, eight feet tall and with a face three feet wide, Bigelow's *Sphinx* is an indelibly American monument that explicitly blends ancient Egyptian and American symbols. The overall effect is what art historian Richard Carrott dubbed "Egyptianizing"—the sculpture does not strive for archaeological verisimilitude, but the combination of Egyptian and non-Egyptian elements nevertheless results in a "total effect [which] echoes an Egyptian feeling or aesthetic."[28] The figure consists of the body of a lion and the head of a woman wearing the Egyptian royal *menes* (headdress) surmounted by the head of an American bald eagle.[29] Around her neck, the *Sphinx* wears an American military medal in the shape of a six-pointed star. The monument sits atop a granite pedestal that includes what Bigelow described as "emblems and inscriptions."[30] Carved in high relief on the southern end of the pedestal is the figure of an Egyptian Lotus (*Nymphaea Lotus*) and on the northern end, the American Water-Lily (*Nymphaea odorata*). The eastern side of the base bears an inscription in Latin, and on the west, the English translation:

AMERICA *CONSERVATA*, AFRICA *LIBERATA* 141

FIGURE 35 Visitors around the Sphinx, c. 1870s. *(Courtesy of Mount Auburn Historical Collections)*

AMERICA CONSERVATA,	AMERICAN UNION PRESERVED,
AFRICA LIBERATA,	AFRICAN SLAVERY DESTROYED,
POPULO MAGNO ASURGENTE,	BY THE UPRISING OF A GREAT PEOPLE,
HEROUM SANGUINE FUSO.	BY THE BLOOD OF FALLEN HEROES.

Never before in the history of the Egyptian Revival were the emblems of American nationalism and Pharaonic Egyptian power so explicitly combined. And yet, with the exception of the medal, the overall absence of martial imagery along with the overtly feminine attributes (the face and flowers) convey the message that this is not so much a *war* memorial as it is a representation of the new nation. Only the inscriptions explicitly convey what it is the *Sphinx* actually commemorates. Upon the monument's completion, Bigelow would make certain that the public understood the symbolic associations (figures 35 and 36).

FIGURE 36 The Sphinx at Mount Auburn Cemetery, 1872. *(Photograph by the author)*

Shortly before the completion of the *Sphinx*, while an air of mystery still shrouded Bigelow's eventual gift to the cemetery, the *Boston Daily Journal* no doubt piqued local curiosity when in anticipation of the unveiling it wrote,

> Death is a mystery, and so is the Sphinx. It was this idea and the wish to perpetuate the memory of the brave young soldiers who went forth to battle for a great cause, and manfully laid down in the embrace of the grim destroyer, which probably actuated one of our oldest and most respected physicians, Dr. Jacob Bigelow, to employ Mr. [Martin] Milmore to cut a colossal statue, representing the mysterious Egyptian monument on the banks of the Nile. . . . This will be the first Sphinx ever wrought in this country of like proportions.

Noting the design of the figure, the *Journal* anticipated the face upon the lion's body to appear "in all the beauty of an Egyptian princess."[31] For the uniqueness of its design, which would set it apart from other examples of Civil War commemoration, and for the anticipated beauty of Milmore's execution of the monument, no doubt the citizens of Boston were curious, if not outright excited, to see the final product.

Once the *Sphinx* was completed and placed in position facing the chapel at Mount Auburn, there was a small unveiling ceremony attended by the

Mount Auburn Cemetery Board of Trustees and a number of Bigelow's friends and family. It was an affair that other monument dedication ceremonies around the country dwarfed by comparison. Unfortunately for Bigelow, at eighty-four years of age he had lost his sight and could not actually see his design, which Milmore had executed so perfectly. As George Ellis would later write in his *Memoir of Jacob Bigelow* following the physician's death in 1879, Bigelow, undeterred by his lack of vision, "wished 'to see it by feeling.' Those who honored him and revered him will always associate the eloquent stone with the scene of his visit to it, when, with others' help, he was raised and aided slowly, inch by inch, to pass his hands over all its members and features."[32]

Despite the rather diminutive gathering, however, the *Sphinx* received much local, and even national, attention by reviewers as a visually striking memorial work of art. Situated as it was in such a prime location at the most famous and visited cemetery in America, the *Sphinx* necessarily became an attraction for thousands of visitors each year. Bigelow made clear with his *Account of the Sphinx* exactly why he designed the monument as he did and what he intended it to represent. Echoing William Dean Howells' words about repetition in the arena of memorial sculptures, Bigelow noted in his *Account*, "The wide range of architectural ideas and combinations exhibited in pillars, pyramids, obelisks, altars, sarcophagi, and mausoleums, have been produced and reproduced in inexhaustible variety. But the more significant creations of expressive sculpture have hitherto been less frequently attempted here, because they are more difficult of satisfactory execution." He conceded that in the United States, "groups of monumental sculpture" had been produced, but nothing on the scale of what could be found on the landscape of the Old World. Regarding such examples, he referred to the colossal lion statues at Waterloo in Belgium (1824–1826) and at Lucerne (1858), which "travelers in Switzerland visit with admiration" (figure 37).[33] No doubt these lions, dedicated to martial valor and symbols of courage, majesty and strength, provided some inspiration to Bigelow in his conception of the *Sphinx*.

Clearly seeking to break from the traditional forms of memorialization in his own country, Bigelow thus sought to introduce a new monumental form to the American commemorative landscape by restoring "for modern application the image of the ancient Sphinx, a form capable of completing, in connection with its pedestal and accessories, the required associations of

144   AMERICA *CONSERVATA*, AFRICA *LIBERATA*

FIGURE 37   Lucerne, Thorwaldsen's Lion, c. 1860–1890. *(Library of Congress)*

repose, strength, beauty, and duration."³⁴ By the time of the *Sphinx*'s completion, Bigelow's admiration for the ancient Egyptians had already been well-established in both his scholarly and civic activities. His gateway to Mount Auburn Cemetery had been instrumental in legitimizing the Egyptian Revival for use throughout the country during the Rural Cemetery Movement. Additionally, Bigelow had served as a member of the second design committee for the Bunker Hill Monument Association, which had voted in favor of the obelisk form for the eventual Bunker Hill Monument.³⁵ Well known among students and scholars for his collected Harvard lectures, *Elements of Technology* (1829) and *The Useful Arts* (1840), Bigelow had long praised the ancient Egyptians for their skill with building and sculpting technologies. Regarding the Sphinx at Giza, he referred to it as an "extraordinary production" and a "wonderful work of art."³⁶ It is therefore not entirely surprising that, with such a record of admiration and emulation, Bigelow would choose for his monument to the Union soldiers a figure derived from his favorite ancient civilization.

With regard to the task of interpreting the *Sphinx*'s combination of imagery and inscriptions, Bigelow controlled, at least initially, the public understanding of the monument. To this end, while Bigelow published his *Account* for distribution among the Trustees and his close acquaintances, the text also appeared in the *Boston Evening Transcript* and the *Lowell Daily Citizen and News*.[37] Reviews of the monument also appeared shortly after its dedication in *The Atlantic Monthly* and *The Ladies' Repository*.[38] *The Atlantic Monthly* was particularly laudatory of the *Sphinx*, first complaining that the "figure of the Union volunteer . . . has become worn by repetition" and that "there would seem to be a doubt whether it furnishes a sufficient reminder to the men of future generations." Noting that such figures only call upon memories of loss, *The Atlantic* considered the *Sphinx* a "more hopeful emblem, inspired by the sense of a noble gain," which "expresses the sum of all."[39] The overall effect of *The Atlantic Monthly*'s words distinctly recalls William Dean Howells' plea to Americans back in 1866 to develop innovative memorial styles and not simply reproduce the typical, well-worn sculptural figures.

In Bigelow's *Account*, which substituted for a formal ceremonial speech to convey the meaning and significance of the monument thus being unveiled, he wrote little about the Civil War. He noted that the war achieved the "greatest moral and social results of modern times," but unlike other contemporary dedicatory remarks, Bigelow did not dwell on the loss of lives suffered during the war, nor did he speak directly about reunion or emancipation.[40] He also completely avoided the increasingly popular theme of white reconciliation, which orators, particularly in the North, encouraged at the dedication ceremonies for other monuments.[41] Bigelow did, however, reflect on *why* he chose a sphinx as the subject for his monument and what he hoped the modern *Sphinx* would convey about the nation as it moved forward into a future of "illimitable progress."[42]

Given most contemporaries' understanding of the female sphinx as originating in Greek mythology, Bigelow offered clarification for visitors to the cemetery by providing first in his *Account* an historical analysis of the *Sphinx*'s derivation, its symbolism, and major examples from antiquity. Echoing his earlier Harvard lectures found in *Elements of Technology* and *The Useful Arts*, Bigelow regarded the colossal Sphinx at Giza as the "most stupendous work of sculpture which the world has seen," and also offered acknowledgement of the "numerous Sphinxes" found in Thebes. He also recalled the Greek myth of Oedipus solving the riddle of the Sphinx and explained that the female Sphinx from Greek mythology connoted a "savage nature" and "self-destruction."[43] Such associations with savagery and self-destruction were already well known. Poems bearing variations of the title

"The Sphinx" appeared from time to time in leading periodicals, including one in *The Atlantic Monthly* published in 1859. The author warns, "Go not to Thebes. The Sphinx is there; And thou shalt see her beauty rare. . . . Oh! Woe to those who fail to read! And woe to him who shall succeed! For he who fails the truth to show; The terror of her wrath shall know."[44] The connection between the Greek Sphinx and the destructiveness of the Civil War were made explicit in a poem entitled "Sphinx and Oedipus" published in the very first issue of *Continental Monthly* toward the beginning of the war. In the poem, the Sphinx's riddle is a demand to know why the North and South have engaged in battle:

> Why poets should sing of this War
> In rapturous anthems of praise,
> I know not. Its meanings so jar,
> Its purpose hath so many ways,
> The SPHINX never readeth the whole.
> 'Tis a riddle propounded to me
> That I am unskillful to tell.
> The Sphinx by the way-side, I see,
> Is watching (I know her so well)
> To mangle us, body and soul.
>
> Is it 'Freedom, that Bondage may live,'
> Which cheers on the North to the fray?
> Is it 'Slavery more Freedom to give,'
> That slogans the Southern foray?
> She asks, and awaits your reply:
> No answer, ye *marshal*-bred bands
> Whose business is murder and blood;
> Ye priests with incarnadined hands;
> Ye peace-men who 'fight for the good;'
> Now solve her this riddle or die!

'Our Flag,' the conservative says,
'Waves over the land of the free;'
God save us!—I think many ways,
But still 'tis a riddle to me,
Whose mystery is hid from the eye;
But Oedipus, showing the souls
All fettered, imbruted and blained,
Who point where its blazonry rolls,
And wail the sad plaint of the chained, -
Asserts, 'There is, somewhere, a lie.'

The message, then, is that the Sphinx knows that the combatants have no answer for her and so she waits at the ready to destroy all those engaged on both sides of the conflict. Ultimately, it is a war without a victor.[45]

In another example, published shortly before the completion of Bigelow's *Sphinx*, a poem entitled "The Sphinx" by M.E.N. Hatheway appeared in *The Atlantic Monthly* in 1871:

She fronts the traveler as he goes,
A power to threaten and beguile;
And fear and love awake before
Her lion strength, her woman smile.

She bids him seek her mystery,
And solve her riddle strange and dim;
With art and wisdom matched against
The doom that waits to conquer him.

But vain the contest and the toil,
The weary heart, the wasted breath;
The mystic meaning still is veiled,
And all endeavor ends in death.

For, should her master-spirit rise
And lay her secret bare and free,
She from her eminence must fall,
And cease from strife, and cease to be.

O life! Whose subtle charm allures,
O life! Whose will inviolate
Forever challenges the soul
To solve the mystery of fate;

And strive where it shall not attain,
And grasp at shadows that elude;
Till, faltering, it quits the chase,
And leaves the tempter unsubdued.[46]

With such embedded negative associations with the female sphinx, Bigelow's choice of a female head atop the lion's body appears curious at first glance. In both *The Useful Arts* and the *Account*, Bigelow commented that Egyptian sphinxes were primarily male and he noted that the Egyptians also crafted female sphinxes, albeit not as regularly. He wrote, "Sphinxes of smaller size, having the head of a woman, are common in Upper Egypt, and, in some instances, rows of these figures appear to have lined the sides of venues a mile or more in length."[47]

To best understand the gendered and racial ramifications of Bigelow's design, the *Account* provides the most revealing statement: "The Sphinx most known in antiquity was an ideal personification of intellect and physical force, expressed by a human head on the body of a lion. It was a favorite emblem in Egypt, and was variously copied by Greeks, Romans, and other nations of later times."[48] The monument's design, which fuses the Anglo head with the lion's body (presumably the most overtly African element), maintains a traditional racial hierarchy even as it envisions a racially united nation. In Bigelow's vision for postwar America, white intellect would lead the nation, while the free black population—the "physical force"—would continue to function as the labor force, the physical muscle. Bigelow's choices of a female face—one clearly derived from Classical sculpture—provides an added layer of gendered as well as racial connotations to his vision.[49]

The face could at once be viewed as the allegorical Columbia, Liberty, Hope or Victory—traditional images, all of which possessed similar classically-derived features—but she could also be viewed as the epitome of Northern white middle class femininity. The nineteenth century ideal of the "domestic angel" of the household, armed with such qualities as Christian piety and moral superiority, she represented both Caucasian superiority in her whiteness and such qualities as peace and benignity in her femininity. Employing the female visage as the literal face of the nation was not unusual. Aside from the traditional use of allegorical figures in American commemorative sculptures, the image of the white American woman as the symbol of the nation would be more fully realized in 1886 with the Statue of Liberty.[50]

Bigelow's comments in the *Account* also provide some insight into how his own perceptions of race and intellectual ability were undoubtedly informed by mid-century ethnological debates: "the ideal image [the sphinx] once created has descended through uncounted ages from barbarism to civilization, assuming in its progress every variety of physiognomy and expression, from the almost Nubian and sometimes brute profile to the most perfect Caucasian face." Concerning Egyptian sculptures, Bigelow argued that even though "African in their locality," they exhibited "many examples of the most perfect intellectual head."[51] Bigelow's subtle use of terminology—the "brute profile" and "intellectual head"—clearly reflects the kinds of physiologically-based racism that had been promoted by the mid-century cranial studies of such men as George Gliddon, Dr. Josiah Nott and Dr. Samuel George Morton, not to mention the centrality of Egypt to mid-century debates over intellectual capacity and race-based slavery. The thrust of these mid-century studies, including Morton's *Crania Aegyptiaca* (1844), Gliddon's *Otia Aegyptiaca* (1849) and Gliddon's, Nott's and Morton's collective monumental work, *Types of Mankind* (1854), involved the study of human crania to disprove any notions regarding the "blackness" of the ancient Egyptians.[52] Echoing Bigelow's own comments regarding the land of the pharaohs, Morton had declared, "Egypt is justly regarded as the parent of civilization, the cradle of the arts, the land of mystery," and he further noted that modern intellectuals debated whether western civilization "had its origin in Egypt or in Ethiopia."[53] The ramifications of such studies for pro-slavery advocates were clear: had the Egyptians been "Africans or even Negroes,"[54] southern white slave owners would be hard-pressed to justify the continued enslavement of African Americans on the basis of mental and intellectual inferiority.

As part of these studies, such men as Morton, Nott and Gliddon offered further commentary on the intellectual abilities of the ancient Egyptians and other Africans based upon visual analyses of their artistic and sculptural productions. The Sphinx at Giza, already known to people around the world and the object of speculative commentaries for centuries, was a troubling specter to these men. Albeit a text principally focused on the crania of North America, Morton offered his assessment of the Sphinx in *Crania Americana* (1839) as a refutation to eighteenth century traveler Volney's observations. According to Morton, Volney "hastily inferred from its flat features and bushy hair, that the Egyptians were real Negroes." Morton refuted such observations with the argument that "these circumstances have no weight." Rather, the sculpture "may have been a shrine of the Negro population of Egypt, who, as traffickers, servants and slaves, were a very numerous body."[55] Reacting to similar observations of the monumental Sphinx, Gliddon argued in his *Otia Aegyptiaca* "[i]t has been the fashion to quote the Sphinx, as an evidence of the Negro tendencies of the ancient Egyptians. They take his *wig* for curly hair—and as the nose is off, of course it is *flat*. . . . But even if the face (which I fully admit) has a strong African cast, it is an almost solitary example, against 10,000 that *are not African*."[56] Published in the years prior to the Civil War, such arguments provided pro-slavery advocates the kind of scholarly and "scientific" support needed to justify the perpetuation of race-based slavery, but they may have also influenced Bigelow as he conceived the design for his own *Sphinx*. Bigelow was well aware of the racial debates and explorations into Egyptological researches during these years, and had even attended George Gliddon's disastrous mummy unwrapping in 1850 at the Tremont in Boston, where the "Theban priestess" ultimately turned out to be a man.[57]

Albeit a man who likely ascribed to Gliddon and Morton's racial theories, Bigelow had never been an outward defender of slavery. George Ellis, his friend and memoirist, claimed on Bigelow's behalf after his death that "He knew that slavery was avenging on us its sum of wrongs, and that only the energy of a mastering force, intelligently and heroically devoted, could crush the evil, and save the nation."[58] Bigelow's conviction that the Civil War had been a moral war, devoted not only to the preservation of the Union but also to the destruction of slavery, was evident from the *Account* and Ellis' reminiscences of his friend. However, Bigelow's racial politics were clearly more complex. Ellis' description casts Bigelow as practically an abolitionist, but such feelings on the physician's part were evidently *post hoc*. In addition to perhaps agreeing with the prevailing ethnological and craniological researches, Bigelow does not appear to have been avowedly anti-slavery until the war actually occurred. Prior to the conflict, while on a trip to Richmond, Virginia in 1852, Bigelow noted with humor in a letter to his wife, Mary, that "Old Virginny is a queen country, swarming with blacks who look lazy & comfortable [. . .] Go every day to the slave market and propose to purchase you a nig if I find one to suit." Rather than seeing the institution of slavery as particularly denigrating to blacks, Bigelow appears to have had greater sympathy for the white Virginians he met, who were "readily communicative on the subject" and who, he felt, "would gladly get rid of their black incubus" if they could.[59] For more than twenty years the Bigelow family maintained strong social ties to the Custis-Lee family of Richmond, which further complicated Bigelow's prewar perceptions of slavery and southern slaveholders.

Once the war began, however, Bigelow became an avowed Unionist, often writing to the *Boston Daily Advertiser* to encourage Northern unity in order to "crush the rebellion." Bigelow's letters in the *Advertiser* made it clear that his attitude toward the South, its people and institutions, had shifted. He wrote in 1862, "We are discovering at last that the South are a dangerous people. Warlike, audacious, needy, unscrupulous, individually disinclined and disqualified for industrial pursuits, but both inclined and qualified for war, rapine, and conquest, their separate existence is incompatible with the peace of the world." Further noting that such types of people had brought upon the Dark Ages of Europe, Bigelow argued, "There is no safety for civilization, liberty, or human progress, but in their absolute suppression."[60] As a response to lagging enthusiasm in the North for the war's continuation, Bigelow also published in the same newspaper a fictional dialogue between Napoleon Bonaparte and "Jeremiah, a Late Citizen of the United States." In the course of the interchange, Napoleon, a representation of Bigelow and his own attitude toward the war, inquires after the progress of the Civil War and offers advice to Jeremiah, who represents the increasing frustration of Northerners when faced with continued military defeat at the hands of the Confederacy. Lamenting to Napoleon, Jeremiah wishes the Constitution had been strong enough to hold the nation together, to which Napoleon responds "Hark'ee, Jeremiah! You have tried Constitution on them long enough: they repudiate it, kick it, spit upon it. They don't want the Constitution, but the "institution" [of slavery]." Jeremiah further complains of "the niggers, the everlasting niggers," not knowing what should be done with this part of the population. But again, Napoleon has a response: "the negroes make good slaves, but better soldiers," noting that blacks had been instrumental in many of the major military victories of the past century, such as in the case of the Haitian Revolution. As for the future of the emancipated race, Napoleon concludes, "A part will be emancipated, a part perhaps exported, or a part perhaps left in the hands of their masters if it should be necessary to save them from idleness and starvation. A restraint will no doubt be put on their excesses."[61] This fictional interchange therefore reflects that while not an advocate of slavery, Bigelow was nevertheless representative of the fact that abolitionism and racism were not mutually exclusive ideologies. Similar to the views of President Abraham Lincoln, Bigelow felt that slavery was inherently immoral, but the races were themselves in no way equal.

It is this overall complexity of Bigelow's personal racial politics that lends a further dimension to his design of the *Sphinx* monument. His choice for the design of the face conveyed popular ideas about white American womanhood, which he hoped, when combined with the body of the powerful lion and iconography derived from ancient Egypt, would be a symbol for the new nation. In Bigelow's words, "It essays to express the present attitude and character of a nation perhaps as far remote in time from the building of the Pyramids as was that event from the earliest constructions attempted by man." America, which had been like the Egypt that held the Hebrews in bondage, was now a new nation rising from the ashes of war. The *Sphinx*, which "has looked backward on unmeasured antiquity, now looks forward to illimitable progress." For Bigelow, the *Sphinx* would stand "as the landmark of a state of things which the world has not before seen, - a great, warlike, and successful nation in the plenitude and full consciousness of its power, suddenly reversing its energies, and calling back its military veterans from bloodshed and victory to resume its still familiar arts of peace and goodwill to man." With such an extraordinary change in the nation's direction, therefore, "What symbol can better express the attributes of a just, calm, and dignified self-reliance than one which combines power with attractiveness, the strength of the lion with the beauty and benignity of woman?"[62]

Despite the monument's intent to celebrate the preservation of the Union and the destruction of slavery, the benign woman so envisaged, given the nineteenth century sculptural tradition to work on Classical models, could not have been anything other than white. The monument would not be a tribute to the sufferings of the past, but a sentinel constantly looking forward to how the nation—now a blended nation of free whites and blacks—would progress. As such, the face of the nation—the population that would continue to dominate—was white, while the free black population, represented by the suggestive references to Africa in the body of the lion, the inscription ("African Slavery Destroyed") and the Egyptian symbols, would continue to labor as the proverbial "muscle" of the nation, free but remaining subsidiary to white leadership. Such racial implications embodied in the unique combination of the *Sphinx*'s white visage with Egyptian and American symbols were not lost on contemporary reviewers. In its review of the monument, *The Atlantic Monthly* duly noted the rendering of the face, "belonging to the noblest type of American womanhood," but then went on to explain the greater significance of the blended symbolism. "She is . . . a wholly new birth, we take it, and her past will date from to-day, — the to-day which has brought the two races, depicted in the African mythic figure and the American face, into such strange and close association."[63] *The Ladies' Repository* was similarly cognizant of the blended imagery, calling the *Sphinx* "a happy symbolic rendering of the union of the American and African races effected by our late war. It tells a marvelous story of the past, yet speaks of a still more marvelous future yet to be realized."[64]

Such optimism about the new relationship between white and black Americans heading into what many imagined would be a glorious future was not entirely uncommon, even during the early 1870s. As historian Nina Silber has observed in *The Romance of Reunion*, northerners "acknowledged the contributions made by different ethnic groups to the Union cause and thus restrained many of the nativist impulses from the 1850s . . . and viewed the men of the ex-slave class not as national outcasts but as loyal, hardworking Americans."[65] The *Sphinx* could then be interpreted as a monument of union—not of reunion by northern and southern whites—but of the anticipated union between white and black Americans, however unequal that relationship might ultimately be. Yet however unbalanced the racial hierarchy might be, as far as Bigelow and contemporary critics were concerned, the *Sphinx* embodied the concept of progress and of the nation moving forward toward the twentieth century. A decade following its dedication, the Reverend Joseph H. Allen echoed Bigelow's own words from the *Account* as he commented, "It is an Egyptian symbol of might and intelligence combined; but, in its human features, modern or American, not brooding on death, but looking forward to the larger life."⁶⁶ Similar to how Bigelow did not dwell on recounting the details of the war itself, neither did the monument exude a sense of lingering on the past. Albeit a form derived from antiquity, Bigelow's Americanized *Sphinx* embodied his perception of the present and future nation.

RIDDLE OF THE SPHINX

Despite Jacob Bigelow's efforts to convey through his *Account* a definitive interpretation of the meaning of the *Sphinx*, it was not long after its unveiling that the public's understanding of the monument began to change. As early as 1878, one year before Bigelow's death, a writer to the *New Hampshire Sentinel* described the monument in a letter to the paper and commented that it had been "the gift of a Boston merchant."⁶⁷ Within Bigelow's immediate social and professional circle, however, the memory of his gift to the cemetery and its broader meaning lingered. This was evident from the obituaries published after his death. The obituary published in *The Medical Record* in 1879 acknowledged Bigelow as "the founder of Mount Auburn Cemetery," as having designed the "stone tower, chapel, gates, and fence," and that the "colossal Sphinx, in granite, was his final gift, and will forever remain a suitable monument to his public spirited labors."⁶⁸ In its memorial to Bigelow, *The Harvard Register* described "that unique and most impressive monument of the civil war, the great Sphinx," as "one of the last active interests of his life."⁶⁹ Yet even the object of these descriptions remained focused on what Bigelow had originally hoped to avoid when he first donated the monument to the cemetery—that, rather than understood as a war memorial and symbol for the postwar nation, it was first and foremost considered *his* monument, and as such, a legacy to his professional and civic activities.

The necessity for Bigelow to remind the public of the *Sphinx*'s meaning became all too clear after his death. No sooner had Bigelow died than the monument became increasingly puzzling to onlookers. As early as 1879, the very year of Bigelow's death, poet Charlotte Fiske Bates (1838–1916) published "The Sphinx at Mount Auburn," a poem that reverted back to earlier conceptions of the destructive female sphinx of ancient Greece:

> How grand she is enthroned among the dead,
> The graves like trophies all about her spread!

Have these not perished as in fable old
With some unfathomed riddle in their hold?

But what the riddle that she now doth ask,
The might of man so fatally to task?
Well may we fancy "What are Life and Death?"
To be the question that has hushed their breath.

Sphinx! Life and Death in thee their type have found,
For so are they in mystic oneness bound;
Fruitful as woman, beautiful as she,
Dread as the lion in his majesty.[70]

No longer expressive of the "benignity of woman" as Bigelow had explained, Bates reinterpreted the *Sphinx* as a queen among the dead, the surrounding graves her trophies; and in the combination of a female head with the lion's body, the *Sphinx* embodied the dualities of life and death.

By the 1880s, with Bigelow no longer alive to reaffirm to observers the meaning of the *Sphinx*, the monument became increasingly enigmatic—even frustrating—to observers and critics alike. The London-based publication, *The Academy* chided, "What a fruitful source of discussion and controversy this curiosity of modern sculpture provides for the archaeologists of the remote future!"[71] A more local voice of consternation came from the *Springfield Republican*, which in a similar tone of confusion and derision, proclaimed "Won't Pharaoh be surprised when he sees the sphinx in Mount Auburn? It will seem more natural to him, however, than to the Puritan forefathers who had no liking for pagan things."[72] By the beginning of the twentieth century, it became clear that not only was the choice of the *Sphinx* for a Civil War memorial considered unusual, but the female face was the most unsettling part of all. In *The New Mediterranean Traveller: A Handbook of Practical Information* (1905), author Daniel Edward Lorenz offered readers a history of the mythical sphinx and of its associations in both ancient Egypt and Greece. Concluding his discussion, Lorenz commented upon the Mount Auburn sculpture: "In one of the most beautiful cemeteries in the United States stands to-day, as a soldier's monument, the image of the youth-devouring female monster of the Grecian myth!" Seemingly unaware of the blended Egyptian symbolism that comprised the monument, Lorenz concluded that he would have preferred to have seen "the Egyptian symbol of immortal life"—in other words, an unadulterated male sphinx—in place of "the Greek Sphinx at Mount Auburn," which could only be considered beautiful "if we are ignorant of its meaning."[73] Lorenz's own ignorance of the monument's symbolism highlights the instability of the *Sphinx*'s ultimate meaning and the rapidity with which, after Bigelow's death, observers forgot the intended function of Bigelow's sentinel in the cemetery.

DEATH AND THE SCULPTOR

Even as the public's understanding of the *Sphinx*'s symbolism faded into obscurity, the monument did more than become just an oddity to be puzzled over by tourists to Mount Auburn. By memorializing the Union soldiers with a monumental sphinx, Bigelow established a precedent whereby Egyptian and Egyptianized sphinxes began to appear within the broader commemorative landscape, particularly within the realm of private memorialization. Beginning in the 1880s and lasting until the early 1930s, members of the industrial capitalist elite began to incorporate sphinxes into their cemetery monuments. These figures began to appear in a variety of guises, including male sphinxes in the purely Egyptian style and Egyptianized female sphinxes with large breasts, either as single monuments or seated in pairs in front of a freestanding Egyptian Revival mausoleum. Perhaps inspired directly or indirectly from the *Sphinx* at Mount Auburn, the earliest examples of private memorial sphinxes involve a solitary figure atop a pedestal. Such is the case with the Lawler Monument in Cincinnati's Spring Grove Cemetery, which actually predates the Mount Auburn *Sphinx* by about two decades, and in the monument for Buffalo grain and malt merchant Edwin Gilbert (1825–1888), whose family burial plot at Forest Lawn Cemetery is marked by an Egyptianized female sphinx, which bears an Anglo-American face and wears the royal *menes* (figure 38).[74]

Later into the twentieth century, guardian sphinxes designed more according to the eighteenth century European Rococo garden sculpture aesthetic appeared flanking the imposing Woolworth mausoleum (1918) in Woodlawn Cemetery in the Bronx, New York; the Winter mausoleum (1931) in Allegheny Cemetery in Pittsburgh, Pennsylvania (figure 39); and the Cardeza-Drake mausoleum (c. 1915) in West Laurel Hill Cemetery, in

FIGURE 38 Edwin Gilbert Monument, Forest Lawn Cemetery, Buffalo, New York, 1888. *(Photograph by Richard Siembab)*

FIGURE 39 Winter Mausoleum Sphinx, Allegheny Cemetery, Pittsburgh, Pennsylvania, 1931. *(Photograph by the author)*

Philadelphia.⁷⁵ Efforts in private memorialization to achieve a sense of archaeological verisimilitude are apparent in the guardian sphinxes that flank the Harper mausoleum (c. 1908–1916) in Cedarville North Cemetery in Cedarville, Ohio and the Tate mausoleum (c. 1915) in Bellefontaine Cemetery in St. Louis, Missouri (figure 40). Clearly carved by the same monument company, the sphinxes flanking both mausoleums appear in the guise of Middle Kingdom pharaoh Amenhetep II—they are overtly masculine and are characterized by their long, heavily carved beards, large noses and oversized ears in imitation of those originally discovered in Egypt.

The most significant work of memorial sculpture to result from the *Sphinx* at Mount Auburn was not, strictly speaking, a cemetery monument. Following the death of sculptor Martin Milmore in 1883 at the young age of thirty-nine, Daniel Chester French (1850–1931), a rising star in the sculptural world, was commissioned to execute a work of sculptural art to be placed over Milmore's burial at Forest Hills Cemetery in Roxbury, Massachusetts. In his effort to adequately memorialize the life of Boston's most beloved sculptor who was cut down in the prime of life, French found inspiration in the *Sphinx* at Mount Auburn and went on to design his award-winning *Death and the Sculptor* (1892). The overall effect of French's work was to ultimately heighten the fame of both sculptors while also renegotiate the public's interpretation of the Mount Auburn *Sphinx*.

French's colossal bronze, initially called the *Milmore Memorial*, garnered a third prize medal at the Paris Salon in 1892, the first such honor for an American sculptor.⁷⁶ In 1893, *Death and the Sculptor* was a feature piece in the art museum at the Columbian Exposition in Chicago and by 1895, art critics recognized the work as French's crowning sculptural achievement. Royal Cortissoz, writing for *The Atlantic Monthly* noted that it was a "most remarkable monument . . . which turns criticism into something not unlike eulogy."⁷⁷ The memorial features a dashing young sculptor working on his masterpiece, an Egyptian sphinx. The figure of Death, executed as a guiding angel with poppies clutched in her right hand, stays the raised hand of the sculptor as he is about to apply his chisel to his work (figure 41). The sphinx, carved in low relief in the background of French's sculpture, is not a copy of the one at Mount Auburn, but the sculptor supposedly chose the subject following a visit to Mount Auburn with his father.⁷⁸

The *Sphinx* monument executed by Milmore was considered by many to be his masterpiece, and the work completed by French, albeit with a

FIGURE 40 Harper Mausoleum Sphinx, Cedarville North Cemetery, Cedarville, Ohio, c. 1908–1916. (*Photograph by Beth Santore*)

FIGURE 41 Daniel Chester French, *Death and the Sculptor/Milmore Memorial*, 1892. (*Photograph by the author*)

different sphinx, nevertheless called to mind the work for which the deceased sculptor was best known. As Cortissoz interpreted the composition, "What he [French] wanted to symbolize was the curtailment by death of any manly life dedicated to plastic art, and to recall in the Sphinx upon which his sculptor is engaged, not the well-known monster which Milmore himself once produced, but the insoluble mystery which stands forever between life and death."[79] Such commentary, which reflected positively on Milmore's achievement, nevertheless reinforced the general ignorance that had developed by this time regarding both the monument's meaning and more especially, Bigelow's role in its creation. William Howe Downes at least acknowledged the *Sphinx*'s function as a war memorial when he noted in 1894 that the "remarkably impressive colossal granite sphinx" facing the chapel had been "modelled [sic] by Martin Milmore as a memorial of the abolition of slavery and the preservation of the Union."[80] This attribution was repeated once again in 1896 in an article on the history of Mount Auburn Cemetery published in *The New England Magazine*, which firmly attributed the *Sphinx* to the work of Milmore, reprinting the inscriptions yet leaving out Bigelow entirely. Hearkening back to the kinds of criticisms against the Egyptian

Revival from earlier in the century, the article also notes, "striking as it is, [the *Sphinx*] seems an inappropriate symbol for a Christian burial place."[81] The *Sphinx* reinterpreted had become, and would remain for much of the twentieth century, a work of art attributed to the skill of Martin Milmore, popularized through the publicity of French's *Death and the Sculptor*, its relationship to Bigelow fading into obscurity.

UNSTABLE SYMBOL

As historian Thomas Brown has noted, the "significance of a [Civil War] monument depended in part on the identity of its sponsors," and more importantly, the "power to instill and dedicate a monument implied authority to shape the public realm and define the conduct that deserved admiration."[82] Jacob Bigelow possessed the power to fund the creation of a public monument and endow it with a particular meaning, but this authority lasted only so long as he continued to live. Given the passage of a relatively short period of time, away from the immediate context of the *Sphinx*'s creation, it quickly became just as enigmatic to its visitors as its predecessors in Egypt. As the work of Sarah J. Purcell on the Bunker Hill Monument has shown, the meanings of public memorials erected in the past "are subject to constant renegotiation."[83] Most Civil War monuments, however—William Dean Howells' dreaded soldier statues and scantily-clad Liberties—appear to have been shielded by the process of renegotiation by the sheer repetition of their designs over the cultural landscape. The creation of similarly-styled monuments, whose designs were agreed upon by monument committees or memorial associations, conveyed a broad cultural consensus as to what the war's significance and legacy entailed. They also adhered to a consistently segregated view of the war and its meaning—the heroism of white soldiers, the appreciation of emancipated slaves, but never the kind of racial cooperation or fusion expressed by Bigelow's *Sphinx*.

It could almost be taken for granted the inherent cultural meaning of the citizen soldier monuments in particular, to the point where, as historian Kirk Savage has argued in *Standing Soldiers, Kneeling Slaves*, "the standardization of the soldier monument . . . industrialized, and cheapened, what was supposed to be the noblest of art forms."[84] In short, the combination of word and image—commemorative inscription and soldier statue—meant that the meaning of these monuments was self-evident. Orators at the unveiling ceremonies reinforced for the public the "official" purpose and meaning of the war, but the monuments themselves were explicit enough in their design that they required no further reaffirmation of how they were supposed to function or what they symbolized in American culture. By contrast, Jacob Bigelow's *Sphinx*, as a singularly unique production in the postwar memorial landscape, was imbued by its creator with a highly complex and nuanced interpretation of the war and the nation itself. The *Sphinx* reflected the beliefs and prejudices, not of the community, but of its creator, yet was presented as a public memorial intended to convey the sentiments of the populace. However, since it lacked the same broad cultural consensus that was so critical to the erection of other Civil War memorials, the long-term meaning of the *Sphinx* was necessarily unstable and open to reinterpretation over time, the role of Bigelow in the monument's genesis largely forgotten or ignored.

CHAPTER 5

American Obelisk: The Washington National Monument

IN AN ARTICLE WRITTEN IN 1879 for the inaugural issue of *The American Art Review* regarding the incomplete Washington National Monument, architect and architectural critic Henry Van Brunt (1832–1903) opened with a sentiment that had existed in the United States since it had won its independence from Great Britain:

> By an act of hardy rebellion against the authority of a mighty nation unjustly exercised, a certain people, after a long and bloody war, were once set aside from the rest of the world to form a true republic; and, because of the wisdom and prudence of its founders, this republic eventually became one of the greatest nations of the earth. There was one, the leader in this rebellion, and chief among these founders by the greatness of his services, the dignity of his character, and the pre-eminence of his virtues, upon whom has been conferred by the common voice of mankind a singular title,—"The Father of his Country."[1]

It was this view of George Washington that had spurred efforts dating as far back as 1783 to erect a national monument in his honor, and the country in 1879 was as yet five years away from completing the stupendous 555-foot tall shaft that stands today in the nation's capital. When it was finally completed in 1884 and dedicated in February 1885, the *New York Times* thus described the structure: "There is at least something characteristically American in this gigantic obelisk, towering above the altitude of the great pyramid and the highest cathedral spires designed by the devout and daring architects of the Middle Ages."[2] Orators at the dedication ceremony hailed the loftiness of the monument as reflective of the loftiness of Washington's unblemished character, that it was a monument to stand the test of time, an achievement in masonry construction of which the nation should be proud. The Washington National Monument was *America's* monument, the tallest man-made structure in the world when it was completed.

The enthusiasm expressed by orators and the press for the completed monument in 1885, however, could not mask the years of frustration and controversy that surrounded its design and construction. As a national monument, dedicated to George Washington but considered an embodiment of the nation itself, the obelisk's journey to completion mirrored in many ways the transformations and ruptures that had taken place within American society and culture during the middle decades of the nineteenth century. Its incomplete state in the years leading up to and including the Civil War was for Americans as tangible a sign as ever of the fractiousness of the Union itself. The need to finish the monument in the war's aftermath became a point of near desperation, as many saw the very pride of the nation invested in whether a monument so conceived and so lofty in purpose could actually be finished. And when it was finally completed and dedicated, Americans during the 1880s entered another era of crisis—not of political or military or even economic crisis, but a crisis of confidence in the architectural aesthetic that had been the standard for over half a century. Architectural eclecticism, with the Egyptian Revival as the key style in American commemorative culture, came under attack as chaotic and bereft of any true taste, style or meaning for the nation and its people. The Washington National Monument would therefore be for art and architectural critics of the 1880s and 1890s a kind of cautionary tale—symbolic of the nation in both the best and worst of ways, and a key example of what *not* to do in future endeavors to memorialize great men and events.

WASHINGTON'S APOTHEOSIS

The desire to erect a national monument to George Washington began as early as 1783 when the Continental Congress "resolved unanimously" to construct an equestrian statue of the General "at the place where the residence of Congress shall be established." Such a monument did not come to pass, nor did any monuments result from Congressional proposals submitted after Washington's death in 1799 and again in 1800.[3] However, similar to the ways in which the Revolutionary War became a mythologized event in United States history, George Washington as *the* Founding Father quickly became after his death a figure that was larger than life, a hero of mythic proportions for the American people. Therefore, when the federal government abandoned plans to erect a memorial to Washington, the individual states took up the cause to honor their *pater patriae*.

Part of the desire to erect a monument rested on the popular apotheosis of Washington after his death. The ascension of Washington to the rank of an immortal occurred in both rhetoric and visual culture upon his death in 1799. In his eulogy to the president, the young Joseph Story—a future jurist and president of Mount Auburn Cemetery—proclaimed that Washington's "deeds are immortal" and "They live in the heart of his country; and his country lives but to celebrate them."[4] Central to the proclamation of Washington's immortality was the notion of his character. In nineteenth century American culture, George Washington the General, more than any other figure from the Revolution, was the embodiment of civic and republican virtue, the ideal to which all patriotic Americans should aspire. Historian Kirk Savage has argued that this process of idolizing the first president was so extreme that "[b]y making Washington's virtues so extraordinary that he surpassed all ancient and modern prototypes, rhetoric threatened to transform him into a demigod, beyond the aspiration of any ordinary individuals."[5] While there were those who were content to simply mourn the loss of the first president, there were others who actively created a vision of Washington as having transcended the bounds of mortality. These diverging trends can be seen in the visual culture of the period, in which there was, on the one hand, the public bereavement of Washington the president as depicted in popular mourning iconography, and on the other, the symbolic apotheosis of Washington the demigod in oil paintings and mass-produced engravings. Art historian Anita Schorsch has argued that the trauma of George Washington's death made mourning iconography both popular and sacred. During the first years of the nineteenth century, images of a grieving figure leaning on a funerary monument to Washington inscribed to his memory appeared in a variety of artistic mediums, including hand-painted miniatures, engravings and samplers. This image, once engrained in the visual culture, continued to appear throughout the first half of the nineteenth century in the material culture of the domestic sphere associated with death and bereavement.[6] Young women continued to stitch samplers depicting such scenes with the names of family members upon the central monuments; families purchased lithographs containing mourning scenes that included space to write the names and death dates of their loved ones; and elaborate mourning jewelry, including rings and pendants, incorporated miniature paintings of this image. The mourning figure with urn and willow would also appear on gravestones carved during the first half of the nineteenth century as well, thus reaffirming the popularity of the iconography within the general population.

More critical to informing the public desire for large monuments in honor of Washington was the depiction of his transformation after death into an immortal. In David Edwin's (1776–1841) oil painting entitled *Apotheosis of Washington* (c. 1800), Washington, garbed in his burial shroud, appears seated in the heavenly sphere, a cherubim flying above to bestow a laurel crown on his head. Washington gestures to Mount Vernon below, while Richard Montgomery and Joseph Warren, Continental Army generals who both died during the war in 1775, offer a gesture of welcome from the background. Another early example of Washington's transformation in art is the commemorative engraving by artist John James Barralet (ca. 1747–1815) entitled *Apotheosis of George Washington* (1802). The image, which due to its popularity went through four printings, features Washington in his funeral clothes being lifted out of his coffin by a winged Father Time and Immortality. The allegorical figures of Faith, Hope and Charity appear at the far left while a grieving Liberty and Native American are situated in the lower register.[7] The popularity of such images was effective in mythologizing the nation's founder as more than a man, and when individual states and communities began efforts to raise monuments to Washington, the theme of immortality became common in project proposals and dedication orations. For example, in 1814 the people of Baltimore accepted a design by architect Robert Mills for a monument that would be dedicated to "the immortal Washington."[8] Seventy years later, when the Washington National Monument was eventually completed, the dedication was made "to the immortal name and memory of George Washington."[9]

One of the earliest efforts to erect a public monument following Washington's death occurred in Massachusetts, when in 1800, the state

Legislature passed a Resolution to erect "a Statue or Monument of Marble" in the state house "with inscriptions and devices adapted to impress a due sense of his sublime virtues, to extend and perpetuate their influence, and to express the publick gratitude for his eminent services."[10] The proposed project remained on hold through the War of 1812 and in 1816 the Massachusetts State Legislature once again initiated plans to erect a monument to George Washington in Boston. Mark Langdon Hill, the chairman of the committee to enact the Legislature's plan, published an article in the *North American Review* in which he weighed the potential designs for the monument. Having eliminated the equestrian statue as too expensive, Hill outlined four remaining possibilities: the pyramid, the obelisk, the triumphal arch and the column. This was the first time that the pyramid and obelisk were taken into consideration as potential styles for a grand public memorial in the United States, but as Hill saw it, it was too difficult to do these forms from ancient Egypt justice given early nineteenth century technologies. He noted that the "only arguments in favour of pyramidal monuments, are their austere simplicity and extreme durability," but asserted that the pyramid "can only be rendered respectable by its size." Unless reproduced with the same proportions as those on the Giza plateau, any other pyramid would be deplorably insignificant by comparison. Hill then went on to consider the obelisk, "another of the inventions of the Egyptians, and which has never been attempted by any other people." The problem he saw with the obelisk could again be blamed on modern technology. Arguing that an obelisk constructed out of multiple blocks would not be durable, Hill maintained "its magnificence mainly consists in its being of one piece." Americans did not possess the quarrying technology necessary to produce their own massive monolith, therefore the obelisk for a monument to Washington was "completely out of the question."[11]

The largest and most well-known monument to Washington that preceded the Washington National Monument was the Baltimore Washington Monument designed by Robert Mills. Designed in 1814 and completed in 1829, the Baltimore monument incorporates a mixture of classical elements. A 140-foot Doric column rises out of an elevated sarcophagic base, and standing atop the entire work is a statue of Washington. Americans and Europeans alike became acquainted with the monument to Washington in Baltimore and acknowledged it as an important example of American monumental architecture. However, there still remained no structure that could be considered a national symbol of gratitude and love for the nation's first president and this caused a certain degree of unease within the populace. It would not be until 1833 that the effort to undertake a national monument project would be undertaken, not by the federal government, but by a group of private citizens.

THE WASHINGTON MONUMENT SOCIETY

The process whereby the Washington National Monument came into being was in many ways similar to the obelisks at Bunker Hill and Groton Heights. The Washington National Monument Society—a local organization promoting itself as a national one—formed in 1833. By 1836, the Society had collected $28,000 and felt ready to receive proposals for a design, one that they hoped would "harmoniously blend durability, simplicity, and grandeur."[12] Among the designs submitted included a plan dated to 1837 by Peter Force (1790–1868) for an immense pyramid (figure 42). By contrast, Thomas M. McClelland of Philadelphia submitted a monument proposal that consisted of a colossal equestrian statue of Washington atop a Gothic triumphal arch. The architect E. Barabino proposed a large column, which in its design was strikingly similar to Robert Mills' Baltimore monument. In 1844, Calvin Pollard (1797–1850) of New York submitted a Gothic design and in the same year, a design sponsored by a Congressional committee consisted of a domed round temple.[13] The Society ultimately appealed to Robert Mills, who had not only designed the Baltimore monument but had also submitted a design in 1825 for the Bunker Hill Monument and been appointed by Andrew Jackson to be the official architect of the United States.

It was clear from his design for the Baltimore Washington Monument that Mills had a predilection for architectural elements derived from antiquity, but as he expressed in a letter accompanying his proposal for the Bunker Hill project in 1825, he had come to prefer the obelisk for large memorial works. He wrote that the obelisk was "peculiarly adapted to commemorate *great transactions*, for its lofty character, [its] great strength, and furnishing a fine surface for inscriptions—There is a degree of lightness and beauty in it that affords a finer relief to the eye than can be obtained in the regular proportioned column."[14] His first attempt at a design for the Washington National Monument was purely Egyptian in inspiration and included, in addition to obelisks, virtually every other Egyptian architectural device as

FIGURE 42 Peter Force, architectural drawing for the Washington Monument, 1837.
(Library of Congress)

well. As described by historian Michael Kammen, the architect, "Envisioned a massive, four-sided rusticated pyramid, a thousand feet square at the base, soaring to a height of 650 feet, and supporting a "collosian" statue of George Washington, the whole thing insanely envisioned as a thousand feet tall. At each corner there would be obelisks 45 feet square and 350 feet tall, with the pyramid separated into seven "grand states of terraces" diminishing in height as they ascended."[15] This initial design reflected the taste of the period on the grandest possible scale with a desire to evoke the same sense of awe and sublimity that only the Great Pyramid itself could rival. The Rural Cemetery Movement, with its attendant use of Egyptian Revival entrance gates and the popularity of family monuments in the forms of Egyptian obelisks, pyramids and mastabas had already become entrenched by the mid-1830s in the Northeast and Mid-Atlantic states. In this first design attempt, then, Mills envisioned a monumental public version of an already popular private memorial style. However, Mills' initial vision was so beyond the limits of nineteenth century technology and available funding that the Society requested a more realistic revision.

Mills' revised monument design, accepted by the Society in 1845 and advertised to the public as the "official" design in 1846, was a structural compromise. Having taken away the idea for a central pyramid, the new monument would instead include a nearly 600-foot tall central obelisk, at the base of which would be a Roman circular temple incorporating the Greek Doric order of columns. Atop the rotunda would be a statue of Washington in a chariot led by six horses (figure 43) As described by the Master Mason Benjamin B. French at the ceremony for the laying of the cornerstone, "A circular colonnade is to form the main feature of the structure, from which, pointing to heaven, will spring a plain obelisk, five hundred feet in height. Near the apex of that obelisk is to be placed, in alto relieve, a single star. Like that star of old, which gathered the wise men at Bethlehem, in Judea, may this be the guiding point to gather together the wise men of this land, should danger ever threaten the existence of our beloved and cherished Union!"[16] Albeit not purely Egyptian in design, the obelisk as the central element conveyed the dominance of the Egyptian over the Greek and Roman architectural influences. In this respect, the new design followed the precedent set by the Bunker Hill and Groton shafts, and thus further strengthened the associations between the Egyptian obelisk and such qualities as morality, civic virtue, and martial valor. Added to these associations was the confirmation of Washington's own immortality as embodied in a monument style already known for its permanence. Further, whereas the obelisks at Bunker Hill and Groton were symbols of American martyrdom, and the monument in Baltimore involved a colossus of Washington in the guise of Cincinnatus, Mills' vision for the National Monument focused on the triumphant heroism of the nation's leader. With the obelisk as the symbol of Washington's immortality, the statue would be, in Savage's view, "suggestive of the triumphant progress to which the monument looked forward."[17] Having accepted Mills' revised design, the Monument Society looked forward to erecting a memorial that would glorify the nation's hero as well as proclaim to all people the future greatness of the United States.

Construction began in 1848, with the ceremony for the laying of the cornerstone held on the Fourth of July. The ceremony in Washington made the one held for the completion of the Bunker Hill Monument pale in comparison. It was attended by President of the United States James Polk and Vice President George Dallas; the president's Cabinet; members of the Senate

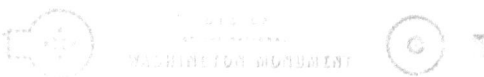

FIGURE 43 Robert Mills, design for the Washington National Monument, lithograph, c. 1846. *(Library of Congress)*

and House of Representatives; representatives from all branches of the military; delegations of visitors from every state and territory; the fire companies of Baltimore and the District of Columbia; members of state and national temperance societies; benevolent societies; literary associations; members of the Monument Society; architect Robert Mills; the Masonic Fraternity; delegations of the Cherokee, Chickasaw, Choctaw, Creek and Sawbridge Indians; and citizens from around the country, "from all political parties; from all professions and occupations; men of all sorts and conditions, and those before whom men of all sorts and conditions bow, as lending the chief ornament and grace to every scene of life."[18] The procession to the site of the monument, which lasted an hour, was, according to the Monument Society, "decidedly the most splendid ever witnessed in Washington."[19]

Robert C. Winthrop (1809–1894), Speaker of the House of Representatives, delivered the dedicatory oration for a future structure that the Monument Society hoped would "endure till time shall be no more."[20] In the course of his address, Winthrop employed language that conveyed the universal obligation of the entire nation to partake in the endeavor to erect the monument: "One monument remains to be reared. A monument which shall bespeak the gratitude, not of States, or of cities, or of governments; not of separate communities, or of official bodies; but of the people, the whole people of the nation:—a National Monument, erected by the citizens of the United States of America." Regarding the date of the ceremony—the Fourth of July—Winthrop declared that it was the most fitting day upon which to lay the cornerstone, as it was "emphatically the people's day."[21] As Winthrop continued, he outlined that the Fourth of July and the character of Washington were not significant to the United States alone—rather, the importance was international as well. "The whole civilized world resounds with American opinions and American principles. Every vale is vocal with them. Every mountain has found a tongue for them."[22] It was therefore incumbent upon the entirety of the American nation to support the construction of the national monument to the memory of George Washington. In Winthrop's eyes, it was also crucial that Washington and his monument serve as an example for those European nations whose people were at that time striving to overthrow their old systems of government.

Central to Winthrop's oration was his exhortation that the ceremony held that day and the monument to be built should bind the citizens of the country through the sentiment of shared brotherhood. Well aware of the social and political disruptions caused by westward expansion and the ongoing issue of slavery, he declared, "Let the column which we are about to construct, be at once a pledge and an emblem of perpetual union! Let the foundations be laid, let the superstructure be built up and cemented, let each stone be raised and riveted, in a spirit of national brotherhood!" Similar to Daniel Webster's allusion to the famed Colossi of Memnon when he delivered his oration at the base of the Bunker Hill Monument in 1843, Winthrop continued, "And may the earliest ray of the rising sun—till that sun shall set to rise no more—draw forth from it daily, as from the fabled statue of antiquity [the Colossi], a strain of national harmony, which shall strike a responsive chord in every heart throughout the Republic!"[23] Through such invocations of national unity and allusions to Egyptian antiquity, Winthrop thus fused the future completion of the monument with the fate of the nation—a fate, he hoped, which would involve the perpetual preservation of the union.

NATIONAL DISGRACE

As construction proceeded, the Washington National Monument Society accepted subscriptions and donations from around the country. Individual states as well as foreign nations contributed stone blocks to be incorporated into the shaft. By 1854, the obelisk, the first component of Mills' design to be undertaken, had risen to a height of 156 feet, but a series of events brought construction to a near-complete halt. In March of that year, vandals from the Know-Nothing Party—a rabidly anti-Catholic, anti-Irish and German immigrant, nationalist political party that experienced a brief period of popularity at this time—broke into the shed that housed the various quarried stones awaiting placement on the monument. They stole the marble slab that had been donated by the Vatican, nicknamed the "Pope's stone" by the press, and destroyed it. This action, which yielded no subsequent prosecution, alienated Catholic Americans and the Roman Catholic Church from the monument project and little enthusiasm emerged from that segment of the population to offer continued support and funds for its construction.[24] To make matters worse, the Know-Nothing Party had taken control of the Monument Society and vowed to only take subscriptions from true "Americans." This proved to be a disastrous policy, for the Society had already expended virtually all of its $230,000 in subscriptions and three years of fundraising by Know-Nothing leadership resulted in the accumulation of only $51.66 in funds.[25] By 1859, what stood on the landscape of the capital was a 170-foot tall stump. The unfinished obelisk remained a stump of increasing infamy for nearly two decades before serious construction resumed and it became an object of national shame and disgrace as well as one of comical derision. Mark Twain, upon seeing it on a trip to Washington in 1867, would describe its appearance as bearing "the aspect of a factory chimney with the top broken off."[26]

As construction came to a stand-still, the ongoing incompletion of the monument became increasingly embarrassing even before the 1860s. The *New York Times* chastised Americans in 1859 for their "patriotic mendicancy" and for remaining "sluggishly indifferent to the disgrace" of leaving the Washington National Monument "miserably incomplete." Appealing to not only the sensibility, but to the national pride of the American people as well, the *Times* exhorted its readers to complete the shaft, since "it cannot remain in its present condition, without making us something more than ridiculous in the eyes of all foreigners who see it, and in our own."[27] In this reading of the situation, then, the meaning of the Washington National Monument was only partially bound to American self-perception; it was also tied to how foreign nations perceived the United States. Failure to complete the monument to America's greatest hero would erode the nation's international reputation. After decades of efforts made by individual citizens and various cultural associations to *prove* to the Old World that the United States possessed all the attributes of an advanced civilization, such a failure would be the most damaging reproof to such pretensions.

By the beginning of the Civil War, the incomplete state of the monument was still a sore point for the nation's pride, but the fact that the country was torn asunder and at war with itself deflected any overtly scornful criticism. Early in the war, there were some states, such as California, which offered donations to the Monument Society as a sign of their fidelity to the Union and hope for the monument's completion once the conflict came to a close.[28] Travelers to Washington D.C. reported back to their local newspapers observations of the Union's capital, and while many felt disappointment upon seeing the monument's unfinished state, they expressed continued hope that it would eventually be completed. One traveler, whose report in 1861 to the *Lowell Daily Citizen* was reprinted in newspapers across the country, offered an observation that cemented the public's view that the fate of the

Washington Monument rested with the fate of the nation. He wrote, "I went to the Washington Monument, situated upon the banks of the beautiful Potomac, and saw the blocks contributed by the many states of this Union, and by many foreign countries. There have been over 200 blocks contributed, nearly all from the states having been put up. The monument is now 175 feet high, and it is intended to carry it up to 600 feet, and from the top one of the most splendid views in the world can be had." Noting the blocks contributed by the various towns, cities and states that were visible in the interior structure as he ascended the staircase, the author commented that the inscriptions "upon the blocks from two states are worthy of remembrance, and I copied them: Louisiana—'Ever faithful to the Constitution and the Union.' Tennessee—'The Federal Union—it must be preserved'." Of the inherent irony conveyed by the inscriptions on these stones, the author dryly noted, "Comment is unnecessary."[29] Many across the country likewise recognized the contrariety embodied in the Louisiana and Tennessee inscriptions, and while the traveler from Lowell offered no explicit comment, others were less reticent. In an article from the *New Hampshire Sentinel* entitled "The Very Stones Cry Out Against Them," the stones themselves were considered the most damning evidence that the South's secession was an act of open rebellion. As the *Sentinel* asked, "Could a more fitting rebuke be administered to these States, which have proved false to these principles, than we have in these words graven upon stone by the authority of the States themselves?"[30]

There were also those who argued that even in its unfinished state, the monument functioned as a representation of the Union's cause. *The Philadelphia Inquirer* urged donations from citizens and soldiers alike with the argument that if "we could see the busy mason on top of the now unsightly shaft," it might serve as "an incentive to the military to protect the spot hallowed by the name of WASHINGTON." The *Inquirer* also noted that, as a symbol of the Union, the monument made for a perfect target: "The monument can be plainly seen from *Munson's Hill*, towering as it does above all the buildings in the city. Let the Rebel cannon take it for a target, but we should have a hundred workmen raising it toward the skies; for while the name of WASHINGTON is revered by an American people it will be protected at whatever cost is necessary."[31] By 1862, virtually no further progress had been made, yet every effort was expended through speeches and the press to rally public support—and money—to resume construction. The Monument Society held a celebration for Washington's birthday at their headquarters in

February, at which Thomas E. Harkins, one of the Society's secretaries, reiterated once again the importance of George Washington to the nation as a reason for the monument's completion: "Build it to the skies, you cannot outreach the loftiness of his principles. Found it upon the massive and enduring rock, you cannot make it more lasting than his fame. Construct it of the purest Parian marble, you cannot make it purer than his life. Exhaust upon it the rules and principles of ancient and modern art, you cannot make it more proportionate than his character."[32] Yet despite every effort to rally support, funding dwindled for the project and by late 1862, there appeared in the press a certain consensus that the Monument Society must "await better times for the resumption and completion of the noble work."[33]

When the war finally did end in April of 1865, construction still did not resume and the press quickly began to see the project as a failure. Calls for a monument to the martyred President Lincoln only made the unfinished state of the Washington Monument more distressing. Within a week of the President's death, the *Daily Constitutional Union* out of Washington, D.C. argued that the monument had been "shamefully neglected."[34] The following month, in May, the *North American* out of Philadelphia responded to calls for a monument to Lincoln by referring to the Washington Monument as a "memorable failure" that "has been heretofore thrust in the faces of all who have endeavored to accomplish such things." The same article went on to bemoan the "everlasting harping on the subject [of the Washington Monument] which is the hobby of so many persons" and concluded that at the very least, the monument could serve as a cautionary tale to the public, "since it serves as a lesson and a warning, to all who undertake such enterprises, against loss of time."[35] This sense of pessimism about the nation's willingness or ability to finish the monument became an oft-repeated theme in the press. *The Daily Picayune* of New Orleans mused "We are inclined to think that many a monument will be completed before this one, if it do not crumble to earth before it is finished," while the *San Francisco Evening Bulletin* chided, "Like the Acropolis at Athens, the monument is now a sow stable." Robert Mills' vision for the monument, with its 600-foot obelisk rising out of a Doric-order rotunda, remained the official design at this time, which only added to the extreme sense of incompleteness of the structure. As it stood, the unfinished obelisk only beckoned comparisons to water tanks, windmills and even prison houses.[36]

Facing such excoriation in the newspapers, the Monument Society appealed to Congress for an appropriation of $300,000 as it had only collected a paltry eleven dollars in donations during the year of 1865.[37] To rally public support and hopefully expedite the further funding and construction process, the Senate even considered the possibility of re-dedicating the monument to the memories of *both* George Washington and Abraham Lincoln.[38] This proposal was ultimately rejected, however, in the feeling that Lincoln, albeit a martyr to the cause of the Union, was not a national figure on par with the nation's *pater patriae*. In February of 1866, in a speech primarily focused toward criticizing the Republicans in Congress, President Andrew Johnson also made an appeal to finish the monument as a sign of the reunification of the Union. Cheers rang out as Johnson declared, "Let it be completed." In a moment of great historical irony, Johnson went on to state, "let me refer to the motto upon the stone sent from my own State [Tennessee]. . . . I stand by that sentiment, and she is willing to stand by it. It was the sentiment enunciated by the immortal Andrew Jackson: 'The Federal Union, it must be preserved'." Upon thus concluding, the people in attendance broke out into wild shouts of applause.[39]

In the midst of the agony of Reconstruction, while President Johnson plead for the monument's completion as a sign of reunion, questions arose over the South's dedication to the monument project given its current state under the dictates of military reconstruction. Concerning the peoples' willingness to offer donations to the work, *The Philadelphia Inquirer* noted, "In the North, something might perhaps be done in furtherance of the object. But in the South, in consequence of the exhaustion not yet recovered from, and a general indisposition to do anything that would contribute to a memorial upon 'Yankee' ground, we presume that it would be difficult to obtain a dollar." Thus openly acknowledging the emotional hostility felt by Southerners, the *Inquirer* warned "The country [must] become settled in its affairs, and something like brotherly feelings be renewed, ere contributions for this memorial or any other which is not strictly sectional, can be expected."[40] Certainly not the first to connect the fate of the monument with the fate of the nation, the *Inquirer* was ultimately prescient in its feeling that the affairs of Reconstruction needed to be settled before any serious progress on a monument, so declared to be a *national* monument, could commence. The 1860s ended with observations made on the increasingly dilapidated appearance of the stump, the continued disgrace that its condition brought down on the nation, and even superstitious claims that the vandalism enacted on the "Pope's stone" in 1854 had cursed the project to never be completed "until this outrage be atoned for."[41] Ultimately, it would not be until the national centennial in 1876—just months before the final end to Reconstruction after the election of Rutherford B. Hayes—that Congress finally stepped in. Effectively taking control of the project away from the Washington National Monument Society in light of its poor leadership and inadequate means of raising funds, Congress pledged federal money along with the Army Corps of Engineers to ensure the monument's ultimate completion.

CASEY AT THE BAT

Once Congress took control of the monument project, a new host of problems emerged. The first concerned the structural integrity of the existing portion of the obelisk. The structure had sat in a state of disrepair for so long, there were questions about whether a modified version of Robert Mills' design, abandoning the rotunda and equestrian statue and thus leaving only the central obelisk, could even be executed. The Army Corps of Engineers examined the portion that had been built and reported that "the foundations were in poor condition and inadequate for the completion of the obelisk as originally designed." However, in October 1877, "the project engineers, under the direction of Col. Thomas Lincoln Casey, decided that with reinforcement of the foundation the monument could be built to its full intended height."[42] In light of this news, the Washington National Monument Society, stripped of its authority but still active in its support of the project, supported the completion of the monument as a single, unadorned obelisk akin to the ones that had been erected earlier in the century.

Even with the Monument Society's approval of the obelisk, however, there developed a heated conflict over proceeding with this design. The aesthetic taste of the 1870s was not what it had been when Robert Mills' design had been adopted in 1845. Private individuals still erected obelisks and other Egyptian Revival monuments in the nation's cemeteries, but by and large, the Egyptian Revival *as a revival* was generally considered *passé* during the 1870s. Even before the Army Corps of Engineers took over construction of the Washington Monument, the press took a stand against Mills' original design. The *New York Times* excoriated the architect's blending of architectural elements in a particularly sarcastic commentary in 1872:

> As is generally known, the plan of the monument is a piecemeal imitation of an Egyptian monolithic obelisk, based upon a curiously-comic Grecian temple. Why the designer contented himself with this incongruous complication of architectural evils, does not appear. He ought to have provided for a series of Gothic flying buttresses, and crowned his obelisk with a Byzantine dome, bearing upon its apex a bronze statue, modeled by Mr. Clarke Mills, and exhibiting the Father of his Country in the act of neatly balancing himself upon his head. The plan would then have had a certain coherence of imbecility, which would have made it absolutely unequaled by anything the world has yet seen in the shape of humorous memorial architecture.[43]

It seems likely that such attitudes influenced the debates over whether or not to proceed with Mills' vision when Congress eventually wrested control of the project away from the Washington National Monument Society. Professional architects were especially vocal about the need to re-envision the structure to better suit the taste of the age. Henry Van Brunt took a particularly vehement and condescending view toward his architectural predecessors, writing, "The original design was conceived at a time when artistic education in America had not been begun." Concerning Mills' original conception for the monument, Van Brunt denounced both the size and architectural eclecticism that were its hallmarks. "Evidently the leading technical motive of the design," he wrote, "is that it shall assert itself as the loftiest structure yet built by the hands of man." Van Brunt went on to describe it as a "Neo-Graeco-Egyptian jumble." Worse, to only build a plain, unadorned obelisk in the style of the Egyptian monoliths would be "a misquotation barbarously misapplied."[44]

Throughout 1877, architects submitted proposals for new designs, the various merits and deficiencies of which were debated in such publications as *The American Art Review*, *The Atlantic Monthly* and the *New York Times*. Generally, most submissions maintained the pre-existing structure as a base for a monumental work of statuary and other architectural adornments. As Van Brunt would despair, "All these designs accept the embarrassing condition of the existing stump of the obelisk, and in various ways aim to give it an architectural development."[45] The only architect who retained a purely

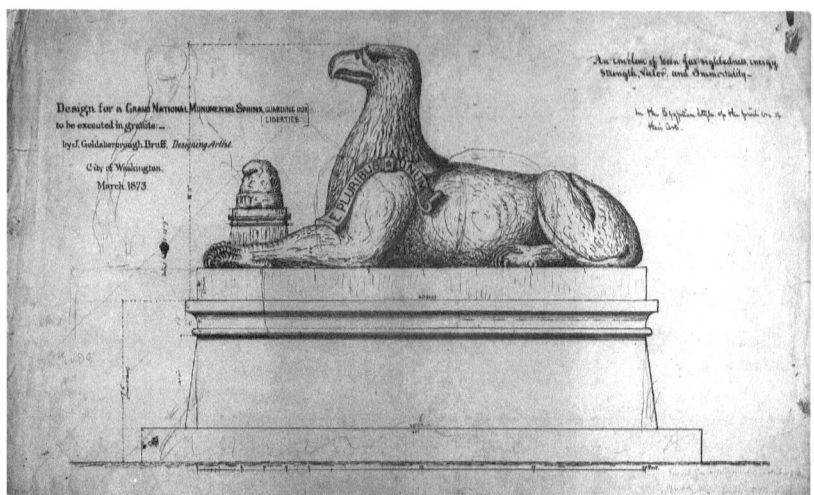

FIGURE 44 Joseph Goldsborough Bruff, design for a grand national monumental Sphinx, guarding our liberties, 1873. *(Library of Congress)*

Egyptian design was topographer and amateur artist Joseph Goldsborough Bruff (1804–1889), who, in 1873, redesigned the obelisk to measure 501 feet in height with colossal granite sphinxes flanking the entrance. Much like Jacob Bigelow had done in his design of the *Sphinx* at Mount Auburn Cemetery, Bruff Americanized his sphinxes. Bruff wrote of his design, "Rendering it in the true Egyptian style, I have nationalized it by the head and breast of our national bird. Such a figure is symbolical of keen far-sightedness, noble aspiration, energy, strength, courage, and immortality."[46] Draped over the shoulder of the sphinx would be a sash emblazoned with E PLURIBUS UNUM. Placed between its feet would be a canopic jar in the shape of a liberty cap and bearing the inscription, LIBERTY (figure 44).[47] Another design submission that likewise retained overtly Egyptianized elements was that submitted by architect Henry R. Searle in 1877. His vision eliminated the Doric rotunda and replaced it with a stepped pyramid design, out of the center of which would emerge a modified version of the obelisk (figure 45).

The widely admired sculptor William Wetmore Story (1819–1895) submitted a design proposal derived from "Florentine and Venetian models" and compared with every other new monument design, this met with greater general approval. Described by "An Architect" for *The Atlantic Monthly*,

FIGURE 45 Henry Robinson Searle, proposed design for the completion of the Washington National Monument, c. 1877. *(Library of Congress)*

Story "incased the existing stump and carried it up with vertical sides to a height of three hundred and fifty feet, including its pyramidal capping. Around the base he has built a square lower story, projecting six or eight feet, against the sides of which he has set four gabled porches a hundred feet high. These porches are carried on a composite order of detached columns, and in the faces of them are niches, in one of which stands a colossal statue of Washington on a high pedestal."

The author proceeded to further describe each story of the newly-conceived shaft, its paneling, cornices, friezes and bronze statuary. Determining overall that the work's "outline is agreeable," possessing a "rather dignified and elegant repose," with "refined and delicate" details, the author ultimately determined that Story's design was disappointing and inappropriate for its purpose. "The grand severity of Washington's character and bearing, the simplicity of the time in which he lived, would be ill commemorated by a monument of such ornate delicacy."[48] Tastes may have changed, but descriptions of George Washington's character as a general and founding father had not. When construction finally resumed in August 1880, the work then undertaken incorporated neither elaborate decorative elements nor any statuary.

In proceeding with the final construction phase, the federal government vested Lieutenant Colonel Thomas Lincoln Casey (1831–1896) of the Army Corps of Engineers with the responsibility of supervising its completion.[49] Originally from New York, Casey had overseen the construction of defensive works on the coast of Maine during the Civil War. During the 1870s, he was transferred to Washington D.C. where, as an administrator in the Army Corps of Engineers, he constructed the last two-thirds of the State, War and Navy Department building, oversaw most of the construction of the Congressional Library, and was engaged in the work on the Washington aqueduct.[50] From 1880 until the setting of the Washington Monument's pyramidion capstone in 1884, Casey approached the monument project as an engineer, not as an architect or aesthete. Having decided that the added elements of the rotunda and chariot statue were not feasible, Casey simplified and re-designed the obelisk so it would follow the same proportions as those found in ancient Egypt. Added to this change was Casey's endeavor to create a national monument that would also function as a modern "technological marvel," complete with a passenger elevator and electric lights—technologies that were still less than a decade old.[51]

In July of 1884, with the monument nearing its completion and standing at a total height of 507 feet, a correspondent for the *Washington Star* interviewed Casey on the details concerning its construction. Not yet open to visitors, the correspondent was invited to ascend with Casey to the top of the structure via the elevator, which had functioned as the primary method for raising the masonry to the summit. Upon describing the impressive array of cables, columns and bracings, the author marveled that "nowhere else on earth does an elevator—balloons excepted—lift one 500 feet from the ground." As Casey relayed to the correspondent, the elevator "easily carries six tons of stone to the top of the monument. After it carries up its last load of material we will have it nicely upholstered and fitted up as a passenger elevator." The marvels did not end there, for the staircase would eventually include electric "incandescent light burners"—in other words, light bulbs—fixed upon the walls to "brilliantly light the stairways" at each platform "for those who will prefer to make the ascent of the monument in that way."[52]

Preceded by the obelisks at Bunker Hill, Groton Heights, and the just-finished Gothicized obelisk at Saratoga, all of which included only an internal staircase, the Washington National Monument set a new standard for both national memorialization and technological achievement. Albeit an engineer and neither an architect nor a designer, Casey remained sensible to the aesthetic significance of the monument. Following its completion, he pronounced it "an obelisk that for grace and delicacy of outline is not excelled by any of the greater Egyptian monoliths, while for dignity and grandeur it surpasses any that can be mentioned."[53] The setting of the capstone was memorialized in an illustration by Sid Nealy for *Harper's Weekly*, the top of which featured portraits of General Gershom Mott, Colonel Thomas Casey (center), and Reuben R. Springer (figure 46). The allusion to ancient Egypt, obvious from the exterior, was reinforced within. Situated above the elevator doors in the interior of the obelisk is a large bronze relief of George Washington in profile, surmounted by a portal akin to those found at Luxor and Karnak, replete with cavetto cornice, touro moulding and winged orb. As a way to Americanize the ancient design, a military star appears in the center of the orb (figure 47). Thus, whereas from the exterior, there appear no designs or symbols to denote the actual meaning of the monument, Washington's semi-divine status to the nation is made explicit in the juxtaposition of the president's profile situated beneath an overtly Egyptian portal. That the Egyptian gateway surrounds the modern elevator is a further

FIGURE 46 Sid H. Nealy, Setting the Capstone, *Harper's Weekly*, Dec. 20, 1884. *(Library of Congress)*

testament to the connection between the superiority and durability of both Egyptian and American technology, a statement that had been lost in the changing tastes of the 1870s.

Even though Casey had clearly taken pride in the Army Corps of Engineers' execution of the work, and the press retained a positive, even relieved, attitude during the final years of its construction, reactions to the completed

FIGURE 47 Detail of elevator door surround, Washington National Monument. *(Library of Congress)*

obelisk before its official dedication were swift and brutal. The *New York Times* was especially cruel to Casey's engineering feat. Standing at 555-feet tall, the Washington National Monument held the distinction of being the tallest manmade structure in the world and would remain so until the completion of the 1,063 foot tall Eiffel Tower in 1889. Gustave Eiffel himself had considered the Washington Monument "remarkable" in its "simplicity and boldness."[54] Yet in December 1884, nearly four decades after the laying of its cornerstone, the *New York Times* simply could not muster any enthusiasm for the obelisk beyond its relief that "The completion of the Washington Monument has at least the advantage of taking that structure off our minds." Acknowledging as the Washington Monument's precedent the monoliths from ancient Egypt, the *Times* noted of its design that it was,

> an imitation of the earliest and rudest form of a monument known in history. We say an imitation because the obelisk was a large and durable stone set on end and inscribed with a statement of the facts, which its erecters desired to make known to posterity. This was not a refined or artistic, but it was a straightforward and sensible, method of commemoration. An imitation of this monolith, built up in small stones and omitting the inscriptions, has no significance whatever, and as a work of art the monument is entitled to neither more nor less consideration than a factory chimney, the ugliness of which is pardoned only for the useful purpose which it subserves.

Thus acknowledging the functionality of the original monoliths, the very engineering and structural compromise that allowed for the vast size of the Washington Monument made it, in the eyes of the *Times*, the exact opposite of functional. Rather, it was merely "a big thing" that "overrode all other considerations" of taste and design. Considered "absurdly unworthy of its subject," the *Times* sarcastically concluded, "we have the sweet consciousness that the Washington Monument is the tallest structure in the world" (figure 48).[55]

THE DESTINY OF THE NATION

Less than three months later, after the monument's formal dedication in February 1885, the enthusiasm expressed at the ceremony for its design filtered into the popular press and so established what would be the official national attitude toward the obelisk—at least for a time. Throughout the dedication, the various speakers referred to the shaft as a "fit" and "appropriate" memorial to Washington. President Chester Arthur proclaimed at its base, "In the completion of this great work of patriotic endeavor there is abundant cause for national rejoicing, for while this structure shall endure it shall be to all mankind a steadfast token of the affectionate and reverent regard in which this people continue to hold the memory of Washington."[56] Coming,

FIGURE 48 Aerial view of the Washington Monument and the White House, Washington, D.C. *(Library of Congress)*

as these words did, from the president himself on such a long-awaited occasion, helped to reinforce the sentiment that the Washington National Monument possessed universal as well as national significance; universal in its recognition around the world and national in its embodiment of American reverence for their Revolutionary hero.

In addition to publishing an account of the dedication ceremonies, the *Times* ran a second article in the same issue, in which it offered extensive praise and admiration for the obelisk. Functioning as an unacknowledged retraction of the derisive statements published earlier in December, the February article reinforced the sentiments declared at the dedication. Whereas previously, the monument's height had been an object of ridicule, it was now a feature worthy of instilling pride in the hearts of all Americans. The *Times* described the obelisk as "characteristically American" and further declared, "Whatever criticisms may be passed upon the design, the fact, pleasing to the patriotic mind, will remain that it overtops every other work of man on the face of the earth."[57] *The Manufacturer and Builder*, an industrial trade journal published from 1869 to 1894, likewise praised the monument as "severely simple and appropriate," and emphasized the overwhelming size of the memorial, commenting, "[n]o idea of its enormous height can be obtained by viewing it from a distance. It is only when one is close up to it that its immensity is properly realized."[58] Similar to descriptions of the monuments at Bunker Hill and Groton Heights, this depiction, which focused on the sheer scale of the obelisk, also contained the same kind of language employed by writers of popular fiction and travel literature to describe the original pyramids and temples in Egypt.

Beyond such commentaries on the size and technological achievement embodied in the Washington Monument, the rhetoric surrounding the monument's formal dedication imbued it with a deeper significance beyond that of memorializing George Washington. Just as during the Civil War, observers had linked the unfinished state of the obelisk to the broken Union and the fate of the monument with the war's outcome, once completed, the shaft had transformed into a tangible beacon that proclaimed "the destiny of the Nation."[59] The Civil War, albeit twenty years' past, was still fresh in the public's memory, its wounds and reconciliations made perpetually visible on the cultural landscape in both the North and South through the erection of local monuments to the soldier dead. Soldier statues, obelisks, and other types of monuments appeared throughout the country, both to mourn the dead and reify the ideals for which each side fought. Especially in the case of the North, monument societies had sought to foster reconciliation and a renewed sense of brotherhood between Union and Confederate veterans by utilizing inscription language on their monuments to promote national unity. However, there still remained a strong sense of sectionalism in the monument-making activities in both sides of the country—more often than not, Union monuments commemorated the efforts of the soldiers who died in "putting down the rebellion," while Confederate monuments aided in establishing a profound and long-lasting rhetoric of the Lost Cause. With such diversity on the local level, the Washington National Monument became for many who witnessed its completion *the* statement of national unity and survival.

Robert C. Winthrop, who had delivered the cornerstone oration thirty-six years earlier, was called upon once again to deliver the dedicatory address. Mindful of his exhortations in 1848, Winthrop commented upon the nature of the Washington Monument as symbolic of a unified nation. Contrasting the nation's obelisk with the Egyptian monoliths, he proclaimed that it was the composite nature of the structure that made the grand monument functionally and symbolically significant to the United States:

> It is not, indeed, as were those ancient obelisks, a monolith, a single stone cut whole from the quarry; that would have been obviously impossible for anything so colossal. Nor could we have been expected to attempt the impossible in deference to Egyptian methods of construction [. . .] America is certainly at liberty to present new models in art as well as government, or to improve upon old ones; and, as I ventured to suggest some years ago, our monument to Washington will be all the more significant and symbolic in embodying, as it does, the idea of our cherished National motto, E PLURIBUS UNUM. That compact, consolidated structure, with its countless blocks, inside and outside, held firmly in position by their own weight and pressure, will be ever an instructive type of the National strength and grandeur which can only be secured by the union of "many in one."[60]

In the case of the earlier obelisks built at Bunker Hill and Groton Heights, the use of multiple stones to complete the projects had simply been a structural compromise. The state of American stonecutting and quarrying technology prohibited the construction of a pure monolith with the dimensions their respective architects and monument associations desired. This clearly remained the case when Robert Mills first designed the Washington National Monument, but at its dedication, Winthrop provided a greater symbolic function by tying its very construction to the national motto—a motto that only remained true *because of* the ultimate preservation of the national Union.

Following the dedication ceremonies, the *New York Times* reaffirmed Winthrop's assessment that the monument's completion could be connected to the Civil War's outcome. As the *Times* observed, "[i]f the Union were to be sundered it need never be finished. It would be more appropriate so, like the broken memorial column that typifies a sundered life and hopes unfulfilled."[61] In other words, had the nation been permanently separated, the incomplete obelisk would have become a perpetual symbol of that division—an enormous cemetery monument to a lost nation. But the completed monument, without any exterior adornment, took on the rhetoric of symbolic unity shared by the states throughout the nation. The republican experiment, having survived the trauma of a bloody civil war, had not only succeeded, but prospered and spread from coast to coast. The very fate of the nation therefore became tied to the hero who represented the ideals of 1776. The government had "assumed to itself the work and the expense of finishing the memorial shaft to him whose anxious and far-seeing fears were no longer to be regarded as justified, and whose faith and hope in the infant nation seemed to be vindicated."[62] Therefore, the Washington Monument was as much a monument to the survival of Washington's political ideals as much as it was a monument to the man himself.

TRANSFORMATION

At first envisioned as a national monument to honor George Washington as the father of his nation, the lengthy process whereby the 555-foot tall obelisk eventually came into being had a transformative effect on the monument's ultimate meaning when it was dedicated in 1885. As a national monument, it would be a destination for American and foreign tourists alike, a symbol of American technological progress while also reflective of a national identity steeped in the ancient past. It would at once glorify the memory of Washington and proclaim both the man and his legacy as eternal, since the obelisk itself was intended to last forever. Additionally, the completion of the monument in and of itself signified the preservation of the Union, the widely perceived endurance of the obelisk again hearkening to the endless future of a united American civilization. Kirk Savage has argued that it is "somehow troubling" that the Washington Monument "should so neatly reconcile so many competing ideals—ancient tradition and modern technology, republican values and national progress, communal harmony and individual enterprise."[63] Yet however much in competition these ideals may have been, they represented the reality of how public figures and the press defined American identity toward the end of the nineteenth century. Albeit a population divided by perceptions of cultural heritage and future progress, the monumental shaft in the nation's capital represented, at least in the official sense, the unity of the republic amidst ongoing cultural conflict. Regardless of how individuals might interpret the obelisk, the symbolism attributed to the monument through the rhetoric of orations and print culture established the official meaning of the structure and reaffirmed the monument's connection to national identity.

As with any public monument, however, the significance of the Washington Monument's design, construction and symbolism remained clear only so long as explanations reaffirming its meaning remained in the public eye. Just as the *Sphinx* at Mount Auburn Cemetery became, after Jacob Bigelow's death, an object before which visitors scratched their heads in confusion and could only wonder at the blend of American and Egyptian imagery, almost as soon as the dedication ceremonies and effusive celebrations over the Washington Monument's completion subsided, the tide turned once again toward criticism of its size and design. When, five months after the dedication, the nation's Civil War hero and president, Ulysses S. Grant died, a movement emerged in favor of a large monument to his memory. Similar to newspaper commentaries at the time of Lincoln's death, the Washington Monument became a cautionary tale against architectural folly. The *North American Review*, responding to calls for a monument to Grant, chastised the Washington Monument with language hauntingly similar to the criticisms of the 1830s and 1840s against the Egyptian Revival's use in cemeteries:

> Then we took a hundred years to build a monument for the great soldier and statesman whom we delight to call the Father of his Country. And at last, produced—what? Something whose inmost significance is essentially *appropriate*? On the contrary, we have dedicated to Washington an obelisk—that symbol which pious worshipers of "bulls and tomcats" upon the Nile had consecrated as the special emblem of Generation, and the particular privilege of certain erotic potentates.[64]

The *North American Review* would not be alone in its criticism of the Washington Monument. Indeed, the last fifteen years of the nineteenth century would not look kindly on obelisks in general, and the Washington Monument in particular. For example, in an 1886 review of public monuments, *The Decorator and Furnisher* offered the following harsh assessment:

> The Washington monument, such a disgracefully long time a-building, satisfies the American ambition for big things, but while it overtops the spires of Cologne Cathedral, of how much greater worth is one of those cathedral spires! The monument is a bare, chimney-like structure that, but for its marble whiteness, might be mistaken at a distance for one of those tall "stocks" that rise into the reek of Glasgow. It has hardly a trace of art about it, except geometrical proportion.

Looking upon the unadorned obelisk as unbefitting the man it commemorated and even the city in which it was built, "the handsomest city on this continent," the review thus concluded that "after waiting for a century for his monument the father of his country should have one 'better worth while' than that which bears his name at present. The material or the nucleus is there; now let it be finished."[65]

Fin-de-siècle criticisms of the Washington Monument often paired it with its smaller counterpart, the Bunker Hill Monument. Physician and poet Oliver Wendell Holmes Sr. (1809–1894), commenting on both structures in 1887, wrote "I own that I think a built-up obelisk a poor affair as compared with an Egyptian monolith of the same form." Of the original Egyptian monuments, Holmes went on to explain, "It was a triumph of skill to quarry, to shape, to transport, to cover with expressive symbols, to erect, such a stone as that which has been transferred to the Thames Embankment, or that which now stands in Central Park. Each of its four sides is a page of history, written so as to endure through scores of centuries." By contrast, "A built-up obelisk requires very little more than brute labor. A child can shape its model from a carrot or a parsnip, and set it up in miniature with blocks of loaf sugar. It teaches nothing, and the stranger must go to his guide-book to know what it is there for." Observing that the Washington Monument from a mile away looked no different from the Bunker Hill Monument a half-mile away, Holmes also expressed doubt as to the durability "of these piecemeal obelisks," relieved that he did not reside near their shadows should an earthquake strike.[66] Thus, without inscriptions, embellishments and obvious outward symbols or reminders to the public of the monuments' meaning, Robert Winthrop's exhortations that the Washington Monument stood as a tangible embodiment of E PLURIBUS UNUM was completely lost. Worse, the exultant claims of the stability and durability of these engineering feats became obscured by the anxiety that a structure so large, composed of multiple blocks, could not endure.

Toward the close of the century, critics remained divided in their views of the monumental obelisks and sought to find a satisfying interpretation for what Americans had reconciled as permanent fixtures on the cultural landscape. Writing in 1894 for *The New England Magazine*, William Howe Downes provided a critical examination of the Washington and Bennington Monuments, with a particular focus on the obelisk at Bunker Hill. Admitting that the Bunker Hill Monument was the "most important monument in Boston, owing to its great size, its lofty and appropriate location, and the historical significance of its commemorative purpose," Downes nevertheless argued in language similar to Holmes' that in comparison to the monoliths of Egypt, it remained lacking. Noting "the perfect purity and balance of their proportions, the subtle and graceful curving lines of their profiles, and the highly decorative character of the elaborate inscriptions" that he considered the hallmark qualities of the original Egyptian obelisks, Downes complained that "none of these features or characteristics are to be found in any of the lofty modern obelisks," with the exception of the Bennington Battle Monument in Vermont. Reminiscent of the *New York Times*' criticisms of the completed Washington Monument in 1884, Downes further noted, "as a merely big thing, the Bunker Hill Monument is to-day much less a marvel than at the time of its completion," admitting that the Washington and Bennington obelisks were superior both in height and quality of construction, albeit "what dignity they possess is entirely due to their exceptional height."[67]

By contrast, F. Marion Crawford, writing in that same year for *The Century*, recaptured the sentiments expressed by Robert Winthrop at the Washington Monument's dedication nearly a decade earlier. Employing language that would evoke in her readers a sense of the sublimity of their nation's grandest monument, Crawford wrote, "The enormous proportions are touched then with a profound mystery; the solidity of the symbol disappears, the greatness of the thought remains, the unending vastness of the idea is overwhelming." Of its multi-stone construction, Crawford waxed poetic, "Block upon block, line by line, it was built up with granite from many States, a union of many into one simple whole, a true symbol of what we Americans are trying to make of ourselves, of our country, and of our beliefs."[68] Blending visions associated with ancient Egypt—its "mystery" and "vastness"—with the enduring principle of the monument, Crawford thus reaffirmed what had gone overlooked in the jumble of aesthetic critiques in the last years of the century: that, as a national monument, the obelisk signified the identity of the nation and its people as multi-faceted and at the same time unified; E PLURIBUS UNUM.

The history of the Washington National Monument is neither short nor straightforward. From its design and construction, to its dedication and public interpretation, the grand obelisk was certainly not without its misinterpretations and critics. As the most well-known example of Egyptian Revival, the monument may be considered the last major expression of the revival as such. Designed at a time when Egyptian-derived architecture possessed the explicit function of linking modern American civilization to antiquity, the importance of this connection had largely faded by the time of the monument's eventual completion and dedication. However, even as it stood as the last major example of Egyptian Revival commemorative architecture, *because* it was the Washington National Monument and not some lesser—either in size or importance—structure, the obelisk in the nation's capital possessed a transformative power on the American perception of Egyptian architecture in general and obelisks in particular. The beginning of the twentieth century would witness a new wave of monument building that would include the construction of several monumental obelisks—one of them outstripping even the Washington Monument in size. By this time, however, whereas the Washington Monument and its predecessors had suffered perpetual comparisons to their ancient counterparts in Egypt, the obelisks of the twentieth century would be considered purely American in character, derived in style from that austere shaft in the nation's capital.

CHAPTER 6

From Egyptian Revival to American Style

THE DECADE OF THE 1880S WAS A TRANSITIONAL PERIOD in a number of ways. First, no sooner did the country celebrate the dedication of the Washington National Monument than American architects and art critics plunged into a series of debates, sparked by calls for a memorial to Ulysses S. Grant, which signaled an emerging rejection of architectural revivalism and a crisis in American aesthetics. Second, after nearly a century of fascination with Egypt, the United States began to transcend the realm of armchair archaeology and amateur enthusiasm to establish a presence within the field of professional Egyptology. The debates and activities of the 1880s and 1890s kept the specter of Egypt—both ancient and modern—in the public eye, which resulted in a continued, if not heightened, fascination in the United States with that country. The first decades of the twentieth century therefore witnessed a widespread new wave of Egyptomania, well before Howard Carter's famous discovery of King Tutankhamen's tomb in 1922 that found expression in museum exhibits, the 1893 World's Columbian Exposition in Chicago, theatrical productions, and the new medium of film.

Even with the disillusionment felt by many architects toward the Egyptian Revival, however, the modern pharaohs of the urban industrial economy commissioned monument companies for their own pyramids, obelisks and temples in the nation's cemeteries. Reflective of the advances in quarrying and manufacturing technology, not to mention the massive expansion in wealth among the capitalist elite, these private monuments were far more lavish and grandiose than their predecessors of the mid-nineteenth century. Within the realm of public commemorative architecture, no fewer than seven monumental obelisks measuring from 100 feet to nearly 600 feet appeared from the beginning of the century through the 1930s. The point of comparison by this time had shifted, for while some drew comparisons to the Egyptian monoliths, most observers scrutinized the new American obelisks according to how they compared to that most "characteristically American" of structures, the Washington National Monument. What this ultimately reveals is that the Washington Monument was transformative in its significance as an example of the Egyptian Revival and its place in American national identity. The twentieth century therefore witnessed the familiar Egyptian forms of the nineteenth century become a decidedly American means of commemorative expression.

"THE ARCHITECTURAL RESULT IS CHAOS"

On July 23, 1885, the nation lost its eighteenth president and hero of the Civil War, Ulysses S. Grant. Even before the funeral took place, a group of "prominent New Yorkers" formed the Grant Monument Association in order to erect a "great national monument."[1] Two months after the Association's establishment, the *North American Review* ran an article entitled "Grant's Memorial: What Shall It Be?" in which a variety of architects and critics offered their voices to the subject. Henry Van Brunt, the architect and prolific writer who had offered his thoughts in 1879 on how the Washington Monument should be completed, wrote "General Grant was as distinctively American as Lincoln. Our monument to his memory should be American." He entreated further that such a monument "be simple, like him, but let the scale of our effort be commensurate with our dignity as a nation."[2] Another contributor, sculptor Wilson McDonald, reflected a greater sense of insecurity regarding America's ability to erect a truly appropriate memorial. "The death of our greatest soldier has given the people of the present generation an opportunity to build a grand monument: we have the wealth, the subject, and the location, but it remains to be seen whether we have the taste, genius, and ability."

With Americans having drawn architectural inspiration from antiquity and foreign lands since the eighteenth century, architects and writers like McDonald began to seriously question whether or not to continue to do so. "The great monuments of the world are before us, from the Pyramids and temples of the Nile to *the matchless Obelisk on the banks of the Potomac*. We can contemplate them all [emphasis added]." This statement is telling in more than one way—McDonald acknowledged the variety of forms available for inspiration, but the most intriguing aspect of his statement is how he divided the Egyptian forms: the pyramids and temples still belonged to the Nile, but the "matchless obelisk" was no longer the ancient monolith; the Washington National Monument had supplanted it as the object for comparison. However, as impressive as even the Washington Monument was, and as varied an architectural palette the great epochs and civilizations of the world offered, McDonald wondered, "Shall we draw upon these great works of past centuries, and upon the experience of older nations, or shall we invent some new style or character of monument which shall be germane to our present civilization and environments; or shall we go back to old Greece, and draw from that pure and ancient fountain of art, as we have drawn upon here for our models of morals, philosophy, and literature"? In McDonald's view, then, the 1880s were a turning point for American architectural design; the death of Grant provided the perfect opportunity to showcase the nation's ability to produce something truly significant and uniquely American. As he concluded, "This generation has the rare opportunity to build a monument to the memory of one of the world's greatest captains, and at the same time to demonstrate that Americans can erect a monument equal if not superior to any of ancient or modern times."[3]

McDonald was not alone in his desire that Americans should begin to innovate in the realm of aesthetic design. Indeed, his comments spoke to a more broadly felt disillusionment with the kind of architectural revivalism that had dominated the American landscape for nearly a century. Critics in the 1880s appeared to be lost on what had prompted their predecessors to opt for Egyptian pyramids and obelisks, Grecian temples and Gothic spires in the first place. Further, they feared the possibility of the Grant memorial becoming a repeat of the Washington Monument, which some commentators clearly viewed as an aesthetic disaster. Art critic Clarence Cook (1828–1900) was especially vehement on this score when he wrote, "So many unfortunate monuments—monuments at once ugly and inappropriate—have been erected to the memory of public men in this country, that it is not possible to hear without apprehension of a project for repeating the experiment in the case of General Grant, especially when we consider the proposed size and cost of the memorial."[4]

In November, art critic Clarence King (1842–1901) anonymously submitted an article for the *North American Review* in which he chastised such calls for something "characteristically American," responding that the only "strictly American" monuments were "Indian earth mounds and Central American buildings."[5] Echoing critiques of the great mounds from earlier in the century, he continued, "The latter are impressive and elaborate enough for a great memorial purpose, but their primitive design and archaic embellishments render them as unfit for nineteenth-century American uses as a Japanese temple or a Cambodian pagoda." Of modern Americans, King could only lament, "We are an unartistic people, with neither an indigenous nor an adopted art language in which to render grand thoughts." Rather, Americans had relied on the styles of other peoples and ages but had been "phenomenally ignorant and obtuse as to the requirements of the styles," and that "We use them only to abuse them; we adopt them only to mutilate and burlesque them [. . .] From Bangor to San Diego we seem never weary of contriving for ourselves belongings which are artistically discordant and customs which are wholly inappropriate." Architectural revivalism, thus spanning the length and breadth of the nation, was effectively a universal folly practiced by all Americans.

King offered, however, more than a castigation of what he saw as a nationally-sanctioned penchant for poor taste in architecture and the decorative arts. Seeking to explain *why* revivalism was so popular, he offered that such eclecticism in taste could be attributed to the very heterogeneity of the American population. "Till there is an American race there cannot be an American style," he offered. Listing the various ethnicities that comprised the American population, King noted that together they may be considered "a people" bound together by a common government. However, such a stew of ethnicities "do not make a *race*, and until they do, all talk of an American style is empty and idle." Any hope for the development of a unique American idiom therefore lay in whether the proverbial melting pot of the United States would actually dissolve the boundaries of race and ethnicity to create a homogeneous nation. King conveyed this hope that once the "composite elements" of the population eventually melted down "into one race alloy . . . belonging to one defined American race, that race will become conscious of its own ideals and aspirations, its own sentiments and emotions, and, as all other great races have done before it, will find its own fit means of expression." In this line of thinking, then, one American race would eventually result in one American style. But until such time, King resolved that architectural eclecticism must remain the order of the day and Americans must use their best judgment to choose the least offensive styles for their current monumental endeavors. To this end, after considering the various stylistic derivations available, King concluded, "What therefore seems to the writer the most fitting tribute of the American people, and the grandest possible monument for General Grant, is a round Roman tomb of noble dimensions treated as to its details in Romanesque style."[6]

Van Brunt affected a similar demeanor of grudging acceptance of the architectural "chaos" he had observed within his own country and projected the hope that "to our successors this inchoate, nebulous mass may resolve itself, not into a style in the historical sense, but into a sort of architectural constellation, in which may be seen, in a manner, some reflection of the spirit of the times in which we live."[7] Thus, for Van Brunt, the best anyone could hope for would be that future generations would learn something from the eclecticism of the nineteenth century and perhaps use it as a cautionary tale of what *not* to do in their own architectural endeavors. *The Century*, by contrast, expressed an irrepressible hope that with the eyes of the world once again watching the American effort to erect yet another national monument, the country would this time get it right: "Its eventual shape will be pictured in every illustrated sheet for the benefit of stay-at-homes, and, before all our other works of art, will attract the feet of those who cross the water. Whatever we build, it will be everywhere known and will be everywhere accepted as the great typical example of American art."[8] Even as various writers continued to debate what kind of monument should be built for Grant, the people of Bennington, Vermont, began construction at last of their Revolutionary War obelisk, which, like so many before it, would be in the shape of an obelisk. Construction began in 1887 amidst this milieu of architectural protest against the Egyptian Revival, and its design drew scorn from the *New York Times* as resembling "that of a cigar flattened on the sides and balanced on the broad end." Even though public opinion of the Bennington Monument's design would eventually soften by the mid-1890s, the obelisk was built at a time, between the completion of the Washington National Monument and the beginning of the Grant Monument, when, as far as critics were concerned, it was not a good idea to opt for the Egyptian Revival style. Rather, it was "The square cigar tower."[9]

As construction on the Bennington Monument proceeded, fundraising and design competitions were held for the Grant Monument. After five years of effort to raise the necessary funds and fielding numerous design submissions—including a design by George W. da Cunha (d.1894) that envisioned a 400-foot obelisk emerging from a double-layered fort—the Grant Monument Association ultimately opted for the design submitted in 1890 by John H. Duncan (1854–1929) of a monumental neoclassical tomb. As described by architectural historian David Kahn, the design incorporated "a 100-square-foot podium with a semicircular apse projecting to the rear" with a "Doric portico" gracing the façade and "piers and Doric columns" continuing around the podium. "On top of the podium a large plain drum supported an Ionic peristyle."[10] Construction began in 1891 and, no doubt to the relief of all involved in the project, the monument was completed in 1897 and marked by a dedication ceremony on April 27 described by the *New York Times* as Grant's "final canonization."[11] As to the memorial's design, it could not help but draw comparisons to the Washington National Monument, albeit so completely different in style. As *The Wheeling Register* out of West Virginia reported, "It is the most imposing mausoleum in the country, outranking in elaborate design and ornamentation even the Washington monument at the capital. Many, however, prefer the simple grandeur of the latter." However, despite whatever disagreements in aesthetic taste reporters may have observed, the *Register* concluded that the Grant monument "is a fitting mark of the nation's appreciation of one of its greatest soldiers and grandest characters."[12] It remains to this day the second largest mausoleum in the western hemisphere, second only to the mausoleum for President James Garfield, located in Lakeview Cemetery in Cleveland, Ohio (figure 49).

Even as the nation's leading architectural critics debated the prevailing architectural trends, the American people experienced a renewed enthusiasm for Egypt, both ancient and modern. The roots of this fervor can be traced to 1877, when the removal of one of the two Alexandrian obelisks to London sparked interest among Americans to acquire a monolith of their own. In New York, Henry B. Stebbins, Commissioner of Public Parks and William H.

FIGURE 49 Grant's Monument, New York, 1892–1897. *(Library of Congress)*

Vanderbilt, who agreed to underwrite the project, began the campaign to acquire an obelisk. In October of that year, the Department of State vested its consul-general in Cairo, E.E. Farman, with the responsibility to begin negotiations with the Egyptian government.[13] Farman presented his case to the Khedive that the United States had been a friend and partner to Egypt whereas England and France, both of which had received obelisks, had been imperial oppressors. Farman also maintained that both England and France had essentially purchased their obelisks, whereas he wanted the Khedive to freely offer one of Egypt's remaining monoliths as a symbol of the mutual friendship that prevailed between the two nations. He would later reflect upon these differences in an article for *The Century*: "The European press of Egypt gave great importance to the fact that the London and Paris obelisks were both given on account of services and favors rendered by the governments of the countries to which they were presented, while there was no pretense of any such consideration for the gift of Cleopatra's Needle to the city of New York."¹⁴ In 1879, the Khedive of Egypt formally offered the second Alexandrian obelisk—Cleopatra's Needle—as a gift to the United States.

In 1881, when the monolith at last reached New York City, massive crowds followed its path toward its final destination in Central Park (figure 50). Elaborate ceremonies attended the obelisk's re-erection and U.S. Secretary of State William M. Evarts delivered the principal oration to a crowd of 20,000. Anthropomorphizing the ancient obelisks, Evarts declared at its base, "How they would smile at modern strength and glory and at the pride of one hundred or one thousand years as indicating strength and permanency and endurance! How they would say [. . .] governments and power of nations are to pass, there is one common grave of ruin in which they are all to be buried."¹⁵ Evarts' language presented a strange reversal of what many Americans had come to expect to hear at the base of their public monuments. Rather than linking the greatness and permanence of American civilization to that of the obelisk, much as other orators had done in prior decades, Evarts reminded his audience that the mightiest of nations—even the United States—would rise and inevitably fall. However, because of the technological genius of the ancient Egyptians, their obelisks, including the one now standing in Central Park, would bear witness to the birth and destruction of nations.

Rather than portend his nation's inevitable decline, New York City's Mayor William Grace offered the more hopeful message that Cleopatra's Needle would "serve to bind us to antiquity."¹⁶ Lieutenant-Commander Henry H. Gorringe (1841–1885), the naval officer who received the commission to engineer the removal and transportation of the obelisk from Egypt to the United States, published the book *Egyptian Obelisks* (1882), which helped spark further public interest in Cleopatra's Needle and the history of obelisks more generally. Praised by *The Century* "as a piece of work on which neither pains nor expense has been spared," *Egyptian Obelisks* outlined the engineering that was necessary to remove Cleopatra's Needle to New York, included an account of the re-erection ceremony with transcriptions of the speeches delivered, and concluded with an "archaeological portion" that explored the history and archaeology of the other known Egyptian obelisks.¹⁷

The publicity of America's acquisition of its first truly significant Egyptian artifact spawned a wave of articles on various subjects associated with both modern and ancient Egypt in the nation's leading periodicals, including

FIGURE 50 Cleopatra's Needle, Central Park, New York. *(Library of Congress)*

the *North American Review*, *Scribner's*, *Harper's New Monthly* and *The Century*.[18] Much of the language about Egypt's ruins and antiquities resembled that which had already been recounted for decades. For example, Francis H. Underwood, writing for *The Atlantic Monthly* in 1880 noted the sublimity of Egyptian architectural endeavors: "The ruins of Egypt, beyond all others on the planet, show grandeur of design with adequate skill and boundless energy in execution. To an Egyptian architect nothing was impossible [. . .] The central idea in Egypt was an all-compelling power, finding expression in original and tremendous forms." Underwood concluded, "It was as if all Egypt, in every reign, had been chiseling the memorials for history. . . . Never was there a people with such an overpowering desire for immortality."[19] American readers by then had long been acquainted with such descriptions. Travel narratives had also been popular, but fewer people were as well versed in descriptions of modern Egypt and Egyptians as they were with those of the pyramids and the Sphinx.

Almost as a corrective, a veritable slew of travel narratives appeared during the 1880s and 1890s that described for American readers the Oriental languor of Cairo and its inhabitants, the comicalities of taking a donkey or camel ride, and of course, the transcendent experience of awe upon witnessing the Pyramids at Giza or the grand temple at Karnak. Constance Fenimore Woolson's account of Cairo in 1890 offered such varying descriptions of the Nilotic land. Of Cairo, she wrote "It is safe to say that to many Americans Cairo is only a confused memory of donkeys and dragomans, mosquitoes and dervishes, and mosques, mosques, mosques!" Despite such apparent chaos, however, Woolson nevertheless went on to describe the city as an absolute Orientalist fantasy: "Her colors are so softly rich, the Saracenic part of her architecture is so fantastically beautiful, the figures in her streets are so picturesque, that one who has an eye for such effects seems to himself to be living in a gallery of paintings without frames, which stretch off in vistas, melting into each other as they go." Her description of the pyramids, by contrast, was reminiscent of those from earlier decades: "There is something in the pyramids which over-awes our boasted civilization." However, whereas earlier travelers had witnessed the pyramids in relative isolation from the modern city, Woolson observed that "modernity is already there. There is a hotel at the foot of Cheops, and one hardly knows whether to laugh or to cry when one sees lawn-tennis going on there daily."[20]

The tourism industry in Egypt, which had its genesis in the years immediately following the Napoleonic campaigns, had become big business by the 1890s. For wealthy, and even for upwardly mobile Americans, travel to Egypt was now a virtual necessity; the experience of riding a camel or donkey in the shadow of the pyramids had somehow become a rite of passage for those who claimed membership to the upper echelons of polite society (figure 51). As Frederic Courtland Penfield, a former U.S. Diplomatic Agent and Consul-General in Egypt, declared in 1899, "The visit to Egypt has become almost as essential to Americans—and fully half of the eight thousand winter visitors are from the States—as the pilgrimage of good Mohammedans to Mecca. The Mohammedans' religion takes them but once to the sacred city of the prophet, but pleasure draws those favored by fortune to the Nile capital time after time."[21] In other words, especially among the emergent and well-established industrial capitalist elite, anyone who was anyone traveled to Egypt.

FIGURE 51 Tourists in front of the Sphinx and Great Pyramid, Giza, c. 1860–1900. *(Library of Congress)*

For those who could not spare the time or money to venture across the Atlantic and Mediterranean to reach the land of the pharaohs, ample opportunities to experience the country's ancient wonders emerged with the establishment of such new cultural institutions as the Boston Museum of Fine Arts and the Metropolitan Museum of Art in New York. From 1888 to 1890, due to the significant contributions made by American donors, the British-led Egypt Exploration Fund delivered a sizable portion of its artifacts discovered from the dig at Bubastis to the Boston Museum of Fine Arts. Describing the objects visitors would see at the "Egypt at Home" exhibit, William C. Winslow intoned, "I am sure that the serene face of Hathor will welcome visitors to the Egyptian rooms with touches of that same witchery that greeted of old millions of devotees and many immortal men of Greece and Rome who paid Bubastis a visit." Winslow assured his readers that the quality and atmosphere of the exhibit was such that it would be just as awe-inspiring were visitors to see the artifacts in their original locale. For Winslow, the exhibit left upon him "an impression to me akin to the awe and wonder that I felt when I entered for the first time an Egyptian temple. Here, too, the archaic creates awe, and the cabalistic excites wonder."[22] Such exhibits therefore purported to recreate the same sense of sublime awe one might experience on a trip to Egypt and opened up the opportunity for Americans of more varied social standing and economic class to see for themselves the wonders of the pharaohs.

In addition to the intellectual environment of the museum, Egypt made further appearances in the popular realm of theatrical productions and fairs. The romance, *Egypt, a Daughter of the Nile*, starring Effie Ellser (who would later transition to film), premiered in 1887. A decade later, in 1898, *The Little Corporal*, a comic opera spoof of Napoleon's campaigns in Egypt, was widely publicized with advertising placards designed by noted illustrator Thomas Nast (figure 52). Recreating the wonders of the ancient and modern world on an even grander stage, the World's Columbian Exposition of 1893 held in Chicago offered visitors the kind of spectacle many had only read about in popular travel narratives—Cairo Street. The 1893 World's Fair was divided into two major sections, the White City and the Midway Plaisance. The White City presented a vision of the magnificence of modern America—its industries, technologies and artistic endeavors. Embodied in its buildings and exhibits was the explicit statement to the millions in attendance of the United States' preeminence in the world. The architectural eclecticism of

FROM EGYPTIAN REVIVAL TO AMERICAN STYLE 207

FIGURE 52 Thomas Nast, *The Little Corporal,* lithograph, c. 1898.
(*Library of Congress*)

the nineteenth century remained alive and well in the White City, as the buildings that housed the various exhibits incorporated every architectural style imaginable. Evocative of its central place in American commemorative culture, there appeared at the north end of the Grand Vista an obelisk, flanked on its four corners by recumbent lions and inscribed with the Fair's purpose, to celebrate the four-hundredth anniversary of Christopher Columbus' voyage to the New World. The Midway Plaisance, by contrast, housed the Fair's entertainments, most popular among them being Cairo Street. Home to jugglers, sword swallowers, donkey boys and dancing girls,

Cairo Street offered a living caricature of every American's Orientalist fantasy. Toward the end of Cairo Street, as a further nod to ancient Egypt, was a reproduction of the Luxor Temple. Obelisks inscribed with the names of Ramesses II and President Grover Cleveland in front of the temple further emphasized the relationship the world's youngest nation claimed to have with the most ancient of them all.[23]

At the 1894 Midwinter Fair held in San Francisco, which organizers sought to model on the Chicago spectacle, ancient Egypt found representation in the fair's Fine Arts Building. As described in *The Magic City*, a folio of images taken from the 1893 and 1894 fairs, the Fine Arts Building was the "gem" of the Midwinter Fair,

> a splendid imitation of the best architecture of Egypt in the days of the Pharaohs. It was designed by Mr. C.C. McDougal, who, before commencing the plans, made an exhaustive study of the ruins of palaces at Philae, Karnak, Luxor and history-preserved Memphis, and then embodied their most striking features in the building. . . . In size it was 120x60, with an extreme height, in the pyramidal dome, of 40 feet. Though constructed of perishable material, in appearance it was as solid as its ancient prototypes, and so handsome, as well as curious, it is a matter of very great regret that it will not endure as a permanent memorial of California's Great Exposition.[24]

In addition to the pyramidal dome, the structure did, indeed, incorporate practically every well-known Egyptian architectural device. Lotus, papyrus and Hathor-headed columns supported the exterior while winged orbs and royal cartouches appeared tucked into cavetto cornices. The building even included winged pharaoh heads atop each corner of the roof (figure 53).

Given the widespread publicity of and enthusiasm for Egypt, it is no wonder then that the United States finally joined the ranks of England, France and Germany in the pursuit of professional Egyptological research. Archaeology as a *science*, as opposed to pot hunting or grave robbing, was still a new field of study. The Archaeological Institute of America dated back only to 1879 and the first issue of *The American Journal of Archaeology* premiered in 1885. As Thomas Ludlow of the AIA explained in that year, "Archaeology . . . has become a science only within a few years, and is a characteristic acquisition of this encyclopaedic [sic] age of patient research and reasoning endeavor—logical, if not always, unhappily, possessing the

FIGURE 53 Fine Arts Building, Midwinter Fair, *The Magic City*, 1894.
(Author's collection)

inspiration attending sincere conviction within narrower bounds."[25] At the time of the AIA's establishment, American archaeological endeavors were primarily oriented toward excavations in North America, Mesopotamia and Greece. It was not until the 1890s, when such wealthy philanthropists as John D. Rockefeller Jr. (1874–1960) and Phoebe Hearst (1842–1919), the mother of publishing magnate William Randolph Hearst, began to fund American digs in Egypt. However, as historian and archaeologist Brian Fagan has explained, given that "Americans were late on the scene," the British, German and French Egyptologists continued to dominate the field until the beginning of World War I.[26]

The expanded American presence in the realm of scholarly Egyptological research could not, and did not, obscure the public's taste for Egyptian themes in popular culture and architecture. The early years of the film industry witnessed the production in 1912 of the first *Cleopatra* film, starring Helen Gardner. Given the romance and intrigue of the subject matter, it went through several more incarnations during the twentieth century, including

Cecil B. Demille's masterpiece, *Cleopatra* (1934); *Caesar and Cleopatra* (1945) starring Claude Rains and Vivien Leigh; and of course, the epic *Cleopatra* (1963) starring Elizabeth Taylor and Richard Burton. The 1915 mystery film, *Lord John in New York*, includes the evil character Dr. Rameses, who attempts to steal a gold-filled mummy. *She* (1917), a film adaptation of a novel of the same name by H. Rider Haggard, is an adventure film set in ancient Egypt. When, beginning in the 1920s, Hollywood emerged as the hub for the American film industry, the era of the lavish movie palace was likewise born. The Egyptian Revival found ample expression in the construction of new theaters designed with an eye for luxury and spectacle. Among the earliest and most impressive examples included Grauman's Egyptian Theater in Hollywood, completed only weeks before Carter's discovery of King Tutankhamen in 1922; Peery's Egyptian Theater in Ogden, Utah, built in 1923 (figure 54); and the Bala Theater (originally opened simply as the Egyptian Theater) in Bala-Cynwyd, Montgomery County, Pennsylvania, built in 1926. This expression of popular Egyptomania in film and film palace lasted well beyond the 1920s, and the popularity of Universal Pic-

FIGURE 54 Peery's Egyptian Theater, Ogden, Utah, 1923. *(Library of Congress)*

tures' *The Mummy* (1932), starring Boris Karloff, further ensured the place of Egyptomania and Mummymania until the present day.

MONUMENTS TO ETERNITY

Given the prevailing enthusiasm for Egypt in both popular and scholarly circles at the fin-de-siècle and early twentieth century, it would have been strange indeed if the Egyptian Revival had disappeared from the commemorative landscape. The comparatively diminutive side-hill tombs of the 1830s–1850s gave way to substantial freestanding mausoleums during the 1890s, many of which took the form of Egyptian temples or pyramids replete with guardian sphinxes, lotus-bedecked urns and columns, and Egyptian-themed stained glass windows. Many of these structures were built even before Carter's discovery in 1922 spurred the biggest wave of Egyptomania since the Napoleonic campaigns. Among these include the pyramidal Egbert Viele mausoleum (c. 1902) located in the West Point Cemetery in New York (figure 55); the Brown mausoleum (c. 1908) at Homewood Cemetery in Pittsburgh (figure 56); the Cardeza-Drake mausoleum (c. 1915) at West Laurel Hill Cemetery in Philadelphia; the Tate mausoleum (c. 1907) at Bellefontaine Cemetery in St. Louis, Missouri; and the Harper mausoleum (c. 1908–1916) at Cedarville North Cemetery in Cedarville, Ohio. In the case of the Browns and the Cardeza-Drakes, they did, in fact, travel to Egypt. Charlotte Drake-Cardeza (1854–1939), first woman to circumnavigate the globe in her own yacht, the *Eleanor*, had also hunted lions on safari in Africa, and tigers and wild boar in India. Perhaps best known for surviving the sinking of the *Titanic* in 1912, she and her son Thomas were aboard that ship on their return from a vacation in Egypt.[27] Among the largest mausoleums built in the Egyptian style include the 45-foot tall Bache mausoleum (c. 1918) at Woodlawn Cemetery in New York, which is an exact reproduction of the Isis Temple on the Island of Philae; and the colossal Woolworth mausoleum (1918), which houses the remains of the five-and-dime innovator (1852–1919) and his family, also at Woodlawn. The twin to the Woolworth mausoleum, completed in 1931, was built for Pittsburgh steel magnate Emil Winter (1857–1935) and resides in that city's Allegheny Cemetery.[28]

More modest examples of the Egyptian Revival appeared as well, including sphinxes atop pedestals, Egyptian sarcophagi and miniaturized versions of the portals that had appeared so regularly as cemetery gateways during the

FIGURE 55 Egbert Viele Mausoleum, U.S. Military Academy Cemetery, West Point, New York, c. 1902. *(Library of Congress)*

FIGURE 56 Brown Mausoleum, Homewood Cemetery, Pittsburgh, Pennsylvania, c. 1908. *(Photograph by the author)*

FIGURE 57 Winslow Monument, Crown Hill Cemetery, Indianapolis, Indiana, c. 1900–1915. *(Photograph by the author)*

mid-nineteenth century (figure 57). And of course, there was the obelisk. By the early twentieth century, various monument companies were publishing fully illustrated catalogues with recommendations as to particular styles and how best to use them. In the case of some monument companies, like the Leland Company in North Carolina, they produced extensive publications that outlined the history and derivation of different monumental forms. Cook and Watkins, a granite works company out of Boston that specialized in granite, marble and statuary, adopted the image of the Sphinx and Pyramids at Giza on its official letterhead (figure 58).[29] J.F. Stanley's *Concerning Memorials: Their Historic Origin and Present Day Adaptations*, published for the Leland Company in 1911, considered the Egyptian obelisk "one of the many examples of the wonderful sense of fine balance in proportions, in which the ancient Egyptians were masters. It is this mastery that turns an otherwise uninteresting, long, rectangular piece of stone into a beautiful memorial." Of the obelisk's use in modern cemeteries, Stanley saw the form as especially desirable "in instances where the plot is restricted in size."[30] Albeit not published for any particular monument company, Henry Bliss' *Memorial Art—Ancient and Modern* (1912) nevertheless offered his recommendations for the use of different monument styles in the modern cemetery. Of the obelisk, Bliss noted, "With its Egyptian significance, 'the power that can recreate,' the obelisk is a most fitting cemetery memorial for those who believe in the Resurrection and future life."[31] Entirely absent were any of the concerns about paganism that had been so prevalent during the mid-nineteenth century.

FIGURE 58 Cook & Watkins Letterhead, 1902. *(Author's collection)*

However, as popular as these styles were in the early decades of the twentieth century, the trend to continue to build large scale individual and family monuments ultimately came to a close by the early 1930s. The deepening of the Great Depression might be considered one factor for the absence of elaborate cemetery monuments, but it was also at this time that the new cemetery landscape, known as the "Memorial Garden," expanded in popularity across the United States. Just as Mount Auburn Cemetery had been the model for the Rural Cemetery Movement in the 1830s, Forest Lawn Memorial Park, established in 1906 in Glendale, California, served as the model for the modern cemeteries of the twentieth century. Designed with the purpose of offering visitors a serene park-like atmosphere, the new memorial parks encouraged uniformity and often required plot owners to use markers that rested flush to the ground. Such restrictions were in part for ease of lawn care, but they also represented the fruition of the late-nineteenth century critics' rejection of eclecticism on the landscape. In their orderly design is also evidence of the rejection of the principles that spawned the Rural Cemetery Movement in the first place—cemeteries like Mount Auburn and Laurel Hill had become, ironically, antiquated; their emphasis on recreating an untouched, "natural" setting for visitors were now considered entirely too wild and unorganized for modern sensibilities. The examples of Egyptian and other revival-inspired monuments and memorials that were constructed during the twentieth century therefore appeared in the nation's older cemeteries that retained adherence to the mid-nineteenth century acceptance of stylistic variety. No such monuments were built in the new memorial parks, which had effectively swept through the nation by the mid-twentieth century.

THE NATION'S MONUMENT

Far more remarkable than the persistence of the Egyptian Revival in the cemetery landscape, however, was the way in which communities across the country continued to opt for the Egyptian Revival—the obelisk, in particular—for public memorial projects. The styles for the grandiose monuments wealthy Americans had erected to house their mortal remains had been chosen either because of personal interest in Egypt or simply as symbols of the vast wealth or power accumulated by their proprietors. It would be safe to say that the Americans who opted for the Egyptian Revival for their private monuments were not striving to make a statement about their nation's relationship to Egypt; if anything, the statement was that they believed themselves to be the economic pharaohs of the industrial capitalist age. By contrast, the communities that erected obelisks as public memorials during the twentieth century were well aware that the style possessed decidedly nationalistic associations.

Located in Sioux City, Iowa, the 100-foot tall obelisk dedicated to the Louisiana Purchase also houses the remains of Sergeant Charles Floyd, the only member of the Lewis and Clark expedition to die along the way. Built in 1900, it was the first monumental obelisk constructed during the twentieth century. In his dedication oration, the Honorable John A. Kasson (1822–1910) offered a lengthy exhortation on the significance of the Louisiana Purchase to the history of the United States, along with an account of the circumstances surrounding the Lewis and Clark Expedition and Floyd's death in 1804. In concluding his address, Kasson spoke of the monument itself. His remarks, which explicitly bind the Floyd obelisk to its Egyptian predecessors, warrant quotation in full:

> The Floyd obelisk reminds me of two others. The first, in Egyptian Thebes, is one of the supreme wonders I have twice voyaged far up the Nile to gaze upon. It is confessedly the beau ideal of its class in material, height and proportions. It is reproduced here more strikingly than in any other work I can call to mind. Spite of earthquake and lightning, tyrants and time, it has stood, wanting eight years, for seven times 500 years. Can you wish anything more than an equal longevity for the companion shaft we have this day dedicated? Thirty-five centuries were a goodly heritage.
>
> The other obelisk of which I am reminded is scarcely inferior to anything but the first. It is the only one of the twelve transported to Rome in her grand era that has never been thrown down. It stands as a memorial of martyrs, of the protomartyrs [sic] under Nero, of the earliest burning of Christians at the stake recorded in a pagan writer. With allusion to those whom this witness saw sealing their testimony with their blood that obelisk is inscribed: "*Christus vivit, Christus regnat, Christus vincit. Christus vindicate suum populum ab omni malo.* Christ lives, Christ reigns, Christ conquers. Christ delivers his people from all evil." May God permit this memorial of ours to be as lasting as Egyptian syenite, and may it forever bear witness to that martyr faith to which we owe our civilization from foundation to topstone.[32]

That the obelisk form was derived from Egypt was self-evident; its qualities of timelessness, which Kasson hoped Sioux City's "companion shaft" would achieve, were so pervasive in the modern era that it was essentially pedestrian knowledge. Kasson's remarks were striking, however, in the way that he dually linked the obelisk with both the technological genius of the ancient Egyptians and with Christian martyrdom; he did *not*, as nineteenth century Americans had done, link the form to pagan beliefs. In a way hearkening back to the commemorative objectives of the obelisks at Bunker Hill and Groton Heights, Kasson linked the obelisk to American sacrifice, except in this case, the willingness for self-sacrifice was explicitly associated with the Christian faith as opposed to patriotism in battle.

Sergeant Floyd had died ninety-six years prior to the construction and dedication of the Sioux City obelisk, and so the dedication of the monument as a memorial to a martyr of westward expansion was an affair rich in meaning for Americans, though absent of the kind of emotion that attends immediate loss. The following year, 1901, *did* bring the nation a deep sense of loss, as an assassin's bullet felled President William McKinley at the Pan-American Exposition in Buffalo, New York. Although the president's body was returned to his home state of Ohio for burial, the people of Buffalo sought to erect their own memorial to his memory. Completed and dedicated September 5, 1907, exactly six years following McKinley's assassination, the 96-foot tall monument features a central obelisk of Vermont marble, with sculptured recumbent lions at each of the four corners of its base (figure 59). Carrere and Hastings, the architects of the Pan-American Exposition, designed the monument, while noted animal sculptor, A. Phimister Proctor, designed and executed the lions. The McKinley Memorial received universal praise at the time of its completion. Art critic E.H. Brush described the entire composition as "giving an impression of mobility and loftiness of character," and that the memorial was "a fitting expression of . . . veneration and affection."[33] *The Architectural Review* described the work as "a model of grave and restrained design."[34]

At its dedication, New York Governor Charles E. Hughes spoke not of the monument's design, but rather its purpose: "In memory of his martyrdom, in memory of an heroic death, in testimony to the futility of insensate envy and the lasting supremacy of law and order, in memory of a worthy life crowned by its sad sacrifice, this monument has been erected."[35] Albeit not considered a national monument, the McKinley Memorial nevertheless became a well-known American obelisk. When Harry Bliss described the obe-

FROM EGYPTIAN REVIVAL TO AMERICAN STYLE 219

FIGURE 59 McKinley Monument, Buffalo, New York, 1901–1907. *(Library of Congress)*

lisk form in his *Memorial Art*, his two examples of the form's use in American public monuments included the Washington National Monument and the McKinley Memorial. Regarding the lions at its base, Bliss offered the following explanatory remarks: "While objection has been made to using the so-called "British" lions with an "Egyptian" obelisk, the lion is really an Egyptian decoration, often used, as were also obelisks, at the entrances to temples. The lions are particularly appropriate in this case, because symbolic of a fallen hero."[36] Whether he was aware of it or not, Bliss' description is evocative of Jacob Bigelow's own allusions to the colossal lions at Waterloo, Belgium and Lucerne, Switzerland in his *Account of the Sphinx at Mount Auburn*.[37]

The twentieth century witnessed the erection of three final monumental obelisks between the completion of the McKinley Memorial and the close of the 1930s, in addition to the completion of the 100-foot tall Chalmette Battle Monument in New Orleans (1840–1908) dedicated to the War of 1812. Albeit far less renowned than a number of other monumental obelisks erected since the nineteenth century, those constructed after the first decade of the twentieth century nevertheless rank among the largest in the country. These are the 351-foot tall Jefferson Davis Monument (1917–1924) located in Fairview, Kentucky, the birthplace of the Confederacy's president; the 220-foot tall New Jersey Veterans' Monument (1928–1930) located in High Point National Park, New Jersey; and the nation's tallest monument, the 567-foot tall San Jacinto Battle Monument (1936–1939) in Austin, Texas.

General Bennett Henderson Young, who was a Louisville lawyer, commander-in-chief of the United Confederate Veterans, and leader of the Jefferson Davis Home Association, initiated the project to erect a monument to mark the birthplace of Davis. Enlisting the aid of the United Daughters of the Confederacy (UDC) for funding, Young oversaw the initial construction of what would eventually be the tallest unreinforced concrete structure in the nation beginning in 1917. The United States' entry into World War I delayed the completion of the monument, which the Association hoped would be a rival to the Washington National Monument. Young, for whom the monument was his passion project, died in 1919, but the UDC took it upon themselves as a point of pride to see the endeavor through to its completion. Some observers considered the lack of controversy surrounding the monument's execution a sign that the nation had at last left the sectionalism of the past behind. One commentator, observing the work then being done on the Davis Monument in 1919 along with other monuments to the Confederacy, noted "the complacency with which the people on one side of the Mason and Dixon's line view the erection of memorials to those on the other side." That there were no Northern protests or efforts to obstruct the monument's completion lent a nationalistic air to the monument, but it became clear that as the obelisk neared its completed height of 351 feet, the state of Kentucky and the South more generally claimed the monument as its very own—a symbol of shared Confederate heritage.[38]

The periodical *Confederate Veteran* published a substantial article on the Davis Monument in 1922, then standing at 216 feet, which revealed great southern pride in the obelisk as well as a tangible sense of competition with the other monumental obelisks. Anticipating the completed memorial to be "one of the most striking . . . ever erected to commemorate Confederate ideals," the *Confederate Veteran* took pride that, unlike the Washington Monument, which "required a government to build it," the monument at Fairview would be "the tribute of the people who loved him [Davis] for his service and sacrifice." Acknowledging that the Washington Monument outstripped the Davis Monument in height, the *Confederate Veteran* nevertheless sought to convey the sense that the obelisk in Kentucky was still superior to that in the nation's capital due to the sentiment that drove its construction. Just as the nation had deified George Washington in the nineteenth century, Davis' apotheosis among Southerners was apparent in the efforts to complete the Kentucky obelisk. As the *Confederate Veteran* concluded, "The courage of Jefferson Davis, his loyalty, patriotism, and nobility of soul are enshrined in every Southern heart. 'His was a magnificent life, so veracious that no man was ever deceived, so intrepid that no duty was ever shirked, and so pure politically that no flaw has ever been found.' Can we then fail to do him justice in this memorial?"[39] When it was eventually completed and dedicated in 1924, the pride of the South in its grand obelisk to their Confederate father was clear. In the days leading up to its dedication, the *Aberdeen American* out of South Dakota declared its completion "the crowning event in the efforts of the southerners who would honor the memory of the confederacy's president."[40] The *Greensboro Record* out of North Carolina boasted that the obelisk was "the highest memorial in the world excepting the Washington Monument, and the highest concrete monument in the world without exception."[41] At its dedication, Dr. Dunbar Rowland of Mississippi declared, "Today witnesses the culmination of loving tributes in the dedication of a memorial which represents the mature thought of a steadfast and loyal people."[42]

The last major monumental obelisk built during the twentieth century also bears the distinction of being the largest in the country, outstripping the height of the Washington National Monument by twelve feet: the San Jacinto Battle Monument near Houston, Texas, dedicated to the centennial of Texas achieving its independence from Mexico (figure 60). Built during the years of the Great Depression, from 1936 to 1939, the monument's construction was undertaken as part of the Public Works Administration under President Franklin Roosevelt's second New Deal program. In its design, the Art Deco monument incorporates two distinctive elements: an architectural base with bronze doors and battered walls, which calls to mind the base of Maximilian Godefroy's Baltimore Battle Monument (1815); and the obelisk, which is topped, not by a pyramidion cap, but by a single massive star, emblematic of the state of Texas. The base houses a museum as well as a theater. Lengthy inscriptions that describe the history of Texas' relationship with Mexico and its eventual independence cover the four exterior sides of the base, with the final statement of the Battle of San Jacinto's significance:

> Measured by its results, San Jacinto was one of the decisive battles of the world. The freedom of Texas from Mexico won here led to annexation and to the Mexican-American War, resulting in the acquisition by the United

States of the states of Texas, New Mexico, Arizona, Nevada, California, Utah and parts of Colorado, Wyoming, Kansas and Oklahoma. Almost one-third of the present area of the American Nation, nearly a million square miles of territory, changed sovereignty.

Carved at the base of the obelisk's shaft are friezes that likewise depict the stages of Texas' history. Upon its completion, the *Dallas Morning News* noted that the monument resembled "the Washington Monument rising from the Lincoln Memorial."[43] Following its dedication, *Life* magazine ran an article entitled "Biggest State Dedicates Nation's Biggest Monument." In the true tradition of everything is bigger in Texas, the very size of the monument appeared to have been the most significant point of pride for the state.[44]

What is most remarkable about the Jefferson Davis Monument and the San Jacinto Battle Monument in the history of the Egyptian Revival is how these structures embody the transformation of the obelisk from an Egyptian monumental form into one that is strictly American. No longer did commentators compare the obelisk with the ancient Egyptian monolith, but rather the Washington National Monument had become the primary example for comparison. The beginning of this transformation could be witnessed with the completion of the McKinley Memorial, as it was doubly linked with the Egyptian monoliths and the Washington Monument. With the subsequent monument projects in Kentucky and Texas, the twentieth century offered clear evidence for the especially transformative nature of the Washington National Monument in American commemorative culture. Even as controversial as that monument's design and construction had been, the agonizing embarrassment in the years leading up to its completion had been miraculously forgotten by the beginning of the new century. Twentieth century Americans, having survived the Civil War and Reconstruction and entered the imperial age with the Spanish-American War, no longer labored to prove the legitimacy of their nation to those of the Old World. The Egyptian Revival *as* a revival dissolved and what was left was simply the American style.

FIGURE 60 Two men in front of San Jacinto Monument, c. 1937. *(Courtesy of the Western History/Genealogy Department, Denver Public Library)*

CODA

The *Broken Obelisk*

NEARLY THIRTY YEARS AFTER THE COMPLETION of the San Jacinto Battle Monument, Abstract Expressionist artist Barnett Newman (1905–1970) executed in an edition of three a monumental architectural sculpture entitled *Broken Obelisk* (1967). The three editions of the sculpture reside at Washington University in Seattle, the Museum of Modern Art in New York and the Rothko Chapel in Houston, Texas. As described by art historian Stephen Polcari, "The sculpture consists of a pyramid topped by a reversed obelisk ascending yet torn, or "broken" at its top. Although it is obviously some kind of symbolic object roughly resembling traditional commemorative monuments of combined pyramid and obelisk, no relevance to any historical experience has been adduced yet by art historians."[1] While the three versions are identical to each other, the *Broken Obelisk* in Houston is the most well-known of the three as it was eventually dedicated in 1971 to Martin Luther King, Jr. In Newman's own view of his work, which he executed in the year of King's death, he noted, "It is concerned with life and I hope I have transformed its tragic content into a glimpse of the sublime."[2]

John and Dominique de Menil, who commissioned artist Mark Rothko (1970) to complete the fourteen paintings that decorate the interior of the non-denominational ecumenical Rothko Chapel, were instrumental in acquiring *Broken Obelisk* for display at the center of the reflecting pool that faces the chapel. The Municipal Commission of the city, however, initially blocked the desired dedication of the sculpture to King's memory in 1969 and justified their decision that as it was "a superb contemporary work [of art]," they did "not wish to bias its reception by the public." Nor did they wish to transform the sculpture into a memorial, which would raise "current political questions."[3] Such objections were eventually overcome and in 1971, the Rothko Chapel was completed and dedicated, and *Broken Obelisk* was officially dedicated as a memorial to Dr. King. Art critic Janet Kutner described both the chapel and *Broken Obelisk* for the *Dallas Morning News* in language that hearkened back to earlier descriptions of Egyptian and Egyptian Revival architecture:

> Simple and elegant in its own way, it [*Broken Obelisk*] seems a glorification of the upward rising spirit, much as the Rothko paintings evoke impressions of life and death and the unfathomed recesses of both. . . . The rusty texture of the metal and the deep glowing or murky colors of the Rothkos each in its way lends an aged and thereby ageless quality rather than a newness. . . . The quality of permanence lent by the Rothko and Newman art is an interesting note on which to found an inter-denominational Chapel which will alternate ritualistic symbols of one faith or another as they are used in various services.[4]

Whether cognizant of the deeper meanings to her allusions to agelessness and permanence, Kutner nevertheless articulated the same sentiment toward Newman's *Broken Obelisk* that had been repeated by orators and architects for nearly two centuries.

In his pairing of the two great orders of Egyptian architectural genius—the pyramid and the obelisk—Newman effectively re-envisioned what had by the twentieth century become the most conventional of American commemorative forms in a most unconventional way. Since the 1790s, Americans had appropriated these and other forms from Egyptian architecture and sculpture as part of a century-long effort to articulate to the rest of the world the nation's identity as the modern beneficiary of antiquity's greatest achievements. Obelisks, pyramids, temples, sphinxes and portals, each repeated across the commemorative landscape in inexhaustible variety, not only reaffirmed the legitimacy of the Egyptian Revival in the United States but transformed it into an inherently American idiom of monumental expression. The obelisk emerged as the preeminent monumental form to symbolize American greatness and achievement as well as martyrdom and defeat. It became the form that could memorialize any and all situations that would require public or private expressions of celebration or grief. It therefore seems altogether fitting that during the most volatile period of American history since Reconstruction, that Barnett Newman's *Broken Obelisk*, which fuses those two most familiar images of the pyramid and obelisk—with the obelisk turned on its head—would be dedicated to a martyr to the Civil Rights Movement, which in every way sought to turn the prevailing social order of the nation on *its* head. It is evocative of a period in American history during which the nation and its people suffered an identity crisis and, much as it had to do during the nineteenth century, sought to find itself once again.

Notes

PREFACE TO THE PAPERBACK EDITION

1. "Nicholas Cage's Pyramid Tomb," Atlas Obscura, https://www.atlasobscura.com/places/nicolas-cage-s-pyramid-tomb.
2. The obelisk to the 2nd Brigade Combat Team may be viewed at the Pennsylvania Military Museum website: https://www.pamilmuseum.org/monuments-shrine.
3. Doreen St. Felix, "Kara Walker's Next Act," https://www.vulture.com/2017/04/kara-walker-after-a-subtlety.html.

INTRODUCTION

1. James Stevens Curl, *The Art & Architecture of Freemasonry*, 2nd ed. (London: B. T. Batsford, 2002), 125.
2. John Ledyard in Edward G. Gray, *The Making of John Ledyard: Empire and Ambition in the Life of an Early American Traveler* (New Haven, CT: Yale University Press, 2007), 182; see also, John A. Wilson, *Signs & Wonders Upon Pharaoh: A History of American Egyptology* (Chicago: University of Chicago Press, 1964), 12–13.
3. "Egyptian Antiquities," *The North American Review* 29, no. 65 (October 1829): 361.
4. Richard G. Carrott, *The Egyptian Revival: Its Sources, Monuments, and Meaning 1808–1858* (Berkeley: University of California Press, 1978), 47.
5. *The Bee* 3, no. 124 (January 1, 1800): 4.
6. "Passages of Eastern Travel," *Harper's New Monthly Magazine* 12, no. 69 (February 1856): 373.
7. Carrott, *Egyptian Revival*, 49–50.
8. M. A. Dodge, "A Day with the Dead" *The Atlantic Monthly* 6, no. 35 (September 1860): 338.
9. Julian Ralph, "Our Exposition At Chicago" *Harper's New Monthly Magazine* 84, no. 500 (January 1892): 214.
10. Amelia B. Edwards, *Pharaohs, Fellahs and Explorers* (New York: Harper & Brothers, 1891), 37–38.
11. Brian Fagan, *The Rape of the Nile: Tomb Raiders, Tourists and Archaeologists in Egypt* (Boulder, CO: Westview Press, 2004), 218.
12. Wilson, *Signs & Wonders*, viii.
13. Hon. Isaac Parker, "Inaugural Address" *North American Review* 3, no. 7 (May 1816): 24.
14. Ibid., 22.
15. Andrew Jackson Downing in James Early, *Romanticism and American Architecture* (New York: A. S. Barnes and Co., 1965), 45.

16. Talbot Hamlin, *Greek Revival Architecture in America* (New York: Dover Publications, 1944), xv. For a more recent, extended discussion of the significance of the Greek Revival, see W. Barksdale Maynard, *Architecture in the United States, 1800–1850* (New Haven: Yale University Press, 2002).

17. Jacob Bigelow, *Elements of Technology, Taken Chiefly from a Course of Lectures Delivered at Cambridge, on the Application of the Sciences to the Useful Arts, Now Published for the Use of Seminaries and Students*, 2nd ed. (Boston: Hilliard, Gray, Little and Wilkins, 1831), 153.

18. James Stevens Curl, *The Egyptian Revival: Ancient Egypt as the Inspiration for Design Motifs in the West* (London: Routledge, 2005), 261.

19. Ibid., 155.

20. Although remarkably little has been written about the Egyptian Revival and Egyptomania in the United States, a number of comprehensive works and essay collections address the subject in the European and more broadly international context. See, for example, James Stevens Curl, *The Egyptian Revival*; also Jean-Marcel Humbert and Clifford Price, eds. *Imhotep Today: Egyptianizing Architecture* (London: University College of London Press, 2003); Sally MacDonald and Michael Rice, eds. *Consuming Ancient Egypt* (London: University College of London Press, 2003); Brian A. Curran, *Obelisk: A History* (Cambridge, MA: The Burndy Library, 2009); Brian Curran, *The Egyptian Renaissance: The Afterlife of Ancient Egypt in Early Modern Italy* (Chicago: The University of Chicago Press, 2007); Jean-Marcel Humbert, *L'Égyptomanie Dans L'Art Occidental* (Paris: ACR Edition Internationale, 1989).

21. For example, see George Gliddon, *Otia Aegyptiaca: Discourses on Egyptian Archaeology and Hieroglyphical Discoveries* (New York: Bartlett and Welford, 1849), 76; Mark Twain, *Innocents Abroad Or, The New Pilgrim's Progress* (1869; repr., New York: The Modern Library, 2003), 476.

22. Joseph Downs, "The Greek Revival in the United States" *The Metropolitan Museum of Art Bulletin* 2, no. 5 (January 1944): 173.

23. Carrott, *Egyptian Revival*, 4.

24. Clay Lancaster, "Oriental Forms in American Architecture 1800–1870," *The Art Bulletin* 29, no. 3 (September 1947): 183.

25. See Carrott, *Egyptian Revival*. Other works that address the subject of the Egyptian Revival in America, either in general or through specific examples, include Scott Trafton, *Egypt Land: Race and Nineteenth Century American Egyptomania* (Durham: Duke University Press, 2004); Elizabeth Broman, "Egyptian Revival Funerary Arts in Green-Wood Cemetery," *Markers XVIII: A Journal for the Association for Gravestone Studies* (2001): 30–67; Peggy McDowell and Richard E. Meyer, *The Revival Styles in American Memorial Art* (Bowling Green, OH: Bowling Green State University Popular Press, 1994); Kirk Savage, "The Self-Made Monument: George Washington and the Fight to Erect a National Memorial," *Winterthur Portfolio* 22, no. 4 (Winter 1987): 225–42; Bernard Kusinitz, "The Enigma of the Colonial Jewish Cemetery in Newport, Rhode Island" *Rhode Island Jewish Historical Notes* 9, no. 3 (November 1985): 225–38; Rochelle S. Elstein, "William Washburn and the Egyptian Revival in Boston," *Old-Time New England, The Bulletin of The Society for the Preservation of New England Antiquities* 70, no. 257 (1980): 63–81; John Zukowsky, "Monumental American Obelisks: Centennial Vistas," *The Art Bulletin*, 58, no. 4 (December 1976): 574–81; Robert L. Alexander, "The Public Memorial and Godefroy's Battle Monument," *The Journal of the Society of Architectural Historians* 17, no. 1 (March 1958): 19–24; Claire Wittler Eckels, "The Egyptian Revival in America" *Archaeology* 3, no. 3 (Autumn 1950): 164–69; Frank J. Roos, "The Egyptian Style" *Magazine of Art* 33 (1940): 218–23, 255, 257.

26. Stephen Polcari, "Barnett Newman's Broken Obelisk," *Art Journal* 53, no. 4 (Winter 1994): 48–55.

CHAPTER 1. THE DREAM OF EGYPT

1. Thomas More in Edith I. Coombs, ed. *America Visited* (New York: Stratford Press, Inc., N.D.), 18–21.

2. Ibid., 27–28.

3. Sydney Smith, review of "Adam Seybert, Statistical Annals of the United States of America," *Edinburgh Review* 33 (Jan. 1820), 69–80, 79–80.

4. Jennifer Speake, ed. *Literature of Travel and Exploration: An Encyclopedia*, vol. 3 (New York: Routledge, 2003), 1197.

5. Frances Trollope in Edith I. Coombs, ed. *America Visited* (New York: Stratford Press, Inc., N.D.), 122–30.

6. Charles Dickens, *American Notes and Pictures From Italy* (New York: Charles Scribner's Sons, N.D.), 296.

7. Ibid., 300.

8. "Civilization: American and European," *The American Whig Review* 3, no. 6 (June 1846): 617.

9. "The Destiny of the Country," *The American Whig Review* 5, no. 3 (March 1847): 231.

10. Sydney Smith, *Edinburgh Review*, 79.

11. "The Destiny of the Country," *The American Whig Review*, 231.

12. "De Tocqueville," *The United States Democratic Review* 21, no. 110 (August 1847): 122.

13. "American Civilization," *The United States Democratic Review* 42, no. 1 (July 1858): 57.

14. "American Civilization," *The Atlantic Monthly* 9, no. 54 (April 1862): 508.

15. "Civilization: American and European," *The American Whig Review* 3, no. 6 (June 1846): 616.

16. Thomas Jefferson, *Notes on the State of Virginia*, ed. William Peden (Chapel Hill: University of North Carolina Press, 1955), 97.

17. Quoted in Nancy Hall Burkett, *Under Its Generous Dome: The Collections and Programs of the American Antiquarian Society* (Worcester, MA: American Antiquarian Society, 1992), 19.

18. "Archaeologica Americana," *North American Review* 12, no. 31 (April 1821): 235.

19. Ibid., 238.

20. "Civilization: American and European," *The American Whig Review*, 616.

21. "Ancient and Modern Civilization," *The United States Democratic Review* 24, no. 131 (May 1849): 449–50.

22. "Sketch of the Rise, Progress, And Influence of the Useful Arts" *The American Whig Review* 5, no. 1 (January 1847): 87.

23. "Egypt Under The Pharaohs," *The International Magazine of Literature, Art, & Science* 2, no. 3 (February 1, 1851): 322.

24. "Great Cities, And Their Fate," *Harper's New Monthly Magazine* 43, no. 258 (November 1871): 904.

25. "Ancient and Modern Civilization," *The United States Democratic Review* 24, no. 131 (May 1849): 457.

26. Ibid., 453.

27. "The Age of Iron and Steam," *Scientific American* 2, no. 39 (June 19, 1847): 309.

28. Ibid., 906.

29. "Ancient and Modern Civilization," *The United States Democratic Review*, 450.

30. Richard G. Carrott, *The Egyptian Revival: Its Sources, Monuments and Meaning, 1808–1858* (Berkeley: University of California Press, 1978), 108.

31. Talbot Hamlin, *Greek Revival Architecture in America* (New York: Dover Publications, Inc., 1944), 5.

32. Caroline Winterer, *The Culture of Classicism: Ancient Greece and Rome in American Intellectual Life, 1780–1910* (Baltimore, MD: The Johns Hopkins University Press, 2002), 19.

33. "The Monuments of Egypt," *The New Englander and Yale Review* 9, no. 33 (February 1851): 1.

34. "Ancient Architecture," *North American Review* 88, no. 183 (April 1859): 347.

35. "Great Cities, And Their Fate," *Harper's New Monthly Magazine*, 906.

36. Ibid., 903.

37. "In Egypt!—Verde Giovane," *The Living Age* 35, no. 440 (October 23, 1852): 159.

38. Herman Melville, *The Writings of Herman Melville*, edited by Harrison Hayford. Volume 15 of *Journals* (Evanston: Northwestern University Press and The Newberry Library, 1989), 75–76.

39. Mark Twain, *Innocents Abroad, Or, The New Pilgrim's Progress* (reprint, New York: The Modern Library, 2003), 473.

40. Melville, *Writings of Herman Melville*, 76.

41. "The Age of Iron and Steam," *Scientific American*, 309.

42. "Great Cities, And Their Fate," *Harper's New Monthly Magazine*, 906.

43. Carrott, *Egyptian Revival*, 133.

44. "The Mississippi River," *Harper's New Monthly Magazine* 33, no. 196 (September 1866): 511.

45. "America in 1846 The Past—The Future," *The United States Democratic Review* 18, no. 91 (January 1846): 58.

46. "The Mississippi River," *Putnam's Monthly Magazine of American Literature, Science & Art* 11, no. 5 (May 1868): 590.

47. Thebes, Cairo, and Karnak, all located in the extreme southern tip of Illinois, are known collectively as "Little Egypt."

48. "The Mississippi River," *Putnam's Monthly Magazine of American Literature, Science, & Art*, 590.

49. "In Egypt!—Verde Giovane," *The Living Age*, 159.

50. Julian Ralph, "Our Exposition At Chicago," *Harper's New Monthly Magazine* 84, no. 500 (January 1892): 212.

51. *The Magic City: A Portfolio of Original Photographic Views of the Great World's Fair and its Treasures of Art, Including a Graphic Representation of the Famous Midway Plaisance, With Graphic Descriptions by America's Brilliant Historical and Descriptive Writer J. W. Buel*, Vol. 1, no. 15 (April 23), (Philadelphia: H. S. Smith and C. R. Graham for Historical Publishing Company, 1894).

52. E. G. Squier, "American Ethnology: Being A Summary of Some of the Results Which Have Followed the Investigation of This Subject," *The American Whig Review* 9, no. 16 (April 1849): 386.

53. The price of admission to P. T. Barnum's museum in New York was $.25, the equivalent of about $7.25 today. Such a price in the mid-nineteenth century would have been exorbitant for the average laborer, especially compared to the price of entry—a nickel—to moving picture Nickelodeons half a century later.

54. That said, European interest in mummies for museum exhibits, study, or to be used in ground up form for medicinal purposes dates back to the sixteenth century. For more on European Egyptomania and mummymania, see Brian Curran, *The Egyptian Renaissance: The Afterlife of Ancient Egypt in Early Modern Italy* (Chicago: University of Chicago Press, 2007); Jean-Marcel Humbert and Clifford Price, eds., *Imhotep Today: Egyptianizing Architecture* (London: University College of London Press, 2003); Jean-Marcel Humbert, *L'Égyptomanie Dans L'Art Occidental* (Paris: ACR Edition Internationale, 1989); Karl H. Dannenfeldt, "Egyptian Mumia: The Sixteenth Century Experience and Debate," *The Sixteenth Century Journal* 16, no. 2 (Summer 1985): 163–80; Karl H. Dannenfeldt, "Egypt and Egyptian Antiquities in the Renaissance," *Studies in the Renaissance* 6 (1959): 7–27.

55. Carrott, *Egyptian Revival*, 34.

56. Susan D. Cowie and Tom Johnson, *The Mummy in Fact, Fiction and Film* (Jefferson, N.C.: McFarland & Company, 2002), 40–49; Belzoni also wrote a detailed account of his ventures, *Narrative of the operations and recent discoveries within the pyramids, temples, tombs, and excavation, in Egypt and Nubia; and of a journey to the coast of the Red Sea, in search of the ancient Berenice; and another to the oasis of Jupiter Ammon* (John Murray, 1820).

57. S. J. Wolfe, *Mummies in Nineteenth Century America: Ancient Egyptians as Artifacts* (Jefferson, NC: McFarland & Company, Inc., 2009), 7–12.

58. Ibid., 14; John A. Wilson, *Signs and Wonders Upon Pharaoh: A History of American Egyptology* (Chicago: University of Chicago Press, 1964), 37.

59. Dylan Bickerstaff, "Examining the Mystery of the Niagara Falls Mummy: The Case Against Rameses I," *KMT: A Modern Journal of Ancient Egypt* 17, no. 4 (Winter 2006–2007): 28.

60. Wolfe, *Mummies in Nineteenth Century America*, 47–48.

61. "Hieroglyphics," *North American Review* 32, no. 70 (January 1831): 96.

62. Alan Rauch, "Preface," in Jane Webb Loudon, *The Mummy! A Tale of the Twenty-Second Century; in Three Volumes* (repr., Ann Arbor: The University of Michigan Press, 1994).

63. Although originally written and published by Gautier in 1840, the story reappeared in English translation in *Harper's New Monthly Magazine* in April, 1871, published under the name H. S. Conant.

64. H. S. Conant, "The Mummy's Foot," *Harper's New Monthly Magazine* 42, no. 251 (April 1871): 750.

65. Albert Smith, "Mr. Grubbe's Night with Memnon," *Putnam's New Monthly Magazine* 10, no. 56 (August 1857): 192–97.

66. Cowie and Johnson, *Mummy in Fact*, 141.

67. Edgar A. Poe, "Some Words With A Mummy," *The American Whig Review* 1, no. 4 (April 1845): 363–71.

68. L. Burke, "Introduction," in George Gliddon, *Otia Aegyptiaca: Discourses on Egyptian Archaeology and Hieroglyphical Discoveries* (New York: Bartlett and Welford, 1849), 5.

69. Wilson, *Signs and Wonders,* 41.

70. "Egypt and America," *Scientific American* 2, no. 12 (December 12, 1846): 90.

71. Gliddon, *Otia Aegyptiaca*, 77.

72. Samuel George Morton, *Crania Aegyptiaca; or, Observations on Egyptian Ethnography, Derived from Anatomy, History and the Monuments* (Philadelphia: John Penington, 1844), 1.

73. Samuel George Morton, *Crania Americana; or, A Comparative View of the Skulls of Various Aboriginal Nations of North and South America: To Which is Prefixed An Essay on the Varieties of the Human Species* (Philadelphia: J. Dobson, 1839), 29.

74. Morton, *Crania Aegyptiaca,* 1.

75. Wolfe, *Mummies in Nineteenth Century America,* 64.

76. This amount works out to a little under $150 dollars today.

77. "Unrolling a Mummy," *Scientific American* 5, no. 35 (May 18, 1850): 274.

78. Ann Fabian, *The Skull Collectors: Race, Science, and America's Unburied Dead* (Chicago: University of Chicago Press, 2010), 110.

79. "That Mummy," *Scientific American* 5, no. 40 (June 22, 1850): 314.

80. "Unrolling the Mummy of a Bishop," *Scientific American* 7, no. 27 (March 20, 1852): 216.

81. Fabian, *Skull Collectors,* 111.

82. Josiah Nott and George Gliddon, *Types of Mankind: Or, Ethnological Researches, Based Upon the Ancient Monuments, Paintings, Sculptures, and Crania of Races, And Upon Their Natural, Geographical, Philological, and Biblical History: Illustrated by Selections from the Inedited Papers of Samuel George Morton, M.D., (Late president of the Academy of Natural Sciences at Philadelphia,) and by Additional Contributions from Prof. L. Agassiz, LL.D.; W. Usher, M.D.; and Prof. H.S. Patterson, M.D.* (Philadelphia: Lippincott, Grambo & Co., 1854).

83. Josiah C. Nott and George R. Gliddon, *Indigenous Races of the Earth; or, New Chapters of Ethnological Enquiry* (Philadelphia: J. B. Lippincot & Co., 1857), 103.

84. Scott Trafton, *Egypt Land: Race and Nineteenth Century American Egyptomania* (Durham, NC: Duke University Press, 2003), 46–47; William Stanton, *The Leopard's Spots: Scientific Attitudes Toward Race in America, 1815–1859* (Chicago: University of Chicago Press, 1960), 158–59.

85. B. G. F., "Who and What are the Negroes?" *The Old Guard* 5, no. 7 (July 1867): 535–36.

86. John P. Jeffries, *The Natural History of the Human Races, With Their Primitive Form and Origin, Primeval Distribution, Distinguishing Peculiarities; Antiquity, Works of Art, Physical Structure, Mental Endowments and Moral Bearing* (New York: Edward O. Jenkins, 1869), 101.

87. Ibid., 357–58.

88. Bruce Kuklik, *Puritans in Babylon: The Ancient Near East and American Intellectual Life, 1880–1930* (Princeton: Princeton University Press, 1996), 102; Wilson, *Signs & Wonders,* viii.

89. William C. Winslow, "Egypt at Home," *The New England Magazine* 8, no. 2 (April 1890): 198–201.

90. Jane G. Austin, "After Three Thousand Years," *Putnam's New Monthly Magazine of American Literature, Science and Art* 12, no. 7 (July 1868): 38–45.

91. Louisa May Alcott, "Lost in a Pyramid, or The Mummy's Curse," *The New World* 1, no.1 (January 16, 1869), repr. John Richard Stephens, ed. *Into the Mummy's Tomb* (New York: Berkley Books, 2001), 33–42.

92. Arthur Conan Doyle, "Lot No. 249. A Story," *Harper's New Monthly Magazine* 85, no. 508 (September 1892): 525–44.

93. Edwin DeLeon, *The Khedive's Egypt, or The Old House of Bondage Under New Masters* (New York: Harper & Brothers, 1878), i.

CHAPTER 2. "THE DEAD SHALL BE RAISED"

1. "Rural Cemeteries," *North American Review* 53, no. 113 (October 1841): 389.

2. Joseph Story, "An Address Delivered on the Dedication of the Cemetery at Mount Auburn, September 24th, 1831" in Jacob Bigelow, *A History of the Cemetery at Mount Auburn* (Boston: James Munro and Company, 1859), 149–50.

3. Ibid., 152–53.

4. Much has been explored in gravestone scholarship on these transitions. Some of the more influential examples include James Deetz, *In Small Things Forgotten: An Archaeology of Early American Life*, rev. ed. (New York: Anchor Books, 1996); James Hijiya, "American Gravestones and Attitudes Toward Death: A Brief History," *Proceedings of the American Philosophical Society* 127, no. 5 (October 14, 1983): 339–63; Allan Ludwig, *Graven Images: New England Stonecarving and Its Symbols, 1650–1815*, 3rd ed. (Hanover, NH: University Press of New England, 1999); Dickran and Ann Tashjian, *Memorials for Children of Change* (Middletown, CT: Wesleyan University Press, 1974); Peter Benes, ed. *Puritan Gravestone Art: The Dublin Seminar for New England Folklife Annual Proceedings, 1976* (Boston: Boston University Press, 1977); James Deetz and Edwin Dethlefsen, "Death's Head, Cherub, Urn and Willow," *Natural History* 76, no. 3 (1967): 29–37.

5. Bigelow, *History of the Cemetery*, 1.

6. Bigelow, *History of the Cemetery*, 154–55.

7. William B .O. Peabody, *Address Delivered at the Consecration of the Springfield Cemetery, September 5th, 1841* (Springfield, IL: Wood and Rupp, 1841), 7.

8. "Rural Cemeteries," *North American Review* 53, no. 113 (October 1841): 388.

9. Nehemiah Cleaveland, *Green-Wood Illustrated, in Highly Finished Line Engraving, From Drawings Taken on the Spot by James Smillie* (New York: R. Martin, 1847), 43.

10. Cornelia M. Walter, *Mount Auburn Illustrated in Highly Finished Line Engraving, from Drawings Taken on the Spot, by James Smillie, With Descriptive Notices by Cornelia W. Walter* (New York: Robert Martin, 1847), 119.

11. By the end of the 1860s, cemetery planners shifted the design from that of an "untouched" or "natural" setting to a more regimented, landscaped "garden" atmosphere. By the beginning of the twentieth century, American cemeteries, many of which at this stage were renamed "memorial gardens," became increasingly simple in design and rigid in the enforcement of rules for monument styles and decorations.

12. Ronald Story, "Class and Culture in Boston: The Athenaeum, 1807–1860," *American Quarterly* 27, no. 2 (May 1975): 178–99.

13. Blanche Linden-Ward, "Strange But Genteel Pleasure Grounds: Tourist and Leisure Uses of Nineteenth Century Rural Cemeteries," in *Cemeteries and Gravemarkers: Voices of American Culture,* ed. Richard Meyer (Logan, UT: Utah State University Press, 1992), 293–328; John F. Sears, *Sacred Places: American Tourist Attractions in the Nineteenth Century* (Amherst: University of Massachusetts Press, 1989), 100.

14. T. D. Woolsey, "Cemeteries and Monuments," *New Englander and Yale Review* 7, no. 28 (November 1849): 491.

15. Bigelow , *History of the Cemetery*, 150.

16. Rev. Pharcellus Church, *An Address delivered at the Dedication of Mount Hope Cemetery, Rochester, Oct. 2, 1838* (Rochester: David Hoyt, 1839), 12.

17. Bigelow, *History of the Cemetery,* 1.

18. Bigelow, *History of the Cemetery,* 152.

19. Church, *Address delivered,* 5.

20. For a broader exploration of these sentimentalizing trends, see Ellen Marie Snyder, "Innocents in a Worldly World: Victorian Children's Gravemarkers" in *Voices of American Culture,* ed. Richard Meyer, 11–30; Deborah A. Smith, "Safe in the Arms of Jesus: Consolation on Delaware Children's Gravestones, 1840–99," *Markers IV: The Journal of the Association for Gravestone Studies* (1987), 85–106; Ann Douglas, "Heaven Our Home: Consolation Literature in the Northern United States, 1830–1880," *American Quarterly* 26, no. 5 Special Issue: Death in America (December 1974): 496–515.

21. Cornelia W. Walter, *Mount Auburn,* 119.

22. *An Address by Rev. Henry Neill and A Poem by Oliver Wendell Holmes. Delivered at the Dedication of the Pittsfield (Rural) Cemetery, September 9th, 1850, With Other Matter and a Map of the Grounds* (Pittsfield, MA: Axtel, Bull and Marsh, 1850), 31–32.

23. Peabody, *Address Delivered,* 14.

24. For more on the early development of the cemetery and its relationship to the Massachusetts Horticultural Society from 1829–1835, see Bigelow, *History of the Cemetery*; Barbara Rotundo, "Mount Auburn Cemetery: A Proper Boston Institution" offprinted from *Harvard Library Bulletin* XXII, no. 3 (July 1974): 268–79; Blanche M. G. Linden, *Silent City on a Hill: Picturesque Landscapes of Memory and Boston's Mount Auburn Cemetery,* rev. ed. (Amherst: University of Massachusetts Press, 2007), 139–72.

25. For more on the design and construction of these features, see Linden, *Silent City on a Hill.*

26. Bigelow, *History of the Cemetery,* 164.

27. Edward Everett, "The Proposed Rural Cemetery" in Jacob Bigelow, *History of Mount Auburn Cemetery,* 138–39.

28. David Charles Sloane, *The Last Great Necessity: Cemeteries in American History* (Baltimore: Johns Hopkins University Press, 1991), 53.

29. Rev. George Putnam, D. D., "Consecration Address," in William A. Crafts, *Forest Hill Cemetery: Its Establishment, Progress, Scenes, Monuments, etc.* (Roxbury, MA: J. Backup, 1855), 66–67.

30. Sloane, *Last Great Necessity,* 85.

31. By their actions, the founders of American rural cemeteries accomplished the same as what had occurred in similarly designed cemeteries throughout Europe. In *The Space of Death: A Study of Funerary Architecture, Decoration, and Urbanism* (Charlottesville: University Press of Virginia, 1983), historian Michel Ragon observed that cemeteries such as Pére Lachaise in Paris are "an idealized double of the city, [which] appears at the same time as a perfect reproduction of the socio-economic order of the living" (39).

32. James Farrell, *Inventing the American Way of Death, 1830–1920* (Philadelphia: Temple University Press, 1980), 110.

33. Conger Sherman, *Guide to Laurel Hill Cemetery, near Philadelphia, 1847* (Philadelphia: C. Sherman, Printer, 1847), 21.

34. In the case of Mount Auburn Cemetery, standard lots of 300 square feet were available for the cost of $150, or fifty cents per square foot, whereas individuals of more humble means could opt for interment in a public lot at the cost of only $12 in 1859; see Bigelow, *History of the Cemetery,* 232–33.

35. For information on early gravestone carving technology, see Theodore Chase and Laurel K. Gabel, *Gravestone Chronicles I* (Boston: New England Historic Genealogical Society, 1997), 5; James Blachowicz, *From Slate to Marble: Gravestone Carving Traditions in Eastern Massachusetts, 1770–1870* (Evanston, IL: Graver Press, 2006). A more comprehensive discussion of these changes appears in Peggy McDowell and Richard E. Meyer, *The Revival Styles in American Memorial Art* (Bowling Green, OH: Bowling Green State University Press, 1994).

36. McDowell and Meyer, *Revival Styles,* 135.

37. Howard Colvin, *Architecture and the After-Life* (New Haven, CT: Yale University Press, 1991), 329.

38. Robert L. Alexander, *The Architecture of Maximilian Godefroy* (Baltimore: Johns Hopkins University Press, 1974), 28, 86–93.

39. *Proceedings of the Bunker Hill Monument Association at the Fifty-Sixth Annual Meeting, June 17, 1879. With the Address of Frederic W. Lincoln* (Boston: Bunker Hill Monument Association, 1879), 24.

40. Jacob Bigelow, *Elements of Technology, Taken Chiefly from a Course of Lectures Delivered at Cambridge, on the Application of the Sciences to the Useful Arts, Now Published for the Use of Seminaries and Students,* 2nd ed. (Boston: Hilliard, Gray, Little and Wilkins, 1831), 132.

41. Jacob Bigelow, *The Useful Arts, Considered in Connexion with the Applications of Science, with Numerous Engravings,* 2nd ed. (New York: Harper & Brothers, Publishers, 1863), 23.

42. "Ancient Architecture," *North American Review* 88, no. 183 (April 1859): 343.

43. Bigelow, *History of the Cemetery,* 26.

44. L. C. Tuthill, *History of Architecture: From The Earliest Times; Its Present Condition in Europe and the United States* (Philadelphia: Lindsay and Blakiston, 1848). Repr. New York: Garland Publishing, Inc., 1988), 44–45.

45. R. A. Smith, *Smith's Illustrated Guide to and through Laurel Hill Cemetery, with a Glance at Celebrated Tombs and Burying-Places, Ancient and Modern—An Historical Sketch of the Cemeteries of Philadelphia—An Essay on Monumental Architecture, and a Tour Up the Schuylkill* (Philadelphia: Willis P. Hazard, Publisher, 1852), 9, 126.

46. "Ancient Architecture," 342.

47. Bigelow, *Elements of Technology,* 3.

48. Bigelow, *History of the Cemetery,* 26.

49. George Gliddon, *Otia Aegyptiaca: Discourses on Egyptian Archaeology and Hieroglyphical Discoveries* (New York: Bartlett and Welford, 1849), 95n.

50. A side-hill tomb is a structure that is built into the side of a hill, with space to hold multiple individuals. These tombs were most commonly built with stone facades and a metal door. Side-hill tombs appear to have been most popular in the years between 1830 and 1860. By contrast, the mausoleum is a freestanding architectural structure with four walls, a roof and a door. Mausoleums often incorporated stained glass windows, and tended to be much larger than the earlier side-hill tombs. Most private family mausoleums appear to have been built in the years between 1880 and 1930.

51. Tuthill, *History of Architecture,* 45.

52. *The Picturesque Pocket Companion and Visitor's Guide Through Mount Auburn* (Boston: Otis, Broaders & Co., 1839), 83.

53. "Rural Cemeteries," 391–92.

54. Nathaniel Dearborn, *A Concise History of, and Guide Through Mount Auburn* (Boston: Nathaniel Dearborn, 1843), 5.

55. It should be noted that while they tended to be nondenominational, nineteenth-century rural cemeteries were designed primarily for the benefit of the Anglo-Protestant population. Catholic and Jewish populations continued to bury the dead in their own faith-based cemeteries, while African Americans were either buried in segregated areas within the rural cemeteries or in their own burying grounds.

56. G. T. C., "Mount Auburn," *The New England Magazine* 7, no. 4 (October 1834): 316, 319.

57. James Gallier, "American Architecture" *North American Review* 43, no. 93 (October 1836): 380, 356.

58. Ibid., 379.

59. "Rural Cemeteries," 411–12.

60. Cleaveland, *Green-Wood Illustrated,* 45–46, 52.

61. Tuthill, *History of Architecture,* 333–34.

62. Walter, *Mount Auburn Illustrated,* 18–19.

63. William A. Crafts, *Forest Hills Cemetery: Its Establishment, Progress, Scenes, Monuments, etc.* (Roxbury, MA: J. Backup, 1855), 79–80.

64. There is a certain irony to the overwhelming popularity of the Gothic Revival of the 1840s–1860s, given the long history of anti-Catholicism in the country. However, as Robin Fleming has aptly argued in her article "Picturesque History and the Medieval in Nineteenth-Century America," *The American Historical Review* 100, no. 4 [October 1995]: 1061–94): "American architects and their patrons were able to ignore Gothic's 'papist' beginnings by relying on a faulty and ahistorical memory of the style's origins," with writers conveying the belief "that the pointed arches and delicate tracery of Gothic had their roots not in the twelfth century or the church but rather in the imitation of groves and bowers under which the Druids performed their sacred rites. According to advocates of this theory, Gothic was an authentic, Teutonic style, gradually tamed and civilized by pious Germanic Christians of unspecified denomination." Therefore, American Protestants of the mid-nineteenth century saw the Gothic style as purely Christian in origin (1062–1063)

65. Smith, *Illustrated Guide,* 125–26.

66. *Forest Lawn: Its History, Dedications, Progress, Regulations, Names of Lot Holders, &c.* (Buffalo, NY: Thomas, Howard & Johnson, 1867), 122.

67. "Cemeteries and Monuments," *The New Englander* 7, no. 28 (November 1849): 489.

68. "Biographical Notice of Mr. Justice Story," *The American Whig Review* 3, no. 1 (January 1846): 68, 79.

69. "A JOY Forever; Requests Amounting to $280,560 Paid to Massachusetts Charitable Institutions," *The New York Times* (May 24, 1872), 2.

70. This cost in today's money would be approximately $17,000, and does not include the construction of the family tomb, which is unknown. According to the perpetual care contract signed by the heirs of Lowell, dated 1882, the monument is described as a granite "12 catacomb unit" with slate shelves in the interior. The cost paid by the Lowell heirs for perpetual care was $1,250 (nearly $28,000 today).

71. Nathaniel Dearborn, *Dearborn's Guide Through Mount Auburn Cemetery* (Boston: Nathaniel S. Dearborn, 1857), 2.

72. Cleaveland, *Green-wood Illustrated,* 8–94; Sherman, *Guide to Laurel Hill,* 24–39.

73. Scott Trafton, *Egypt Land: Race and Nineteenth Century American Egyptomania* (Durham, NC: Duke University Press, 2004), 157; Carrott, *The Egyptian Revival,* 91–96.

74. Trafton, *Egypt Land,* 162.

75. Denison Olmstead in Henry H. Townshend, *The Grove Street Cemetery: A Paper Read Before The New Haven Colony Historical Society, October 27, 1947* (New Haven, CT: New Haven Colony Historical Society, 1947), 19.

76. These cemeteries include the Old Granary Burying Ground (1840) in Boston; the Jewish Touro Cemetery (1843) in Newport, Rhode Island; Mount Hope Cemetery (1838) in Rochester, New York; Westminster Cemetery (1813–1815) in Baltimore, Maryland; the Odd Fellows Cemetery (1849) in Philadelphia; Cypress Grove Cemetery in New Orleans (1840). Nor was the use of biblical quotes intended for the unexecuted Egyptian Revival gateway designs for Laurel Hill Cemetery (1836) in Philadelphia and Greenmount Cemetery (1845) in Baltimore.

77. Gliddon, *Otia Aegyptiaca,* 95n.

78. Joshua Segal, *The Old Jewish Cemetery of Newport: A History of North America's Oldest Extant Jewish Cemetery* (Nashua, NH: Jewish Cemetery Publishing, LLC, 2007), 31–36.

79. Mary Louise Christovich et al., *New Orleans Architecture: The Cemeteries* (Gretna, LA: Pelican, 1971), 97.

80. Robert Florence, *New Orleans Cemeteries: Life in the Cities of the Dead* (New Orleans, LA: Batture Press, 1997), 115.

81. Twentieth-century Egyptian Revival manifested to a far greater extent in popular culture than had its expression in the previous century. During the second major Egyptian Revival, the style appeared in the construction of movie theaters, zoos, and even department stores—a reflection of changing patterns of American national and consumer identity.

82. *The Stranger's Guide in Philadelphia and Its Environs. Including Laurel Hill, Woodlands, Monument, Odd Fellows', and Glenwood Cemeteries* (Philadelphia: Lindsay & Blakiston, 1852), 231.

CHAPTER 3. REVOLUTIONARY MONUMENTS

1. Jacob Bigelow, *Elements of Technology, Taken Chiefly from a Course of Lectures Delivered at Cambridge, on the Application of the Sciences to the Useful Arts,* 2nd ed. (Boston: Hilliard, Gray, Little and Wilkins, 1831), 133.

2. Jacob Bigelow, *The Useful Arts, Considered in Connexion with the Applications of Science; with Numerous Engravings, Vol. I* (New York: Harper & Brothers, Publishers, 1863), 27.

3. Beginning with George Washington (d. 1799), a pair of obelisks flanks the "new" burial vault for the first president and his family, constructed on the grounds of Mount Vernon in 1831, whereas a sizable obelisk marks the burial of Thomas Jefferson (d. 1826) at Monticello Cemetery. As with Jefferson's burial, a single obelisk marks the burial of James Madison (d. 1836) in Montpelier, Virginia. In the case of Andrew Jackson (d. 1845), the monument located near The Hermitage includes an obelisk within a Doric-columned cupola. Martin Van Buren's (d. 1862) body is marked by an obelisk in Kinderhook Reformed Cemetery in Kinderhook, New York, and an imposing sixty-foot obelisk surmounts the tomb of William Henry Harrison (d. 1841) in North Bend, Ohio. Millard Fillmore's (d. 1874) grave is marked by a red granite obelisk at Forest Lawn Cemetery in Buffalo, New York, and Franklin Pierce's (d. 1869) obelisk is topped with a Gothic-style cross. In the case of Abraham Lincoln (d. 1865), the martyr president's mausoleum (dedicated 1874) at Oak Ridge Cemetery in Springfield, Illinois, is surmounted by a massive 117-foot obelisk. The last president whose grave is marked by an obelisk is Lincoln's successor, Andrew Johnson (d. 1875), whose monument consists of a marble obelisk topped with an eagle and flag; it is located at the Andrew Johnson National Cemetery in Greeneville, Tennessee. Due to their public stature, the graves of the presidents exist in a liminal zone between public and private and, like the monumental obelisks dedicated in honor of the Revolutionary War, the presidents' burial markers reinforced the connection between the obelisk form and memorial activities.

4. Paul Shackel, *Myth, Memory, and the Making of the American Landscape* (Gainesville: University Press of Florida, 2001), 3.

5. The following inscription appears at the base of the plaque: INVENIT ET SCULPSIT. PARISIIS. J. J. CAFFIERI SCULPTOR. REGIUS ANNO DOMINI. MDCCLXXVII.

6. For a more extended discussion of this monument and the role of Montgomery in the American Revolution, see Sally Webster, "Pierre-Charles L'Enfant and the Iconography of Independence," *Nineteenth-Century Art Worldwide: A Journal of Nineteenth-Century Visual Culture* 7, no. 1 (Spring 2008): n.p.

7. Mark Langdon Hill, "Monument to Washington," *North American Review* 2, no. 6 (March 1816): 334–35.

8. Jacob Bigelow, "Bigelow's *Elements of Technology*," *North American Review* 30, no. 67 (April 1830): 348.

9. John Zukowsky, "Monumental American Obelisks: Centennial Vistas," *The Art Bulletin* 58, no. 4 (December 1976): 579.

10. Daniel Webster, *The Bunker Hill Monument, Adams and Jefferson: Two Orations* (Boston: Houghton, Mifflin and Company, 1893), 15.

11. William Willder Wheildon, *Memoir of Solomon Willard: Architect and Superintendent of the Bunker Hill Monument* (Boston: 1865), 71.

12. Charles Griswold, "An Address in Commemoration of the Lives and Services of Ledyard and his Brave Associates, Who Fell at Groton Heights Sept. 6, 1781, in Defence of Their Country, Delivered at Groton, (Conn.) September 6th, 1826, on the Laying of the Corner Stone of a Monument to Their Memory." (New London: J. B. Clapp, 1826), 4.

13. Horatio Greenough in George Washington Warren, *The History of the Bunker Hill Monument Association* (Boston: James R. Osgood & Co., 1877), 159.

14. However, as will be explored in Chapters 5 and 6, later obelisks *would* glorify particular individuals, as in the case of George Washington, Abraham Lincoln, William McKinley, and Jefferson Davis.

15. Robert L. Alexander, "The Public Memorial and Godefroy's Battle Monument," *The Journal of the Society of Architectural Historians* 17, no. 1 (March 1958): 19.

16. Daniel Webster in Warren, *History of the Bunker Hill*, 40.

17. Warren, *History of the Bunker Hill*, 37.

18. Webster in Warren, *History of the Bunker Hill*, 41.

19. "Groton Heights" reprinted in Hezekiah Niles and William Ogden Niles, *Niles' Weekly Register* V (Baltimore: The Franklin Press, 1826), 76.

20. Groton Monument Association, *Proceedings of 6 September 1825*, n.p. (Bill Memorial Library, Groton, CT).

21. Daniel Webster in William Wilder Wheildon, *Memoir of Solomon Willard: Architect and Superintendent of the Bunker Hill Monument* (Boston: 1865), 61–62.

22. *The Orations on Bunker Hill Monument, The Character of Washington, and The Landing At Plymouth by Daniel Webster* (New York: American Book Company, 1894), 16.

23. Ibid., 21.

24. Ibid., 42.

25. Ibid., 22–23.

26. Wheildon, *Memoir of Solomon Willard*, 76.

27. Solomon Willard in Wheildon, *Memoir of Solomon Willard*, 79.

28. "Bunker's Hill," *Middlesex Gazette* 41, no. 3013 (May 24, 1826): 3.

29. Kirk Savage, *Monument Wars: Washington, D.C., the National Mall, and the Transformation of the Memorial Landscape* (Berkeley: University of California Press, 2009), 1.

30. "Bunker Hill Monument," *Essex Register* 27, no. 63 (August 6, 1827), 3.

31. "Charlestown—November 22," *Bangor Weekly Register* 12, no. 48 (November 28, 1827): 3.

32. "Bunker Hill Monument," *Newburyport Herald* (March 21, 1828), 2.

33. *New Bedford Mercury* 22, no. 11 (September 19, 1828), 2.

34. "Bunker Hill," *Baltimore Patriot & Mercantile Advertiser* 33, no. 42 (February 18, 1829): 2.

35. Edward Everett, *Orations and Speeches on Various Occasions*, vol. I (Boston: Little, Brown & Company, 1850), 354–56.

36. "Bunker Hill Monument," *The Daily Atlas* 10, no. 258 (April 30, 1842): 2.

37. "Bunker-Hill," *Boston Courier* 16, no. 1894 (June 16, 1842): 2.

38. The monument was actually completed on July 23, 1842, but the dedication ceremony was not held until this later date.

39. *The Orations on Bunker Hill* (1894), 18.

40. "The Bunker Hill Celebration," repr. in *The [Baltimore] Sun* 13, no. 28 (June 17, 1843), 2.

41. *The Orations on Bunker Hill* (1894), 47.

42. Constance Fenimore Woolson, "Cairo in 1890," *Harper's New Monthly Magazine* 83, no. 497 (October 1891): 671.

43. *The Orations on Bunker Hill* (1894), 47.

44. Ibid., 47–48.

45. "To the Editor of the Transcript," *Boston Evening Transcript*, 15, no. 4385 (November 9, 1844): 2.

46. Edward Everett, *Orations and Speeches on Various Occasions*, vol. III (Boston: Little, Brown & Company, 1870), 3.

47. "Revolutionary Monument," *New London Gazette* 61, no. 3208 (May 4, 1825): 3.

48. *New York Spectator* 28, no. 3 (August 2, 1825).

49. "Groton Hill" repr. in *Newburyport Herald* 29, no. 37 (August 5, 1825): 2.

50. "Battle of Groton Heights," *American Mercury* 42, no. 2147 (August 23, 1825): 2.

51. Groton Monument Association, *Proceedings of the 6th Sept. 1825*, n.p. (Bill Memorial Library, Groton, CT).

52. Griswold, "Address in Commemoration," 3.
53. Ibid., 7.
54. Ibid., 15.
55. Ibid., 14–15.
56. Ibid., 17.
57. Ibid., 11.
58. Ibid., 18.
59. Charles Allyn, *The Battle of Groton Heights: A Collection of Narratives, Official Reports, Records, Etc. of the Storming of Fort Griswold, The Massacre of Its Garrison, The Burning of New London by British Troops Under the Command of Brig.-Gen. Benedict Arnold, on the 6th of September, 1781* (New London: Charles Allyn, 1882), 177.
60. "Groton Monument," *The New-London Gazette* 68, no. 3520 (April 27, 1831): 3.
61. Zukowsky, "Monumental American Obelisks," 574.
62. "Groton Monument," *The New-London Gazette* (April 27, 1831), 3.
63. Ibid.
64. "Groton Monument," *Columbian Register* (August 17, 1850), 3.
65. *The Constitution* 15, no. 758, (July 7, 1852): 2.
66. Lafayette S. Foster in *The Groton Centennial to be Celebrated September 6, 1881, Under the Patronage of the state of Connecticut and of the United States* (New Haven: Tuttle, Morehouse & Taylor, 1881), 16.
67. Ibid., 16.
68. "State New's" *New Haven Evening Register* 41, no. 65 (March 25, 1881): 4.
69. "State Correspondence," *New Haven Evening Register* 41, no. 118 (May 21, 1881): 4.
70. "Groton Massacre," *New York Herald* 247 (September 4, 1881, 12.
71. Sarah J. Purcell, "Commemoration, Public Art, and the Changing Meaning of the Bunker Hill Monument" *The Public Historian* 25, no. 2 (Spring 2003): 65.
72. James M. Mayo, *War Memorials As Political Landscape: The American Experience and Beyond* (New York: Praeger Publishers, 1988), 126.
73. Stereoview from the America Illustrated Series, Boston & Suburbs, "Bunker Hill Monument," c.1860–1910.

CHAPTER 4. AMERICA *CONSERVATA*, AFRICA *LIBERATA*

1. Jacob Bigelow, *An Account of the Sphinx at Mount Auburn* (Boston: Little, Brown, and Company, 1872), 5.
2. Although there were no sphinxes as public memorials prior to 1872, one example exists of a sphinx used in the United States for the sake of private memorialization: the Lawler Monument, which dates to around 1850 and is located in Cincinnati's Spring Grove Cemetery.
3. Bigelow, *An Account of the Sphinx*, 7.
4. Ibid., 13.
5. Thomas J. Brown, *The Public Art of Civil War Commemoration: A Brief History with Documents* (Boston: Bedford/St. Martin's, 2004), 25.
6. John R. Neff, *Honoring the Civil War Dead: Commemoration and the Problem of Reconciliation* (Lawrence: University of Kansas Press, 2005), 1.
7. Mount Auburn Cemetery Board of Trustees Meeting Minutes, April 3, 1865. Mount Auburn Cemetery Archives.
8. For more detail on monument association and LMA activities in the North and South, see Kirk Savage, *Standing Soldiers, Kneeling Slaves: Race, War, and Monuments in Nineteenth Century America* (Princeton, NJ: Princeton University Press, 1997); Paul Shackel, *Memory in Black and White: Race, Commemoration, and the Post-Bellum Landscape* (Walnut Creek, CA: Alta Mira Press, 2003); Thomas J. Brown, *The Public Art of Civil War Commemoration: A Brief History with Documents* (Boston: Bedford/St. Martin's, 2004); John R. Neff, *Honoring the Civil War Dead: Commemoration and the Problem of Reconciliation* (Lawrence, KS: The University of Kansas Press, 2005); Cynthia Mills

and Pamela Simpson, eds. *Monuments to the Lost Cause: Women, Art, and the Landscapes of Southern Memory* (Knoxville, TN: The University of Tennessee Press, 2003); William Blair, *Cities of the Dead: Contesting the Memory of the Civil War in the South, 1865–1914* (Chapel Hill: The University of North Carolina Press, 2004); Caroline E. Janney, *Burying the Dead But Not the Past: Ladies' Memorial Associations and the Lost Cause* (Chapel Hill: The University of North Carolina Press, 2008).

9. Brown, *Public Art*, 38–39.

10. Neff, *Honoring the Civil War Dead*, 5.

11. Solomon Lincoln, "Address Delivered at the Dedication of the Soldiers' and Sailors' Monument in Hingham, June 17, 1870," in *The Town of Hingham in the Late Civil War*, ed. by Fearing Burr and George Lincoln (Hingham, 1876), 40–41.

12. Frederick O. Prince in Dedication of the Monument on Boston Common Erected to the Memory of the Men of Boston Who Died in the Civil War (Boston, 1877), 120.

13. Ibid., 123.

14. Mount Auburn Cemetery Board of Trustees Meeting Minutes, March 6, 1865 to January 8, 1866. Mount Auburn Cemetery Archives. Although no documentary evidence explains why the board would abandon the project, Mount Auburn Cemetery Archives curator, Meg Winslow, has speculated that it may have been connected to legislation passed by the Board of Trustees that restricted or prohibited the erection of nonfunerary monuments by anyone other than actual plot owners. Blanche Linden alludes to "controversy over corporate funding of historical statuary" during the 1850s as well as to the possibility that a number of trustees may have "considered sufficient the monument erected by the Company of Independent Cadets in 1867." However, because the board abandoned plans for a monument in 1866, this latter theory seems unlikely. See Blanche Linden, *Silent City on a Hill*, 231–32.

15. *Dedication of the Monument on Boston Common Erected to the Memory of the Men of Boston Who Died in the Civil War* (Boston: Boston City Council, 1877), 11–15.

16. Ibid., 91; 86.

17. Janney, *Burying the Dead*, 95–97.

18. For a more comprehensive discussion of the *Shaw Memorial* in Boston, see Martin H. Blatt, Thomas J. Brown, and Donald Yacovone, eds. *Hope & Glory: Essays on the Legacy of the 54th Massachusetts Regiment* (Amherst: University of Massachusetts Press, 2001).

19. *Proceedings at the Dedication of the Soldiers' and Sailors' Monument, in Providence* (Providence: A. Crawford Greene, Printer to the State, 1871), 4.

20. William Dean Howells, "Question of Monuments" *The Atlantic Monthly* 17, no. 103 (May 1866): 647.

21. Mount Auburn Cemetery Board of Trustees Meeting Minutes, December 14, 1870. Mount Auburn Cemetery Archives.

22. Mount Auburn Cemetery Board of Trustees Meeting Minutes, August 9, 1871 and September 18, 1871. Mount Auburn Cemetery Archives.

23. Bigelow, *An Account of the Sphinx*, 5.

24. Jacob Bigelow, Boston, to John T. Bradlee, Esq., Boston, 25 October, 1872, Mount Auburn Cemetery Archives, Cambridge, MA.

25. Jacob Bigelow, Boston, to John T. Bradlee, Esq., Boston, 1 November, 1872, Mount Auburn Cemetery Archives, Cambridge, MA.

26. Transl.: "Jacob Bigelow made it and dedicated it"; the north face of the base is inscribed "Martin Milmore Sculptor Boston 1872"; Jacob Bigelow, Boston, to John T. Bradlee, Boston, 25 October 1872, Mount Auburn Cemetery Archives, Cambridge, MA; Jacob Bigelow, Boston, to John T. Bradlee, Boston, 1 November 1872, Mount Auburn Cemetery Archives, Cambridge, MA; see also, Blanche Linden, *Silent City on a Hill*, 234.

27. Jacob Bigelow, Boston, to John T. Bradlee, Esq., Boston, 28 October, 1872, Mount Auburn Cemetery Archives, Cambridge, MA.

28. Richard G. Carrott, *The Egyptian Revival*, 61.

29. In traditional Egyptian sculpture, the royal *menes* would be surmounted by the head of a serpent, such as a cobra or asp.

30. Bigelow, *An Account of the Sphinx*, 4.

31. "Boston and Vicinity: Memorial Statues" *Boston Daily Journal* (March 11, 1872), 4.

32. George E. Ellis, *Memoir of Jacob Bigelow, M.D., LL.D.* (Cambridge, MA: John Wilson & Son, 1880), 71.

33. Bigelow, *An Account of the Sphinx*, 6–7.

34. Ibid., 7–8.

35. Ellis, *Memoir of Jacob Bigelow*, 59.

36. Jacob Bigelow, *The Useful Arts, Considered in Connexion With the Applications of Science* (Boston: Marsh, Capen, Lyon and Wedd, 1840), 25.

37. "An Account of the Sphinx at Mount Auburn," *Boston Evening Transcript* (Aug. 27, 1872), 3; "The Sphinx at Mount Auburn," *Lowell Daily Citizen and News* (Feb. 14, 1873), 1.

38. "Art," *The Atlantic Monthly* 31, no. 183 (Jan. 1873): 114–16; Rev. E. Wentworth, ed., "Art Notes," *The Ladies' Repository*, 31 (Cincinnati: Hitchcock and Walden, 1873): 227–30.

39. "Art," 116.

40. Bigelow, *An Account of the Sphinx*, 5.

41. This theme has been covered in details by historians of the Civil War and Reconstruction; see, Nina Silber, *The Romance of Reunion: Northerners and the South, 1865–1900* (Chapel Hill: The University of North Carolina Press, 1993); David W. Blight, *Race and Reunion: The Civil War in American Memory* (Cambridge: The Belknap Press of Harvard University Press, 2001).

42. Bigelow, *An Account of the Sphinx*, 13.

43. Ibid., 8–10.

44. "The Sphinx," *The Atlantic Monthly* 3, no. 20 (June, 1859): 724.

45. "Sphinx and Oedipus," *Continental Monthly: Devoted to Literature and National Policy* 1, no. 1 (Jan. 1862): 63.

46. M. E. N. Hatheway, "The Sphinx," *The Atlantic Monthly* 28, no. 169 (November, 1871): 563.

47. Bigelow *The Useful Arts*, 26.

48. Bigelow, *An Account of the Sphinx*, 8.

49. Kirk Savage, in *Standing Soldiers, Kneeling Slaves*, 8–15, contends that classicism informed virtually all sculptural work in America during the nineteenth century; the classical tradition defined beauty and perfection as well as whiteness, and so even in monuments that referred to slavery and emancipation, the body of the "Negro," as the antithesis of classical whiteness, was virtually impossible to depict as it might "ultimately change the face of the nation," 19.

50. The United States has not been alone in this practice. Since the sixteenth century, nations have commonly employed the female image to personify the body politic, both positively and negatively. See Nancy Isenberg, "Death and Satire: Dismembering the Body Politic," in *Mortal Remains: Death in Early America,* ed. Nancy Isenberg and Andrew Burstein (71–90) (Philadelphia: University of Pennsylvania Press, 2003).

51. Bigelow, *An Account of the Sphinx*, 10–11.

52. A number of works have provided extended discussions of these publications and contemporary debates concerning the race of the Egyptians, including William Stanton, *The Leopard's Spots: Scientific Attitudes Toward Race in America, 1815–1859* (Chicago: The University of Chicago Press, 1960); Bruce Dain, *A Hideous Monster of the Mind: American Race Theory in the Early Republic* (Cambridge, MA: Harvard University Press, 2002); C. Wyatt Evans, *The Legend of John Wilkes Booth: Myth, Memory, and a Mummy* (Lawrence, KS: University of Kansas Press, 2004); Scott Trafton, *Egypt Land: Race and Nineteenth-Century American Egyptomania* (Durham, NC: Duke University Press, 2004); Ann Fabian, *The Skull Collectors: Race, Science, and America's Unburied Dead* (Chicago: The University of Chicago Press, 2010).

53. Morton, *Crania Aegyptiaca*, 1.

54. George Gliddon, *Otia Aegyptiaca: Discourses on Egyptian Archaeology and Hieroglyphical Discoveries* (Philadelphia: John Penington, 1849), 77.

55. Samuel George Morton, M.D., *Crania Americana: or, A Comparative View of the Skulls of Various Aboriginal Nations of North and South America: To Which is Prefixed an Essay on the Varieties of the Human Species* (Philadelphia: J. Dobson, 1839), 29.

56. Gliddon, *Otia Aegyptiaca,* 76.
57. Stanton, *Leopard's Spots,* 146.
58. Ellis, *Memoir of Jacob Bigelow,* 70.
59. Jacob Bigelow, Richmond, to Mary Scollay Bigelow, Boston, May 5, 1852, *Family Papers of Jacob Bigelow,* Massachusetts Historical Society, Boston, MA.
60. "The Dark Side, The Bright Side, The Practicable Side," repr. Jacob Bigelow, *Modern Inquiries: Classical, Professional, and Miscellaneous* (Boston: Little, Brown and Company, 1867), 371.
61. "Dialogue Between Napoleon the First, and Jeremiah, a Late Citizen of the United States," *Boston Daily Advertiser* (August 11, 1862), repr. Jacob Bigelow, *Modern Inquiries,* 365–70.
62. Bigelow, *An Account of the Sphinx,* 12–14.
63. "Art," 116.
64. "Art Notes," 227.
65. Silber, *Romance of Reunion,* 125.
66. Rev. Joseph H. Allen, "Mount Auburn Cemetery," *The Harvard Register* 3, no. 7 (Cambridge: Moses King, Publisher, 1881): 370.
67. "Letter from the Bay State," *New Hampshire Sentinel* (September 12, 1878), 2.
68. "Obituary: Jacob Bigelow, M.D., LL.D.," *The Medical Record,* vol. 15 (New York: William Wood and Company, 1879), 167.
69. Rev. Joseph H. Allen, "Mount Auburn Cemetery," *The Harvard Register* 3, no. 7 (Cambridge: Moses King, Publisher, 1881): 370.
70. Charlotte Fiske Bates, *Risk, and Other Poems* (Cambridge, MA: John Wilson and Son, 1879), 20.
71. "Notes on Art and Archaeology," *The Academy* 28, no. 703 (October 24, 1885): 280.
72. "Note and Comment," *Springfield Republican* (Aug. 13, 1886), 4.
73. Daniel Edward Lorenz, *The New Mediterranean Traveller: A Handbook of Practical Information* (New York: Fleming H. Revell Company, 1905), 279.
74. Richard O. Reisem et al. *Field Guide to Forest Lawn Cemetery, Buffalo, New York* (Buffalo, NY: Forest Lawn Heritage Foundation, 1998), 12.
75. Large-breasted female sphinxes appeared during the eighteenth century as part of the broad array of rococo garden sculpture, as was the case in the Belvedere gardens in Vienna and in the gardens of Veitshöchheim (1763–1775) near Würzburg. As described by historian James Curl, these figures resembled "courtesans from a Rococo *Salon.*" See James Stevens Curl, *The Egyptian Revival: Ancient Egypt as the Inspiration for Design Motifs in the West* (London: Routledge, 2005), 150.
76. Michael Richman, "The Early Public Sculpture of Daniel Chester French," *American Art Journal* 4, no. 2 (November 1972): 113–14.
77. Royal Cortissoz, "New Figures in Literature and Art," *The Atlantic Monthly* 75, no. 448 (February 1895): 228.
78. Richman, *Early Public Sculpture,* 114n.
79. Cortissoz, "New Figures," 228.
80. William Howe Downes, "Monuments and Statues in Boston," *The New England Magazine* 17, no. 3 (November 1894): 371.
81. Frank Foxcroft, "Mount Auburn," *The New England Magazine* 20, no. 4 (June 1896): 428.
82. Brown, *Public Art,* 22.
83. Sarah J. Purcell, "Commemoration, Public Art, and the Changing Meaning of the Bunker Hill Monument," *The Public Historian* 25, no. 2 (Spring 2003): 55.
84. Savage, *Standing Soldiers, Kneeling Slaves,* 192.

CHAPTER 5. AMERICAN OBELISK

1. Henry Van Brunt, "The Washington Monument," *The American Art Review* 1, no. 1 (November 1879): 7.
2. "The Washington Monument," *New York Times* (February 22, 1885), 6.

3. Robert Belmont Freeman, Jr., "Design Proposals for the Washington National Monument," *Records of the Columbia Historical Society, Washington, D.C. 49* (1973/1974): 151–52.

4. Joseph Story in Andrew Burstein, "Immortalizing the Founding Fathers: The Excesses of Public Eulogy." In *Mortal Remains: Death in Early America,* ed. Nancy Isenberg and Andrew Burstein (Philadelphia: University of Pennsylvania Press, 2003), 94.

5. Kirk Savage, "The Self-Made Monument: George Washington and the Fight to Erect a National Memorial," *Winterthur Portfolio* 22, no. 4 (Winter 1987): 227.

6. Anita Schorsch, "A Key to the Kingdom: The Iconography of a Mourning Picture," *Winterthur Portfolio* 14, no. 1 (Spring 1979): 60.

7. Phoebe Lloyd Jacobs, "John James Barralet and the Apotheosis of George Washington," *Winterthur Portfolio* 12 (1977): 115.

8. "Miscellany from the Baltimore Federal Gazette," *The Boston Weekly Messenger* 3, no. 38 (July 8, 1814): 4.

9. "Marking a People's Love: Dedication of the Washington Monument," *New York Times* (February 22, 1885), 3.

10. Quoted in Mark Langdon Hill, "Monument to Washington," *North American Review* 3, no. 8 (July 1816): 340.

11. Ibid., 334–35.

12. Freeman, Jr., "Design Proposals," 153; Frederick L. Harvey, *History of the Washington National Monument and the Washington National Monument Society,* (Washington, DC, 1902), 18.

13. Ibid., 153–62.

14. Robert Mills in Rhodri Windsor Liscombe, *Altogether American: Robert Mills, Architect and Engineer, 1781–1855* (New York: Oxford University Press, 1994), 140.

15. Michael Kammen, *Visual Shock: A History of Art Controversies in American Culture* (New York: Alfred A. Knopf, 2006), 12–13.

16. Benjamin B. French, Esquire, in *Oration Pronounced by the Honorable Robert C. Winthrop, Speaker of the House of Representatives of the United States, on the 4th of July, 1848, on the Occasion of Laying the Corner-Stone of the National Monument to the Memory of Washington* (Washington: J. & G. S. Gideon, Printers, 1848), 44–45.

17. Savage, "The Self-Made Monument," 234.

18. *Oration* (1848), 13.

19. "Introduction" in *Oration* (1848), 7.

20. Ibid.

21. *Oration* (1848), 10.

22. Ibid., 17.

23. *Oration* (1848), 34.

24. Harvey, *History of the Washington,* 49–56.

25. Savage, "The Self-Made Monument," 235.

26. Mark Twain in Freeman, Jr., "Design Proposals," 168.

27. "The Washington Monument," *New York Times* (September 3, 1859), 4.

28. *The Sun* [Baltimore] 49, no. 1 (May 20, 1861): 4.

29. "Camp of the Sixth Regiment," *Lowell Daily Citizen* 11, no. 1601(July 18, 1861): 2.

30. "The Very Stones Cry Out Against Them," *New Hampshire Sentinel* 63, no. 40 (October 3, 1861), 1.

31. "The Washington Monument," *The Philadelphia Inquirer* (September 25, 1861), 1.

32. "Washington Monument Association," *The Philadelphia Inquirer* (February 25, 1862), 8.

33. "The Washington Monument," *The Philadelphia Inquirer* (October 25, 1862), 3.

34. *Daily Constitutional Union* [Washington, D.C.] 4, no. 119 (April 21, 1865): 2.

35. "The Lincoln Monument," *North American* [Philadelphia] 97, no. 26513 (May 30, 1865): 2.

36. "The Washington Monument," *The Daily Picayune* [New Orleans] (July 29, 1865), 1; "Views of the National Capital—No. 2," *San Francisco Evening Bulletin* 20, no. 118 (August 24, 1865): 1; "The Washington Monument," *Dallas Weekly Herald* 13, no. 18 (January 20, 1866): 4.

37. "Washington Items," *Albany Evening Journal* (November 1, 1865), 2.
38. *New York Herald Tribune* 25, no. 7703 (December 14, 1865): 6.
39. "The President's Position," *Albany Evening Journal* (February 23, 1866), 2.
40. "The National Washington Monument," *The Philadelphia Inquirer* (August 4, 1866), 4.
41. "The National Washington Monument," *The Philadelphia Inquirer* (July 18, 1867), 4; "The Shame of It," *The Weekly Patriot* [Harrisburg, PA] 16, no. 38 (December 31, 1868): 2.
42. Freeman, Jr., "Design Proposals," 170–72.
43. "The Washington Monument," *New York Times* (December 19, 1872), 4.
44. Van Brunt (1879a), "The Washington Monument," 9–11.
45. Henry Van Brunt, "The Washington Monument (Concluded)" *The American Art Review* 1, no. 2 (December 1879): 63.
46. J. Goldsborough Bruff in Freeman, Jr., "Design Proposals," 179.
47. Canopic jars are figural jars that were originally used in ancient Egypt to hold the internal organs of a mummified person. Imsety, the human-headed deity, holds the liver. Hapy, the baboon-headed deity, holds the lungs. Duamutef, the jackal-headed deity, holds the stomach. Qebehsenuef, the falcon-headed deity, holds the intestines.
48. An Architect, "The Washington Monument, and Mr. Story's Design" *The Atlantic Monthly* 43, no. 258 (April 1879): 525–26.
49. Savage, "The Self-Made Monument," 237–38.
50. Henry L. Abbot, "Memoir of Thomas Lincoln Casey, 1831–1896," read before the National Academy of Sciences (April 21, 1897), 128.
51. Savage, "The Self-Made Monument," 238.
52. "The Tallest in the World," *Washington Star* (July 26, 1884), repr. in *New York Times* (July 28, 1884), 8.
53. "Marking a People's Love: Dedication of the Washington Monument," *New York Times* (February 22, 1885), 3.
54. William A. Eddy, "The Highest Structure in the World," *The Atlantic Monthly* 63, no. 380 (June 1889): 721.
55. "The Washington Monument," *New York Times* (December 7, 1884), 8.
56. "Marking a People's Love: Dedication of the Washington Monument," 3.
57. "The Washington Monument," *New York Times* (February 22, 1885), 6.
58. "The Completion of the Washington Monument," *The Manufacturer and Builder* 17, no. 3 (March 1885): 66.
59. "The Washington Monument" *New York Times* (February 22, 1885), 6.
60. *The Dedication of the Washington National Monument, with the Orations by Hon. Robert C. Winthrop and Hon. John W. Daniel.* February 21, 1885. Published by Order of Congress (Washington, 1885), 52–53.
61. "The Washington Monument," *New York Times* (February 22, 1885), 6.
62. Ibid.
63. Savage, "The Self-Made Monument," 241.
64. "Style and the Monument" 141, no. 348 *North American Review* (November 1885): 444–45.
65. "Our Public Monuments," *The Decorator and Furnisher* 8, no. 2 (May 1886): 39.
66. Oliver Wendell Holmes, "One Hundred Days in Europe," *The Atlantic Monthly* 60, no. 360 (October 1887): 468.
67. William Howe Downs, "Monuments and Statues in Boston," *The New England Magazine* 17, no. 3 (November 1894): 354–55.
68. F. Marion Crawford, "Washington As A Spectacle," *The Century* 48, no. 4 (August 1894): 495.

CHAPTER 6. FROM EGYPTIAN REVIVAL TO AMERICAN STYLE

1. David M. Kahn, "The Grant Monument," *The Journal of the Society of Architectural Historians* 41, no. 3 (October 1982): 212. It should be noted that Grant and his wife resided in New York at

the time of his death, and evidently wanting to be buried together, Grant eschewed burial in either Arlington National Cemetery or the West Point Cemetery (the location of his alma mater).

2. Henry Van Brunt in "Grant's Memorial: What Shall It Be?" *North American Review* 131, no. 346 (September 1885): 283; 286.

3. Wilson McDonald in "Grant's Memorial: What Shall It Be?" 288–90.

4. Clarence Cook in "Grant's Memorial: What Shall It Be?" 291.

5. "Style and the Monument," *North American Review* 141, no. 348 (November 1885): 443. In Samuel Franklin Emmons, *Biographical Memoir of Clarence King, 1842–1901* (Washington, DC: Judd & Detweiler, Inc., 1907), a paper read before the National Academy of Sciences in 1903, Emmons claimed that although submitted anonymously, the article was "known by friends of Mr. King to have been written by him" (55).

6. "Style and the Monument," 443–53.

7. Henry Van Brunt, "On the Present Condition and Prospects of Architecture," *The Atlantic Monthly* 57, no. 341 (March 1886): 374.

8. "Topics of the Time: The Grant Memorial," *The Century* 31, no. 6 (April 1886): 957.

9. "The Bennington Monument," *New York Times* (3 July 1887).

10. Kahn, "The Grant Monument," 218; 226–27.

11. Kahn, "The Grant Monument," 231; *New York Times* (April 25 1897), 2.

12. "Grant Day in New York," *The Wheeling Register* 35, no. 289 (April 28, 1897), 4.

13. L. C. Wright, *United States Policy Toward Egypt, 1830–1914* (New York: Exposition Press, 1969), 155.

14. E. E. Farman, "The Negotiations for the Obelisk" *The Century* 24, no. 6 (October 1882): 889.

15. William M. Evarts in Henry H. Gorringe, *Egyptian Obelisks* (New York: G. P. Putnam's Sons, 1882), 52.

16. William R. Grace in Gorringe, *Egyptian Obelisks*, 53.

17. "Gorringe's 'Egyptian Obelisks,'" *The Century* 24, no. 6 (October 1882): 947. For further history of Cleopatra's Needle in New York, see Martina D'Alton, *The New York Obelisk, or How Cleopatra's Needle Came to New York and What Happened When It Got There* (New York: The Metropolitan Museum of Art, 1993).

18. For example, see Richard A. Proctor, "The Pyramid of Cheops," *The North American Review* 136, no. 316 (March 1883): 257–70; Edward L. Wilson, "Finding Pharaoh" *The Century Magazine* 34, no. 1 (May 1887): 3–10; Edward L. Wilson, "The Great Pyramid" *Scribner's Magazine* 3, no. 1 (January 1888): 41–64; Amelia B. Edwards, "Bubastis: An Egyptian Historical Society," *The Century* 39, no. 3 (January 1890): 323–49; William C. Wilson, D.D., D.C.L., LL.D., "Egypt At Home," *The New England Magazine* 8, no. 2 (April 1890): 198–217; W. St. Chad. Boscawen, "Egypt and Chaldea in the Light of Recent Discoveries," *Harper's New Monthly Magazine* 88, no. 524 (January 1894): 190–205; Madam Adam, "France and England in Egypt," *The North American Review* 159, no. 452 (July 1894): 34–46; Frederic Courtland Penfield, "Sidelights on the Exploitation of Egypt," *The North American Review* 159, no. 455 (October 1894): 479–90; Frederic Courtland Penfield, "Contemporary Egypt," *The North American Review* 161, no. 464 (July 1895): 13–25; R. Talbot Kelly, "An Artist Among the Fellaheen," *The Century Magazine* 55, no. 6 (April 1898): 878–87; Benjamin Ide Wheeler, "The Seven Wonders of the World: The Great Pyramids of Egypt," *The Century Magazine* 56, no. 1 (May 1898): 107–9.

19. Francis H. Underwood, "Egypt Under the Pharaohs," *The Atlantic Monthly* 45, no. 269 (March 1880): 315–16.

20. Constance Fenimore Woolson, "Cairo in 1890," *Harper's New Monthly Magazine* 83, no. 497 (October 1891): 651; 671. The second half of Woolson's travel narrative appeared the following month as "Cairo in 1890" *Harper's New Monthly Magazine* 83, no. 497 (November 1891): 828–55.

21. Frederic Courtland Penfield, "In Fascinating Cairo," *The Century Magazine* 58, no. 6 (October 1899): 811.

22. Winslow, "Egypt at Home," 198; 201.

23. Marie-Stéphanie Delamaire, "Searching for Egypt: Egypt in 19th Century American World Exhibitions," in *Imhotep Today: Egyptianizing Architecture,* ed. Jean-Marcel Humbert and Clifford Price (London: University College of London Press, 2003), 130.

24. *The Magic City: A Portfolio of Original Photographic Views of the Great World's Fair and its Treasures of Art, Including a Graphic Representation of the Famous Midway Plaisance, With Graphic Descriptions by America's Brilliant Historical and Descriptive Writer J. W. Buel* 1, no. 15 (April 23), (Philadelphia: H.S. Smith and C.R. Graham for Historical Publishing Company, 1894), 17.

25. Thomas W. Ludlow, "Archaeological Study in America," *The Century Magazine* 30, no. 4 (August 1885): 652.

26. Brian Fagan, *The Rape of the Nile: Tomb Raiders, Tourists and Archaeologists in Egypt* (Boulder, CO: Westview Press, 2004), 246.

27. John McClenahan, *Singular Philadelphians* (Richmond, VA: Dietz Press, 1999), 16.

28. Edward F. Bergman, *Woodlawn Remembers: Cemetery of American History* (Utica, NY: North Country Books, 1988), 27; Peggy McDowell and Richard E. Meyer, *The Revival Styles in American Memorial Art* (Bowling Green, OH: Bowling Green State University Popular Press, 1994), 158.

29. Cook & Watkins, Boston, to Mount Auburn Cemetery Association, Cambridge, 1 May, 1902 (Mount Auburn Cemetery Archives, Cambridge, MA).

30. J. F. Stanley, *Concerning Memorials: Their Historic Origin and Present Day Adaptations* (Salisbury, NC: The Leland Company—South, 1911), 8.

31. Henry A. Bliss, *Memorial Styles—Ancient and Modern* (Buffalo, 1912), 184.

32. John A. Kasson in *Report of the Floyd Memorial Association* (Sioux City: Press of Perkins Bros., 1897), 85.

33. E. H. Brush, "McKinley Memorials in Sculpture" in *The American Review of Reviews* 36, ed. by Albert Shaw (July-December 1907): 469–70.

34. "Current Periodicals," *The Architectural Review* 14, no. 11 (November 1907): 230.

35. Charles Evans Hughes, *Addresses of Charles Evans Hughes, 1906–1916,* intro. by Jacob Gould Schurman, 2nd ed. (New York: G. P. Putnam's Sons, 1916), 254.

36. Bliss, *Memorial Styles,* 181–82.

37. Jacob Bigelow, *An Account of the Sphinx at Mount Auburn* (Boston: Little, Brown and Company, 1872), 6–7.

38. Joy M. Giguere, "'Young and Littlefield's Folly': Fundraising, Confederate Memorialization, and the Construction of the Jefferson Davis Monument in Fairview, Kentucky, 1907–1924," Register of the Kentucky Historical Society 115, No. 1 (Winter 2017), 39-73; *Twenty-Fourth Annual Report of the American Scenic and Historic Preservation Society,* 1919 (Albany: J. B. Lyon Company, 1919), 195.

39. "The Jefferson Davis Memorial," *Confederate Veteran* 30, no. 11 (November 1922): 405.

40. "Davis Memorial to be Dedicated at Fairview, Ky," *Aberdeen American* (June 4, 1924), 3.

41. "Dedicate Monument to President of Confederacy," *Greensboro Daily* (June 7, 1924), 1.

42. Quoted in "Shaft is Dedicated to Jefferson Davis," *Dallas Morning News* (June 8, 1924), 1.

43. "San Jacinto Museum Rites Set Two Days," *Dallas Morning News* (April 16, 1939), 15.

44. "Biggest State Dedicates Nation's Biggest Monument," *Life* (May 8, 1939), 26–27.

CODA

1. Stephen Polcari, "Barnett Newman's Broken Obelisk," *Art Journal* 53, no. 4, *Sculpture in Postwar Europe and America, 1945–1959* (Winter 1994), 48.

2. Barnett Newman in Polcari, "Barnett Newman's Broken Obelisk," 48.

3. "Sculpture Dedication to Dr. King Rejected," *Dallas Morning News* (June 24, 1969), 14.

4. Janet Kutner, "Art: Last Rothko Works in Chapel," *Dallas Morning News* (March 14, 1971), 5.

Bibliography

Abbot, Henry L. "Memoir of Thomas Lincoln Casey, 1831–1896." Read before the National Academy of Sciences. April 21, 1897.

"An Account of the Sphinx at Mount Auburn." *Boston Evening Transcript* (August 27, 1872), 3.

Adam, Madam. "France and England in Egypt." *The North American Review* 159, no. 452 (July 1894): 34–46.

An Address by Rev. Henry Neill and A Poem by Oliver Wendell Holmes. Delivered at the Dedication of the Pittsfield (Rural) Cemetery, September 9th, 1850, With Other Matter and a Map of the Grounds. Pittsfield, MA: Axtel, Bull and Marsh, 1850.

"The Age of Iron and Steam." *Scientific American* 2, no. 39 (June 19, 1847): 309.

Alcott, Louisa May. "Lost in a Pyramid, or The Mummy's Curse." *The New World* 1, no. 1 (January 16, 1869): 33–42. Reprinted in John Richard Stephens, ed. *Into the Mummy's Tomb.* New York: Berkley Books, 2001,

Alexander, Robert L. *The Architecture of Maximilian Godefroy.* Baltimore, MD: Johns Hopkins University Press, 1974.

———. "The Public Memorial and Godefroy's Battle Monument." *The Journal of the Society of Architectural Historians* 17, no. 1 (March 1958): 19–24.

"Alexis de Tocqueville." *The Atlantic Monthly* 8, no. 49 (November 1861): 551–58.

Allegheny Cemetery: Historical Account of Incidents and Events Connected with its Establishment. Charter and Supplemental Acts of Legislation. Reports of 1848 and 1857. Proceedings of Corporators, June 21, 1873. *Rules, Regulations, &c. List of Officers, Managers and Corporators to Date. Remarks on the Ornamentation and Arrangement of Cemeteries. Funeral Oration of Wilson McCandless, Esq. On Commodore Barney and Lieut. Parker.* Pittsburgh, PA: Bakewell & Marthens, 1873.

Allen, Rev. Joseph H. "Mount Auburn Cemetery." *The Harvard Register* 3, no. 7. Cambridge, MA: Moses King, Publisher, 1881.

Allyn, Charles. *The Battle of Groton Heights: A Collection of Narratives, Official Reports, Records, Etc. of the Storming of Fort Griswold, The Massacre of Its Garrison, The Burning of New London by British Troops Under the Command of Brig.–Gen. Benedict Arnold, on the 6th of September, 1781.* New London: Charles Allyn, 1882.

"American Civilization." *The Atlantic Monthly* 9, no. 54 (April 1862): 502–11.

"American Civilization." *The United States Democratic Review* 42, no. 1 (July 1858): 50–58.

"America in 1846 The Past – The Future." *The United States Democratic Review* 18, no. 91 (January 1846): 57–65.

"Ancient and Modern Civilization." *The United States Democratic Review* 24, no. 131 (May 1849): 449–60.

"Ancient Architecture." *North American Review* 88, no. 183 (April 1859): 341–49.

"Archaeologica Americana." *North American Review* 12, no. 31 (April 1821): 235–56.

An Architect. "The Washington Monument, and Mr. Story's Design." *The Atlantic Monthly* 43, no. 258 (April 1879): 524–27.

"Art." *The Atlantic Monthly* 31, no. 183 (January 1873): 114–16.

Austin, Jane G. "After Three Thousand Years." *Putnam's New Monthly Magazine of American Literature, Science and Art* 12, no. 7 (July 1868): 38–45.

Bates, Charlotte Fiske. *Risk, and Other Poems*. Cambridge, MA: John Wilson and Son, 1879.

"Battle of Groton Heights." *American Mercury* 42, no. 2147 (August 23, 1825): 2.

The Bee 3, no. 124 (January 1, 1800): 4.

Belzoni, Giovanni. *Narrative of the operations and recent discoveries within the pyramids, temples, tombs, and excavation, in Egypt and Nubia; and of a journey to the coast of the Red Sea, in search of the ancient Berenice; and another to the oasis of Jupiter Ammon*. John Murray, 1820.

Bender, Thomas. "The 'Rural' Cemetery Movement: Urban Travail and the Appeal of Nature." *The New England Quarterly* 47, no. 2 (June 1974): 196–211.

Benes, Peter, ed. *Puritan Gravestone Art: The Dublin Seminar for New England Folklife Annual Proceedings, 1976*. Boston: Boston University Press, 1977.

"The Bennington Monument." *New York Times*, July 3, 1887.

Bergman, Edward F. *Woodlawn Remembers: Cemetery of American History*. Utica, NY: North Country Books, 1988.

B. G. F., "Who and What are the Negroes?" *The Old Guard* 5, no. 7 (July 1867): 535–43.

Bickerstaff, Dylan. "Examining the Mystery of the Niagara Falls Mummy: The Case Against Rameses I." *KMT: A Modern Journal of Ancient Egypt* 17, no. 4 (Winter 2006–2007): 26–34.

Bigelow, Jacob. *An Account of the Sphinx at Mount Auburn*. Boston: Little, Brown, and Company, 1872.

———. "Bigelow's *Elements of Technology*." *North American Review* 30, no. 67 (April 1830): 337–60.

Bigelow, Jacob, Boston, to J. T. Bradlee, Esquire, Cambridge, 23 July 1872. Mount Auburn Cemetery Archives, Cambridge, MA.

Bigelow, Jacob, Boston, to J. T. Bradlee, Esquire, Cambridge, 25 August 1872. Mount Auburn Cemetery Archives, Cambridge, MA.

Bigelow, Jacob, Boston, to J. T. Bradlee, Esquire, Cambridge, 25 October 1872. Mount Auburn Cemetery Archives, Cambridge, MA.

Bigelow, Jacob, Boston, to J. T. Bradlee, Esquire, Cambridge, 28 October 1872. Mount Auburn Cemetery Archives, Cambridge, MA.

Bigelow, Jacob, Boston, to J. T. Bradlee, Esquire, Cambridge, 1 November 1872. Mount Auburn Cemetery Archives, Cambridge, MA.

Bigelow, Jacob, Richmond, to Mary Scollay Bigelow, Boston, 5 May 1852, *Family Papers of Jacob Bigelow*, Massachusetts Historical Society, Boston, MA.

———. *Elements of Technology, Taken Chiefly from a Course of Lectures Delivered at Cambridge, on the Application of the Sciences to the Useful Arts, Now Published for the Use of Seminaries and*

Students, 2nd ed. Boston: Hilliard, Gray, Little and Wilkins, 1831.

———. *A History of the Cemetery at Mount Auburn.* Boston: James Munro and Company, 1859.

———. *Modern Inquiries: Classical, Professional, and Miscellaneous.* Boston: Little, Brown and Company, 1867.

———. *The Useful Arts, Considered in Connexion With the Applications of Science.* Boston: Marsh, Capen, Lyon and Wedd, 1840.

———. *The Useful Arts, Considered in Connexion with the Applications of Science, with Numerous Engravings,* 2nd ed. New York: Harper & Brothers, Publishers, 1863.

"Biggest State Dedicates Nation's Biggest Monument." *Life* (May 8, 1939): 26–27.

"Biographical Notice of Mr. Justice Story." *The American Whig Review* 3, no. 1 (January 1846): 68–82.

Blachowicz, James. *From Slate to Marble: Gravestone Carving Traditions in Eastern Massachusetts, 1770–1870.* Evanston, IL: Graver Press, 2006.

Blair, William. *Cities of the Dead: Contesting the Memory of the Civil War in the South, 1865–1914.* Chapel Hill: The University of North Carolina Press, 2004.

Blatt, Martin H., Thomas J. Brown, and Donald Yacovone, eds. *Hope & Glory: Essays on the Legacy of the 54th Massachusetts Regiment.* Amherst: University of Massachusetts Press, 2001.

Blight, David W. *Race and Reunion: The Civil War in American Memory.* Cambridge: The Belknap Press of Harvard University Press, 2001.

Bliss, Henry A. *Memorial Styles – Ancient and Modern.* Buffalo, 1912.

Boscawen, W. St. Chad. "Egypt and Chaldea in the Light of Recent Discoveries." *Harper's New Monthly Magazine* 88, no. 524 (January 1894): 190–205.

"Boston and Vicinity: Memorial Statues." *Boston Daily Journal* (March 11, 1872): 4.

Brier, Bob. "Saga of Cleopatra's Needles." *Archaeology* 55, no. 6 (November/December 2002): 48–54.

Broman, Elizabeth. "Egyptian Revival Funerary Arts in Green-Wood Cemetery." *Markers XVIII: A Journal for the Association for Gravestone Studies* (2001): 30–67.

Brown, Thomas J. *The Public Art of Civil War Commemoration: A Brief History with Documents.* Boston: Bedford/St. Martin's, 2004.

Brush, E. H. "McKinley Memorials in Sculpture." In *The American Review of Reviews,* edited by Albert Shaw, 36 (July–December 1907): 469–70.

"Bunker-Hill." *Boston Courier* 16, no. 1894 (June 16, 1842): 2.

"Bunker Hill." *Baltimore Patriot & Mercantile Advertiser* 33, no. 42 (February 18, 1829): 2.

"The Bunker Hill Celebration." Reprinted in *The [Baltimore] Sun* 13, no. 28 (June 17, 1843): 2.

"Bunker Hill Monument." *The Daily Atlas* 10, no. 258 (April 30, 1842): 2.

"Bunker Hill Monument." *Essex Register* 27, no. 63 (August 6, 1827): 3.

"Bunker's Hill." *Middlesex Gazette* 41, no. 3013 (May 24, 1826): 3.

"Bunker Hill Monument." *Newburyport Herald* (March 21, 1828): 2.

Burr, Fearing, and George Lincoln. *The Town of Hingham in the Late Civil War.* Hingham, 1876.

"Camp of the Sixth Regiment." *Lowell Daily Citizen* 11, no. 1601(July 18, 1861): 2.

Carrott, Richard G. "The Architect of the Pennsylvania Fire Insurance Building." *The Journal of the Society of Architectural Historians* 20, no. 3 (October 1961): 138–39.

———. *The Egyptian Revival: Its Sources, Monuments, and Meaning 1808–1858.* Berkeley: University of California Press, 1978.

"Charlestown – November 22." *Bangor Weekly Register* 12, no. 48 (November 28, 1827): 3.

Chase, Theodore, and Laurel K. Gabel. *Gravestone Chronicles I*. Boston: New England Historic Genealogical Society, 1997.

Christovich, Mary Louise, ed. *New Orleans Architecture: The Cemeteries*. Gretna, LA: Pelican, 1971.

Church, Rev. Pharcellus. *An Address delivered at the Dedication of Mount Hope Cemetery, Rochester, Oct. 2, 1838*. Rochester: David Hoyt, 1839.

"Civilization: American and European." *The American Whig Review* 3, no. 6 (June 1846): 611–25.

Cleaveland, Nehemiah. *Green-Wood Illustrated, in Highly Finished Line Engraving, From Drawings Taken on the Spot by James Smillie*. New York: R. Martin, 1847.

Colvin, Howard. *Architecture and the After-Life*. New Haven, CT: Yale University Press, 1991.

"The Completion of the Washington Monument." *The Manufacturer and Builder* 17, no. 3 (March 1885): 66.

Conant, H. S. "The Mummy's Foot." *Harper's New Monthly Magazine* 42, no. 251 (April 1871): 749–53.

The Constitution 15, no. 758 (July 7, 1852): 2.

Cook & Watkins, Boston, to Mount Auburn Cemetery Association, Cambridge, 1 May, 1902. Mount Auburn Cemetery Archives, Cambridge, MA.

Coombs, Edith I., ed. *America Visited*. New York: Stratford Press.

Cortissoz, Royal. "New Figures in Literature and Art." *The Atlantic Monthly* 75, no. 448 (February 1895): 228.

Cowie, Susan D., and Tom Johnson. *The Mummy in Fact, Fiction and Film*. Jefferson, NC: McFarland & Company, 2002.

Crafts, William A. *Forest Hill Cemetery: Its Establishment, Progress, Scenes, Monuments, etc.* Roxbury, MA: J. Backup, 1855.

Crawford, F. Marion. "Washington As A Spectacle." *The Century* 48, no. 4 (August 1894): 483–96.

Curl, James Stevens. "The Architecture and Planning of the Nineteenth-Century Cemetery." *Garden History* 3, no. 3 (Summer 1975): 13–41.

———. *The Art & Architecture of Freemasonry*, 2nd ed. London: B. T. Batsford, 2002.

———. *The Egyptian Revival: Ancient Egypt as the Inspiration for Design Motifs in the West*. London: Routledge, 2005.

Curran, Brian. *The Egyptian Renaissance: The Afterlife of Ancient Egypt in Early Modern Italy*. Chicago, IL: The University of Chicago Press, 2007.

———. *Obelisk: A History*. Cambridge, MA: The Burndy Library, 2009.

"Current Periodicals." *The Architectural Review* 14, no. 11 (November 1907): 230.

Daily Constitutional Union [Washington, D.C.], 4, no. 119 (April 21, 1865): 2.

Dain, Bruce. *A Hideous Monster of the Mind: American Race Theory in the Early Republic*. Cambridge, MA: Harvard University Press, 2002.

D'Alton, Martina. *The New York Obelisk, or How Cleopatra's Needle Came to New York and What Happened When It Got There*. New York: The Metropolitan Museum of Art, 1993.

Dannenfeldt, Karl H. "Egypt and Egyptian Antiquities in the Renaissance." *Studies in the Renaissance* 6 (1959): 7–27.

———. "Egyptian Mumia: The Sixteenth Century Experience and Debate." *The Sixteenth Century Journal* 16, no. 2 (Summer 1985): 163–80.

Darnall, Margarett J. "The American Cemetery as Picturesque Landscape: Bellefontaine Cemetery, St. Louis." *Winterthur Portfolio* 18, no. 4 (Winter 1983): 249–69.

"Davis Memorial to be Dedicated at Fairview, Ky." *Aberdeen American* (June 4, 1924), 3.

de Tocqueville, Alexis. *Democracy in America and Two Essays on America*. Repr. New York: Penguin Books, 2003.

"De Tocqueville." *The United States Democratic Review* 21, no. 110 (August 1847): 115–24.

Dearborn, Nathaniel. *A Concise History of, and Guide Through Mount Auburn*. Boston: Nathaniel Dearborn, 1843.

"Dedicate Monument to President of Confederacy." *Greensboro Daily* (June 7, 1924), 1.

Dedication of the Monument on Boston Common Erected to the Memory of the Men of Boston Who Died in the Civil War. Boston, 1877.

The Dedication of the Washington National Monument, with the Orations by Hon. Robert C. Winthrop and Hon. John W. Daniel. February 21, 1885. Washington: Published by Order of Congress, 1885.

Deetz, James. *In Small Things Forgotten: An Archaeology of Early American Life*. Rev. ed. New York: Anchor Books, 1996.

Deetz, James, and Edwin Dethlefsen, "Death's Head, Cherub, Urn and Willow." *Natural History* 76, no. 3 (1967): 29–37.

DeLeon, Edwin. *The Khedive's Egypt, or The Old House of Bondage Under New Masters*. New York: Harper & Brothers, 1878.

"The Destiny of the Country." *The American Whig Review* 5, no. 3 (March 1847): 231–40.

Dickens, Charles. *American Notes and Pictures From Italy*. New York: Charles Scribner's Sons, N.D.

Dodge, M. A. "A Day with the Dead." *The Atlantic Monthly* 6, no. 35 (September 1860): 326–42.

Douglas, Ann. "Heaven Our Home: Consolation Literature in the Northern United States, 1830–1880." *American Quarterly* 26, no. 5 Special Issue: Death in America (December 1974): 496–515.

Downes, William Howe. "Monuments and Statues in Boston." *The New England Magazine* 17, no. 3 (November 1894): 353–72.

Downs, Joseph. "The Greek Revival in the United States." *The Metropolitan Museum of Art Bulletin* 2, no. 5 (January 1944): 173–76.

Doyle, Arthur Conan. "Lot No. 249. A Story." *Harper's New Monthly Magazine* 85, no. 508 (September 1892): 525–44.

Early, James. *Romanticism and American Architecture*. New York: A. S. Barnes, 1965.

Eckels, Claire Wittler. "The Egyptian Revival in America." *Archaeology* 3, no. 3 (Autumn 1950): 164–69.

Eddy, William A. "The Highest Structure in the World." *The Atlantic Monthly* 63, no. 380 (June 1889): 721.

Edwards, Amelia B. "Bubastis: An Egyptian Historical Society." *The Century* 39, no. 3 (January 1890): 323–49.

———. *Pharaohs, Fellahs and Explorers*. New York: Harper & Brothers, 1891.

"Egypt and America." *Scientific American* 2, no. 12 (December 12, 1846): 90.

"Egypt Under The Pharaohs." *The International Magazine of Literature, Art, & Science* 2, no. 3 (February 1, 1851): 323–26.

"Egyptian Antiquities." *The North American Review* 29, no. 65 (October 1829): 361–89.

Ellis, George E. *Memoir of Jacob Bigelow, M.D., LL.D.* Cambridge, MA: John Wilson & Son, 1880.

Elstein, Rochelle S. "William Washburn and the Egyptian Revival in Boston." *Old-Time New England, The Bulletin of The Society for the Preservation of New England Antiquities* 70, no. 257 (1980): 63–81.

Emmons, Samuel Franklin. *Biographical Memoir of Clarence King, 1842–1901.* Washington, DC: Judd & Detweiler, 1907.

Etlin, Richard. "Landscapes of Eternity: Funerary Architecture and the Cemetery, 1793–1881." *Oppositions: A Journal for Ideas and Criticism in Architecture* 8 (Spring 1977): 22.

Evans, C. Wyatt. *The Legend of John Wilkes Booth: Myth, Memory, and a Mummy.* Lawrence, KS: University of Kansas Press, 2004.

Everett, Edward. *Orations and Speeches on Various Occasions*, vol. I. Boston: Little, Brown & Company, 1850.

———. *Orations and Speeches on Various Occasions*, vol. III. Boston: Little, Brown & Company, 1870.

Fabian, Ann. *The Skull Collectors: Race, Science, and America's Unburied Dead.* Chicago: University of Chicago Press, 2010.

Fagan, Brian. *The Rape of the Nile: Tomb Raiders, Tourists and Archaeologists in Egypt.* Boulder, CO: Westview Press, 2004.

Farman, E. E. "The Negotiations for the Obelisk." *The Century* 24, no. 6 (October 1882): 879–89.

Farrell, James. *Inventing the American Way of Death, 1830–1920.* Philadelphia: Temple University Press, 1980.

Faust, Drew Gilpin. *This Republic of Suffering: Death and the American Civil War.* New York: Alfred A. Knopf, 2008.

Fleming, Robin. "Picturesque History and the Medieval in Nineteenth-Century America." *The American Historical Review* 100, no. 4 (October 1995): 1061–1094.

Florence, Robert. N*ew Orleans Cemeteries: Life in the Cities of the Dead.* New Orleans: Batture Press, 1997.

Folsom, C. S., Superintendent's Office, Mount Auburn, to John T. Bradlee, Esq., Cambridge, 4 December 1871.

Folsom, C. S., Superintendent's Office, Mount Auburn, to John T. Bradlee, Esq., Cambridge, 5 December 1871. Mount Auburn Cemetery Archives, Cambridge, MA.

Folsom, C. S., Superintendent's Office, Mount Auburn, to John T. Bradlee, Esq., Cambridge, 6 November 1871. Mount Auburn Cemetery Archives, Cambridge, MA.

Folsom, C. S., Superintendent's Office, Mount Auburn, to John T. Bradlee, Esquire (Chairman of the Subcommittee on the Sphinx), Cambridge, 29 February 1872. Mount Auburn Cemetery Archives, Cambridge, MA.

Folsom, C. W., Superintendent's Office, Mount Auburn, to John T. Bradlee, Esq., Cambridge, 2 September 1871. Mount Auburn Cemetery Archives, Cambridge, MA.

Forest Hills Cemetery: Its Establishment, Progress, Scenery, Monuments, Etc. Boston: Damrell & Moor & George Coolidge, 1858.

Forest Lawn: Its History, Dedications, Progress, Regulations, Names of Lot Holders, &c. Buffalo: Thomas, Howard & Johnson, 1867.

Foxcroft, Frank. "Mount Auburn." *The New England Magazine* 20, no. 4 (June 1896): 419–38.

Francaviglia, Richard V. "The Cemetery as an Evolving Cultural Landscape." *Annals of the Association of American Geographers* 61, no. 3 (September 1971): 501–09.

Freeman, Jr., Robert Belmont. "Design Proposals for the Washington National Monument." *Records of the Columbia Historical Society, Washington, D.C.* 49 (1973/1974): 151–86.

French, Stanley. "The Cemetery as Cultural Institution: The Establishment of Mount Auburn and the "Rural Cemetery" Movement." *American Quarterly* 26, no. 1 (March 1974): 37–59.

Gallier, James. "American Architecture." *North American Review* 43, no. 93 (October 1836): 356–84.

Gliddon, George. *Otia Aegyptiaca: Discourses on Egyptian Archaeology and Hieroglyphical Discoveries.* New York: Bartlett and Welford, 1849.

Gorringe, Henry H. *Egyptian Obelisks.* New York: G. P. Putnam's Sons, 1882.

"Gorringe's 'Egyptian Obelisks'." *The Century* 24, no. 6 (October 1882): 947.

"Grant Day in New York." *The Wheeling Register* 35, no. 289 (April 28, 1897): 4.

"Grant's Memorial: What Shall It Be?" *North American Review* 131, no. 346 (September 1885): 276–77.

Gray, Edward G. *The Making of John Ledyard: Empire and Ambition in the Life of an Early American Traveler.* New Haven: Yale University Press, 2007.

"Great Cities, And Their Fate." *Harper's New Monthly Magazine* 43, no. 258 (November 1871): 903–14.

Griswold, Charles. "An Address in Commemoration of the Lives and Services of Ledyard and his Brave Associates, Who Fell at Groton Heights Sept. 6, 1781, in Defence of Their Country, Delivered at Groton, (Conn.) September 6th, 1826, on the Laying of the Corner Stone of a Monument to Their Memory." New London: J.B. Clapp, 1826.

The Groton Centennial to be Celebrated September 6, 1881, Under the Patronage of the state of Connecticut and of the United States. New Haven, CT: Tuttle, Morehouse & Taylor, 1881.

"Groton Heights." Reprinted in Hezekiah Niles and William Ogden Niles, *Niles' Weekly Register,* vol. V. Baltimore: The Franklin Press, 1826.

"Groton Hill." Reprinted in *Newburyport Herald* 29, no. 37 (August 5, 1825), 2.

"Groton Massacre." *New York Herald* 247 (September 4, 1881), 12.

"Groton Monument." *Columbian Register* (August 17, 1850), 3.

"Groton Monument." *The New-London Gazette* 68, no. 3520 (April 27, 1831): 3.

Groton Monument Association, Proceedings of 6 September 1825, n.p. Bill Memorial Library, Groton, CT.

G. T. C., "Mount Auburn." *The New England Magazine* 7, no. 4 (October 1834): 316–20.

Hall Burkett, Nancy. *Under Its Generous Dome: The Collections and Programs of the American Antiquarian Society.* Worcester, MA: American Antiquarian Society, 1992.

Hamlin, Talbot. *Greek Revival Architecture in America.* New York: Dover Publications, 1944.

———. "The Greek Revival in America and Some of its Critics." *The Art Bulletin* 24, no. 3 (September 1942): 244–58.

Harvey, Frederick L. *History of the Washington National Monument and the Washington National Monument Society.* Washington, DC, 1902.

Hatheway, M. E. N. "The Sphinx." *The Atlantic Monthly* 28, no. 169 (November 1871): 563.

Haynes, Joyce. "America's Earliest Egyptian Collection at the Peabody Essex Museum, Salem." *KMT: A Modern Journal of Ancient Egypt* 11, no. 2 (Summer 2000): 30–41.

"Hieroglyphics." *North American Review* 32, no. 70 (January 1831): 95–127.

Hijiya, James. "American Gravestones and Attitudes Toward Death: A Brief History." *Proceedings of the American Philosophical Society* 127, no. 5 (October 14, 1983): 339–63.

Hill, Mark Langdon. "Monument to Washington." *North American Review* 2, no. 6 (March 1816): 329–41.

Holmes, Oliver Wendell. "One Hundred Days in Europe." *The Atlantic Monthly* 60, no. 360 (October 1887): 343–56.

Howells, William Dean. "Question of Monuments." *The Atlantic Monthly* 17, no. 103 (May 1866): 646–49.

Hughes, Charles Evans. *Addresses of Charles Evans Hughes, 1906–1916: With an Introduction by Jacob Gould Schurman*, 2nd ed. New York: G.P. Putnam's Sons, 1916.

Humbert, Jean-Marcel. *L'Égyptomanie Dans L'Art Occidental*. Paris: ACR Edition Internationale, 1989.

Humbert, Jean-Marcel, and Clifford Price, eds. *Imhotep Today: Egyptianizing Architecture*. London: University College of London Press, 2003.

"In Egypt! – Verde Giovane" *The Living Age* 35, no. 440 (Oct. 23, 1852): 159–60.

Internment Record for Lot No. 529, Kirk Boott Tomb, 1836. Mount Auburn Cemetery Archives, Cambridge, MA.

Internment Record for Lot No. 693, Joy Family Tomb, 1839. Mount Auburn Cemetery Archives, Cambridge, MA.

Isenberg, Nancy, and Andrew Burstein, eds. *Mortal Remains: Death in Early America*. Philadelphia: University of Pennsylvania Press, 2003.

Jacobs, Phoebe Lloyd. "John James Barralet and the Apotheosis of George Washington." *Winterthur Portfolio* 12 (1977): 115–37.

Janney, Caroline E. *Burying the Dead But Not the Past: Ladies' Memorial Associations and the Lost Cause*. Chapel Hill: The University of North Carolina Press, 2008.

"The Jefferson Davis Memorial." *Confederate Veteran* 30, no. 11 (November 1922): 405.

Jefferson, Thomas. *Notes on the State of Virginia*. Edited by William Peden. Chapel Hill: University of North Carolina Press, 1955.

Jeffries, John P. *The Natural History of the Human Races, With Their Primitive Form and Origin, Primeval Distribution, Distinguishing Peculiarities; Antiquity, Works of Art, Physical Structure, Mental Endowments and Moral Bearing*. New York: Edward O. Jenkins, 1869.

"A JOY Forever; Requests Amounting to $280,560 Paid to Massachusetts Charitable Institutions." *The New York Times* (May 24, 1872), 2.

Kahn, David M. "The Grant Monument." *The Journal of the Society of Architectural Historians* 41, no. 3 (October 1982): 212–31.

Kammen, Michael. *Visual Shock: A History of Art Controversies in American Culture*. New York: Alfred A. Knopf, 2006.

Kelly, R. Talbot. "An Artist Among the Fellaheen." *The Century Magazine* 55, no. 6 (April 1898): 878–87.

Kidney, Walter C. *Allegheny Cemetery: A Romantic Landscape in Pittsburgh*. Pittsburgh: Pittsburgh History & Landmarks Foundation, 1990.

King, Moses. *Mount Auburn Cemetery*. Cambridge, MA: Moses King, Publisher, 1883.

Kuklik, Bruce. *Puritans in Babylon: The Ancient Near East and American Intellectual Life, 1880–1930*. Princeton: Princeton University Press, 1996.

Kusinitz, Bernard. "The Enigma of the Colonial Jewish Cemetery in Newport, Rhode Island." *Rhode Island Jewish Historical Notes* 9, no. 3 (November 1985) 225–38.

Kutner, Janet. "Art: Last Rothko Works in Chapel." *Dallas Morning News* (March 14, 1971), 5.

Lamia, Stephen, curator. *Egypt: The Source and The Legacy*. Sarah Lawrence College Art Gallery, 13 February–22 April, 1990.

Lancaster, Clay. "Oriental Forms in American Architecture 1800–1870." *The Art Bulletin* 29, no. 3 (September 1947): 183–93.

Lears, T. J. Jackson. *No Place of Grace: Antimodernism and the Transformation of American Culture, 1880–1920,* 2nd ed. Chicago: University of Chicago Press, 1994.

"Letter from the Bay State." *New Hampshire Sentinel* (September 12, 1878), 2.

Lincoln, Levi. "An Address Delivered on the Consecration of the Worcester Rural Cemetery, September 8, 1838." Boston: Dutton & Wentworth, Printers, 1838.

"The Lincoln Monument." *North American* [Philadelphia] 97, no. 26513 (May 30, 1865): 2.

Linden, Blanche M. G. *Silent City on a Hill: Picturesque Landscapes of Memory and Boston's Mount Auburn Cemetery.* Rev. ed. Amherst: University of Massachusetts Press, 2007.

Liscombe, Rhodri Windsor. *Altogether American: Robert Mills, Architect and Engineer, 1781–1855.* New York: Oxford University Press, 1994.

Lorenz, Daniel Edward. *The New Mediterranean Traveller: A Handbook of Practical Information.* New York: Fleming H. Revell Company, 1905.

Loudon, Jane Webb. *The Mummy! A Tale of the Twenty-Second Century; in Three Volumes*, repr. Ann Arbor: The University of Michigan Press, 1994.

Ludlow, Thomas W. "Archaeological Study in America." *The Century Magazine* 30, no. 4 (August 1885): 652–53.

Ludwig, Allan. *Graven Images: New England Stonecarving and Its Symbols, 1650–1815*, 3rd. ed. Hanover, NH: University Press of New England, 1999.

MacDonald, Sally and Michael Rice, eds. *Consuming Ancient Egypt*. London: University College of London Press, 2003.

The Magic City: A Portfolio of Original Photographic Views of the Great World's Fair and its Treasures of Art, Including a Graphic Representation of the Famous Midway Plaisance, With Graphic Descriptions by America's Brilliant Historical and Descriptive Writer J. W. Buel, 1, no. 15 (April 23). Philadelphia: H.S. Smith and C.R. Graham for Historical Publishing Company, 1894.

"Marking a People's Love: Dedication of the Washington Monument." *New York Times* (February 22, 1885), 3.

Maynard, W. Barksdale. *Architecture in the United States, 1800–1850*. New Haven: Yale University Press, 2002.

Mayo, James M. *War Memorials As Political Landscape: The American Experience and Beyond.* New York: Praeger Publishers, 1988.

McDowell, Peggy, and Richard E. Meyer. *The Revival Styles in American Memorial Art*. Bowling Green, OH: Bowling Green State University Popular Press, 1994.

McClenahan, John. *Singular Philadelphians*. Richmond, VA: Dietz Press, 1999.

Melville, Herman. *The Writings of Herman Melville*. In Journals, vol 15. Edited by Harrison Hayford. *Journals*. Evanston: Northwestern University Press and The Newberry Library, 1989.

Meyer, Richard, ed. *Cemeteries and Gravemarkers: Voices of American Culture.* Logan, UT: Utah State University Press, 1992.

Miller II, J. Jefferson. "The Designs for the Washington Monument in Baltimore." *The Journal of the Society of Architectural Historians* 23, no. 1 (March 1964): 19–28.

Mills, Cynthia and Pamela Simpson, eds. *Monuments to the Lost Cause: Women, Art, and the Landscapes of Southern Memory.* Knoxville, TN: The University of Tennessee Press, 2003.

"Miscellany from the Baltimore Federal Gazette." *The Boston Weekly Messenger* 3, no. 38 (July 8, 1814): 4.

"The Mississippi River." *Harper's New Monthly Magazine* 33, no. 196 (September 1866): 511–17.

"The Mississippi River." *Putnam's Monthly Magazine of American Literature, Science & Art* 11, no. 5 (May 1868): 590–601.

"The Monuments of Egypt." *The New Englander and Yale Review* 9, no. 33 (February 1851): 1–14.

Morton, Samuel George. *Crania Aegyptiaca; or, Observations on Egyptian Ethnography, Derived from Anatomy, History and the Monuments*. Philadelphia: John Penington, 1844.

———. *Crania Americana; or, A Comparative View of the Skulls of Various Aboriginal Nations of North and South America: To Which is Prefixed An Essay on the Varieties of the Human Species*. Philadelphia: J. Dobson, 1839.

Mount Auburn Cemetery Board of Trustees Meeting Minutes, 6 March 1865 to 18 September 1872. Mount Auburn Cemetery Archives, Cambridge, MA.

Mt. Auburn Memorial Vol. 1 (15 June 1859 – 1 June 1860). Mount Auburn Cemetery Archives, Cambridge, MA.

"The National Washington Monument." *The Philadelphia Inquirer* (August 4, 1866), 4.

"The National Washington Monument." *The Philadelphia Inquirer* (July 18, 1867), 4.

Neff, John R. *Honoring the Civil War Dead: Commemoration and the Problem of Reconciliation*. Lawrence: University of Kansas Press, 2005.

New Bedford Mercury 22, no. 11 (September 19, 1828): 2.

New London County Historical Society, Letterhead, 1881. Bill Memorial Library, Groton, CT.

New York Herald Tribune 25, no. 7703 (December 14, 1865): 6.

New York Spectator 28 (August 2, 1825): 3.

New York Times (April 25, 1897), 2.

Nicholls, Dale Reeves. *Egyptian Revival Jewelry & Design*. Altglen, PA: Schiffer Publishing Ltd, 2006.

"Note and Comment." *Springfield Republican* (Aug. 13, 1886), 4.

"Notes on Art and Archaeology." *The Academy* 28, no. 703 (October 24, 1885): 280.

Nott, Josiah, and George Gliddon. *Indigenous Races of the Earth; or, New Chapters of Ethnological Enquiry*. Philadelphia: J. B. Lippincot & Co., 1857.

———. *Types of Mankind: Or, Ethnological Researches, Based Upon the Ancient Monuments, Paintings, Sculptures, and Crania of Races, And Upon Their Natural, Geographical, Philological, and Biblical History: Illustrated by Selections from the Inedited Papers of Samuel George Morton, M.D., (Late president of the Academy of Natural Sciences at Philadelphia,) and by Additional Contributions from Prof. L. Agassiz, LL.D.; W. Usher, M.D.; and Prof. H.S. Patterson, M.D.* Philadelphia: Lippincott, Grambo & Co., 1854.

"The Obelisks of Egypt." *The International Magazine of Literature, Art, & Science* 4, no. 4 (November 1851): 469–71.

"Obituary: Jacob Bigelow, M.D., LL.D." *The Medical Record*, vol. 15. New York: William Wood and Company, 1879.

Oration Pronounced by the Honorable Robert C. Winthrop, Speaker of the House of Representatives of the United States, on the 4th of July, 1848, on the Occasion of Laying the Corner-Stone of the National Monument to the Memory of Washington. Washington: J. & G.S. Gideon, Printers, 1848.

The Orations on Bunker Hill Monument, The Character of Washington, and The Landing At Plymouth by Daniel Webster. New York: American Book Company, 1894.

"Our Public Monuments." *The Decorator and Furnisher* 8, no. 2 (May 1886): 39.

Pantazzi, Michael, curator. *Egyptomania*. National Gallery of Canada, 17 June–18 September 1994.

Parker, Hon. Isaac. "Inaugural Address." *North American Review* 3, no. 7 (May 1816): 11–27.

"Passages of Eastern Travel." *Harper's New Monthly Magazine* 12, no. 69 (February 1856): 224–34.

Peabody, William B. O. *Address Delivered at the Consecration of the Springfield Cemetery, September 5th, 1841*. Springfield: Wood and Rupp, 1841.

Pendleton's Lithograph. *Mount Auburn Cemetery* (lithograph), N.D. Mount Auburn Cemetery Archives, Cambridge, MA.

Penfield, Frederic Courtland. "Contemporary Egypt." *The North American Review* 161, no. 464 (July 1895): 13–25.

———. "In Fascinating Cairo." *The Century Magazine* 58, no. 6 (October 1899): 811–32.

———. "Sidelights on the Exploitation of Egypt." *The North American Review* 159, no. 455 (October 1894): 479–90.

Perpetual Care Contract for Lot No. 35, Coffin Family Tomb, 1881. Mount Auburn Cemetery Archives, Cambridge, MA.

Perpetual Care Contract for Lot No. 245, Lowell Family Tomb, 1882. Mount Auburn Cemetery Archives, Cambridge, MA.

Perpetual Care Contract for Lot No. 529, Boott Family Tomb, 1887. Mount Auburn Cemetery Archives, Cambridge, MA.

Perpetual Care Contract for Lot No. 693, Joy Family Tomb, 1869. Mount Auburn Cemetery Archives, Cambridge, MA.

The Picturesque Pocket Companion and Visitor's Guide Through Mount Auburn. Boston. Otis, Broaders & Co., 1839.

Poe, Edgar Allan. "Some Words With A Mummy." *The American Whig Review* 1, no. 4 (April 1845): 363–71.

Polcari, Stephen. "Barnett Newman's Broken Obelisk." *Art Journal* 53, no. 4 (Winter 1994): 48–55.

"The President's Position." *Albany Evening Journal* (February 23, 1866), 2.

"Principle Entrance to Mt. Auburn" (lithograph), 1849. Mount Auburn Cemetery Archives, Cambridge, MA.

Proceedings at the Dedication of the Soldiers' and Sailors' Monument, in Providence. Providence: A. Crawford Greene, Printer to the State, 1871.

Proceedings of the Bunker Hill Monument Association at the Fifty-Sixth Annual Meeting, June 17, 1879. With the Address of Frederic W. Lincoln. Boston: Bunker Hill Monument Association, 1879.

Proctor, Richard A. "The Pyramid of Cheops." *The North American Review* 136, no. 316 (March 1883): 257–70.

Purcell, Sarah J. "Commemoration, Public Art, and the Changing Meaning of the Bunker Hill Monument." *The Public Historian* 25, no. 2 (Spring 2003): 55–71.

Ragon, Michel. *The Space of Death: A Study of Funerary Architecture, Decoration, and Urbanism*. Charlottesville: University Press of Virginia, 1983.

Ralph, Julian. "Our Exposition At Chicago." *Harper's New Monthly Magazine* 84, no. 500 (January 1892): 205–14.

Record Sheet with Family Interment List for Lot No. 529, Boott Family Tomb, 1836–1877. Mount Auburn Cemetery Archives, Cambridge, MA.

Rees, Joan. "The American Campaign of Amelia B. Edwards to Promote the Egypt Exploration Society." *KMT* 13, no. 4 (Winter 2002–2003): 80–84.

Reisem, Richard O. et al. *Field Guide to Forest Lawn Cemetery, Buffalo, New York*. Buffalo: Forest Lawn Heritage Foundation, 1998.

Report of the Floyd Memorial Association. Sioux City, IA: Press of Perkins Bros., 1897.

"Revolutionary Monument." *New London Gazette* (May 4, 1825), 61: no. 3208, 3.

Richman, Michael. "The Early Public Sculpture of Daniel Chester French." *American Art Journal* 4, no. 2 (November 1972): 113–14.

Rockett, William. "The Egyptian Revival." *Aramco World Magazine* (January-February 1982): 12–19.

Roos, Frank J. "The Egyptian Style." *Magazine of Art* 33 (1940): 218–23, 255, 257.

Rotundo, Barbara. "Mount Auburn Cemetery: A Proper Boston Institution." Off-printed from *Harvard Library Bulletin* XXII, no. 3 (July 1974): 268–79.

———. "Mount Auburn: Fortunate Coincidences and an Ideal Solution." *Journal of Garden History* 4, no. 3 (July–September 1984): 255–67.

"Rural Cemeteries." *North American Review* 53,113 (October 1841): 385–412.

"San Jacinto Museum Rites Set Two Days." *Dallas Morning News* (April 16, 1939), 15.

Savage, Kirk. *Memorial Wars: Washington, D.C., the National Mall, and the Transformation of the Memorial Landscape*. Berkeley: University of California Press, 2009.

———. "The Self-Made Monument: George Washington and the Fight to Erect a National Memorial." *Winterthur Portfolio* 22, no. 4 (Winter 1987): 225–42.

———. *Standing Soldiers, Kneeling Slaves: Race, War, and Monuments in Nineteenth Century America*. Princeton, NJ: Princeton University Press, 1997.

Scharf, Frederic A. "The Garden Cemetery and American Sculpture: Mount Auburn." *The Art Quarterly* 24 (Spring 1961): 80–88.

Schorsch, Anita. "A Key to the Kingdom: The Iconography of a Mourning Picture." *Winterthur Portfolio* 14, no. 1 (Spring 1979): 41–71.

Schuyler, David. "The Evolution of the Anglo-America Rural Cemetery: Landscape Architecture as Social and Cultural History." *Journal of Garden History* 4, no. 3 (July–September 1984): 291–304.

"Sculpture Dedication to Dr. King Rejected." *Dallas Morning News* (June 24, 1969), 14.

Sears, John F. *Sacred Places: American Tourist Attractions in the Nineteenth Century*. Amherst: University of Massachusetts Press, 1989.

Segal, Joshua. *The Old Jewish Cemetery of Newport: A History of North America's Oldest Extant Jewish Cemetery*. Nashua, NH: Jewish Cemetery Publishing, LLC, 2007.

Shackel, Paul. *Memory in Black and White: Race, Commemoration, and the Post-Bellum Landscape*. Walnut Creek, CA: Alta Mira Press, 2003.

———. *Myth, Memory, and the Making of the American Landscape*. Gainesville: University Press of Florida, 2001.

"Shaft is Dedicated to Jefferson Davis." *Dallas Morning News* (June 8, 1924), 1.

"The Shame of It." *The Weekly Patriot* [Harrisburg, PA] 16, no. 38 (December 31, 1868), 2.

Sherman, Conger. *Guide to Laurel Hill Cemetery, near Philadelphia, 1847*. Philadelphia: C. Sherman, Printer, 1847.

Silber, Nina. *The Romance of Reunion: Northerners and the South, 1865–1900*. Chapel Hill: The University of North Carolina Press, 1993.

Singley, B.L. Stereoview card "1858 – The Lion of Lucerne, Switzerland." Headville, PA: Keystone View Company, Manufacturers and Publishers, 1896.

"Sketch of the Rise, Progress, And Influence of the Useful Arts." *The American Whig Review* 5, no. 1 (January 1847): 87–96.

Sloane, David Charles. *The Last Great Necessity: Cemeteries in American History*. Baltimore, MD: Johns Hopkins University Press, 1991.

Smith, Albert. "Mr. Grubbe's Night with Memnon" *Putnam's New Monthly Magazine* 10, no. 56 (August 1857): 192–97.

Smith, Deborah A. "Safe in the Arms of Jesus: Consolation on Delaware Children's Gravestones, 1840–99." *Markers IV: The Journal of the Association for Gravestone Studies* (1987): 85–106.

Smith, R. A. *Smith's Illustrated Guide to and through Laurel Hill Cemetery, with a Glance at Celebrated Tombs and Burying-Places, Ancient and Modern – An Historical Sketch of the Cemeteries of Philadelphia – An Essay on Monumental Architecture, and a Tour Up the Schuylkill*. Philadelphia: Willis P. Hazard, Publisher, 1852.

Smith, Robert C. "Two Centuries of Philadelphia Architecture 1700–1900." *Transactions of the American Philosophical Society*, New Series, 43, no. 1 (1953): 289–303.

Smith, Sydney. Review of "Adam Seybert, Statistical Annals of the United States of America." *Edinburgh Review* 33 (January 1820): 69–80.

Speake, Jennifer, ed. *Literature of Travel and Exploration: An Encyclopedia*, vol. 3. New York: Routledge, 2003.

"The Sphinx." *The Atlantic Monthly* 3, no. 20 (June 1859): 724.

"Sphinx and Oedipus." *Continental Monthly: Devoted to Literature and National Policy* 1, no. 1 (January 1862): 63.

"The Sphinx at Mount Auburn." *Lowell Daily Citizen and News* (Feb. 14, 1873), 1.

Squier, E. G. "American Ethnology: Being A Summary of Some of the Results Which Have Followed the Investigation of This Subject." *The American Whig Review* 9, no. 16 (April 1849): 385–99.

Stanley, J. F. *Concerning Memorials: Their Historic Origin and Present Day Adaptations*. Salisbury, NC: The Leland Company – South, 1911.

Stanton, William. *The Leopard's Spots: Scientific Attitudes Toward Race in America, 1815–1859*. Chicago: University of Chicago Press, 1960.

"State Correspondence." *New Haven Evening Register* 41, no. 118 (May 21, 1881): 4.

"State New's." *New Haven Evening Register* 41, no. 65 (March 25, 1881): 4.

Story, Ronald. "Class and Culture in Boston: The Athenaeum, 1807–1860." *American Quarterly* 27, no. 2 (May 1975): 178–99.

The Stranger's Guide in Philadelphia and Its Environs. Including Laurel Hill, Woodlands, Monument, Odd Fellows', and Glenwood Cemeteries. Philadelphia: Lindsay & Blakiston, 1852.

"Style and the Monument." *North American Review* 141, no. 348 (November 1885): 443–53.

The Sun [Baltimore] 49, no. 1 (May 20, 1861): 4.

"The Tallest in the World." *Washington Star* (July 26, 1884). Reprinted in *New York Times* (July 28, 1884), 8.

Tashjian, Dickran and Ann. *Memorials for Children of Change*. Middletown, CT: Wesleyan University Press, 1974.

"That Mummy." *Scientific American* 5, no. 40 (June 22, 1850): 314.

"Topics of the Time: The Grant Memorial." *The Century* 31, no. 6 (April 1886): 953–57.

"To the Editor of the Transcripts" *Boston Evening Transcript* 15, no. 4385 (November 9, 1844): 2.

Townshend, Henry H. *The Grove Street Cemetery: A Paper Read Before The New Haven Colony Historical Society, October 27, 1947.* New Haven: New Haven Colony Historical Society, 1947.

Trafton, Scott. *Egypt Land: Race and Nineteenth Century American Egyptomania.* Durham: Duke University Press, 2004.

Tuthill, L. C. *History of Architecture: From The Earliest Times; Its Present Condition in Europe and the United States.* Philadelphia: Lindsay and Blakiston, 1848. Reprinted by New York: Garland Publishing, 1988.

Twain, Mark. *Innocents Abroad, Or, The New Pilgrim's Progress*, reprint. New York: The Modern Library, 2003.

Twenty-Fourth Annual Report of the American Scenic and Historic Preservation Society, 1919. Albany: J.B. Lyon Company, 1919.

Underwood, Francis H. "Egypt Under the Pharaohs." *The Atlantic Monthly* 45, no. 269 (March 1880): 315–27.

"Unrolling a Mummy." *Scientific American* 5, no. 35 (May 18, 1850): 274.

"Unrolling the Mummy of a Bishop." *Scientific American* 7, no. 27 (March 20, 1852): 216.

Upton, Dell. "The Urban Cemetery and the Urban Community: The Origin of the New Orleans Cemetery." *Perspectives in Vernacular Architecture*, 7, Exploring Everyday Landscapes. (1997): 131–45.

Van Brunt, Henry. "On the Present Condition and Prospects of Architecture." *The Atlantic Monthly* 57, no. 341 (March 1886): 374–84.

"The Very Stones Cry Out Against Them," *New Hampshire Sentinel* 63, no. 40 (October 3, 1861), 1.

"Views of the National Capital – No. 2." *San Francisco Evening Bulletin* 20, no. 118 (August 24, 1865): 1.

Walter, Cornelia M. *Mount Auburn Illustrated in Highly Finished Line Engraving, from Drawings Taken on the Spot, by James Smillie, With Descriptive Notices by Cornelia W. Walter.* New York: Robert Martin, 1847.

Ward, Pearl L. "The Tourist Scene in Egypt During the 19th & Early 20th Centuries." *KMT: A Modern Journal of Ancient Egypt* 11, no. 3 (Fall 2000): 70–81.

Warren, George Washington. *The History of the Bunker Hill Monument Association.* Boston: James R. Osgood & Co., 1877.

———. *The History of the Bunker Hill Monument Association During the First Century of the United States of America.* Boston: John R. Osgood and Company, 1876.

———. *Memoir of Solomon Willard: Architect and Superintendent of the Bunker Hill Monument.* Boston, 1865.

"Washington Items." *Albany Evening Journal* (November 1, 1865), 2.

———. "The Washington Monument." *The American Art Review* 1, no. 1 (November 1879): 7–12.

———. "The Washington Monument (Concluded)." *The American Art Review* 1, no. 2 (December 1879): 57–65.

"The Washington Monument." *The Daily Picayune* [New Orleans] (July 29, 1865), 1.

"The Washington Monument." *Dallas Weekly Herald* 13, no. 18 (January 20, 1866): 4.

"The Washington Monument." *New York Times* (September 3, 1859), 4.

"The Washington Monument." *New York Times* (December 19, 1872), 4.

"The Washington Monument." *New York Times* (December 7, 1884), 8.

"The Washington Monument." *New York Times* (February 22, 1885), 6.

"Washington Monument Association." *The Philadelphia Inquirer* (February 25, 1862), 8

"The Washington Monument." *The Philadelphia Inquirer* (October 25, 1862), 3.

"The Washington Monument." *The Philadelphia Inquirer* (September 25, 1861), 1.

Webster, Daniel. *The Bunker Hill Monument, Adams and Jefferson: Two Orations*. Boston: Houghton, Mifflin and Company, 1893.

Webster, Sally. "Pierre-Charles L'Enfant and the Iconography of Independence." *Nineteenth-Century Art Worldwide: A Journal of Nineteenth-Century Visual Culture* 7, no. 1 (Spring 2008), np.

Wentworth, Rev. E., ed. "Art Notes." *The Ladies' Repository* 31. Cincinnati: Hitchcock and Walden, 1873: 227–30.

Wheeler, Benjamin Ide. "The Seven Wonders of the World: The Great Pyramids of Egypt." *The Century Magazine* 56, no. 1 (May 1898): 107–09.

Wheildon, William Willder. *Memoir of Solomon Willard: Architect and Superintendent of the Bunker Hill Monument*. Boston, 1865.

Wilson, Edward L. "Finding Pharaoh." *The Century Magazine* 34:1 (May 1887), 3–10.

———. "The Great Pyramid." *Scribner's Magazine* 3, no. 1 (January 1888): 41–64.

Wilson, John A. *Signs & Wonders Upon Pharaoh: A History of American Egyptology*. Chicago: University of Chicago Press, 1964.

Wilson, Susan. *Garden of Memories: A Guide to Historic Forest Hills*. Forest Hills Educational Trust, 1998.

Wilson, D.D., D.C.L., LL.D., William C. "Egypt At Home." *The New England Magazine* 8, no. 2 (April 1890): 198–217.

Winslow, William C. "Egypt at Home." *The New England Magazine* 8, no. 2 (April 1890): 198–217.

Winterer, Caroline. *The Culture of Classicism: Ancient Greece and Rome in American Intellectual Life, 1780–1910*. Baltimore: The Johns Hopkins University Press, 2002.

Wischnitzer, Rachel. "Thomas U. Walter's Crown Street Synagogue, 1848–49." *The Journal of the Society of Architectural Historians* 13, no. 4 (December 1954): 29–31.

Wolfe, S. J. *Mummies in Nineteenth Century America: Ancient Egyptians as Artifacts*. Jefferson, NC: McFarland & Company, Inc., 2009.

Woolsey, T. D. "Cemeteries and Monuments." *New Englander and Yale Review* 7, no. 28 (November 1849): 489–501.

Woolson, Constance Fenimore. "Cairo in 1890." *Harper's New Monthly Magazine* 83, no. 497 (October 1891): 651–74.

———. "Cairo in 1890." *Harper's New Monthly Magazine* 83, no. 497 (November 1891): 828–55.

Wright, L. C. *United States Policy Toward Egypt, 1830–1914*. New York: Exposition Press, 1969.

Zukowsky, John. "Monumental American Obelisks: Centennial Vistas." *The Art Bulletin* 58, no. 4 (December 1976): 574–81.

Index

Page numbers in **boldface** refer to illustrations.

Agassiz, Louis, 42, 233n82
Alcott, Louisa May, 46, 233n91
allegorical figures, 10, 22, 62, 72, 81, 130, 135, 137, 149, 166. See also Statue of Liberty
American Antiquarian Society, 22, 104, 231n17
American exceptionalism, 21, 25
Archaeological Institute of America, 208
archaeology, 16, 195, 202, 208, 229n11, 230n21, 230n25, 233n68, 234n4, 236n49, 242n54, 243n71; American digs in Egypt, 209. See also Egyptology
architectural eclecticism. See architectural revivalism
architectural revivalism, 5–11, 60, 72–73, 76, 87, 89, 195, 206–7, 216: criticisms of eclecticism, 15, 73, 164, 179, 197–200; Gothic Revival, 7, 11, 26, 57, 60, 72–73, 75, 75, 77, 81, 87–88, 96, 128, 168, 179, 183, 197, 236n64, 238n3; Greek Revival, 5–7, 9, 12, 60, 64–65, 77, 170, 229n16, 230n22, 231n31 ; as reflection of American heterogeneity, 10, 198. See also Egyptian Revival
Arnold, Benedict, 105, 116, 119, 240n59. See also Groton Monument
Arthur, Chester, 186
Austin, Henry, 81, **82**

Baltimore Battle Monument. See Godefroy, Maximilian

Batterson, J.G., 136
Belzoni, Giovanni Battista, 8, 33, 232n56
Bennington Battle Monument, 14, 94, 97, **97**, 122, 192–93, 199–200, 246n9
Bigelow, Jacob, 42, **64**, 242n32, 242n35, 243n58, 243–68; Bunker Hill Monument Design Committee, 63, 144; burial reform, 52; Elements of Technology, 7, 64, 68, 91, 102, 144–45, 229n17, 236n40, 236n47, 237n1, 238n8; A History of the Cemetery of Mount Auburn, 55, 65, 234n2, 234nn5–6, 234n15, 234nn17–18, 235n24, 235nn26–27, 235n34, 236n43, 236n48; Mount Auburn chapel, 57, 128; Mount Auburn gateway, 63, 65–66, 68, 70–71, 73–74; Mount Auburn round tower, 57; as president of Mount Auburn Cemetery Association, 15, 57; as promoter of Egyptian Revival, 7, 64–65, 70, 90; racial attitudes, 148–52, 243nn59–61; as renaissance man, 57, 63; Rural Cemetery Movement, 7, 55, 57; and the Sphinx at Mount Auburn, 15, 127–29, 134, 139–45, 147–48, 152–56, 160–62, 180, 191, 219, 240n1, 240nn3–4, 241nn21–27, 241n30, 242nn33–34, 242n37, 242n40, 242nn42–43, 242n48, 242n51, 243n62, 247n37; The Useful Arts, 65, 91, 144–45, 148, 236n41, 238n2, 242n36, 242n47
Bonaparte, Napoleon: campaigns in Egypt 2, 8, 17–18, 48, 60, 205, 211; fictional representation of, 151–52, 206, **207**, 243n61. See also hieroglyphics

266 INDEX

Boott, Kirk, 77, **78**

Boston Athenaeum, 103

Bradlee, John T., 139, 241nn24–27

Bradlee, Joseph P., 77, **78**

Bradlee, Josiah, 77

Broken Obelisk, 12, 225–27, 230n26, 247nn1–4

Bruff, Joseph Goldsborough, 180, **180**, 245n46

Bulkeley, Charles, 117. See also Groton Monument

Bunker Hill Monument, 14, 62, 92, 94, **94**, 98, 100, 102, 105, 122–23, 161, 168, 170, 183, 189, 192–93, 218, 238n9, 238n11, 239nn26–46, 240n71: Association, 63, 98, 103–4, 106, 109, 117, 120, 235n39, 238n13; comparisons with Egyptian architecture, 107–8, 114–15, 133, 188; construction delays, 108–10; cornerstone ceremony, 106–8, 120, 238n10; dedication, 112, **113**, 114, 133, 173, 238nn16–17, 239n18, 239nn21–25; Ladies' auxiliary association, 110; and Manifest Destiny, 103–2; as a national symbol, 114–15; Second Committee on the Design, 63, 108, 144; souvenirs from, 125, **125**, 126, 240n73. See also Everett, Edward; Greenough, Horatio; memorials; Mills, Robert; Revolution, American; Webster, Daniel; Willard, Solomon

burying grounds. See graveyards

Caffieri, J.J., 98, 238n5

canopic jars, 180, 245n47

Casey, Thomas Lincoln, 245n50; background, 182; completion of Washington Monument, 178, 182–85, **184**

cemeteries: Allegheny Cemetery (Pittsburgh), 156, **157**, 211; Bellefontaine Cemetery (St. Louis), 158, 211; Cedarville North Cemetery (OH), 158, **159**, 211; Cypress Grove Cemetery (New Orleans), 87, 237n76; as cultural institutions, 14, 49–50, 53–54, 90, 104; design, 13, 49–50, 54, 57, 59–60, 65, 90; Dorchester North Burying Ground (Boston), 87, **89**; as escape from urban environment, 55–56; Finn's Point National Cemetery (NJ), 137; Forest Hills Cemetery (Roxbury, MA), 58, 74, **75**, 81–82, 87, 104, 158, 236n63; Forest Lawn Cemetery (Buffalo), 76, 156, **157**, 238n3, 243n74; Forest Lawn Memorial Park (Glendale, CA), 216; Green Mount Cemetery (Baltimore), 87; Green-Wood Cemetery (NY), 53, 73, 81, 230n25, 234n9, 236n60, 237n72; Grove Street Cemetery (New Haven, CT), 81–82, **82**, 84, 86, 237n75; Hollywood Cemetery (Richmond, VA), 134–35, **136**, 137; Homewood Cemetery (Pittsburgh), 211, **213**; Lakeview Cemetery (Cleveland), 200; Laurel Hill Cemetery (Philadelphia), 59, 67, 76, 81, 87, 216, 235n33, 236n45, 237n72, 237n76, 237n82; Mikveh Israel Cemetery (Philadelphia), 85; Mount Auburn Cemetery (Cambridge, MA), 9, 13–15, 42, 49–51, 53, 55, 57–58, 60, 62–63, 65, **66**, **69**, 70–74, 76–77, **78–80**, 81, 84, 87, 104, 127–29, 131, 134, **141**, 142, **142**, 143–44, 154–56, 158, 160, 165, 180, 191, 216, 219, 234n2, 234n10, 235n21, 235n24, 235nn26–27, 235n34, 236n52, 236n54, 236n56, 236n62, 237n71, 240n1, 240nn3–4, 240n7, 241n14, 241nn21–27, 242nn33–34, 242n37, 242n40, 243n62, 243n66, 243n69, 243n81, 247n29, 247n37; Mount Hope Cemetery (Rochester), 54–55, 87, 234n16, 237n76; Mount View Cemetery (Pekin, NY), 137; Oakland Cemetery (Atlanta), 137; Old Burying Ground (Farmington, CT), 84, **84**, 86; Old Granary Burying Ground (Boston), 83, **83**, 86, 237n76; Père-Lachaise Cemetery (Paris), 53, 60, 235n31; Pittsfield Rural Cemetery (Pittsfield, MA), 56, 235n22; Riverside Cemetery (Cornish, ME), 87; Spring Grove Cemetery (Cincinnati), 129, 156, 240n2; Springfield Cemetery (Springfield, MA), 52, 54, 234n7; St. Roch Cemetery/Campo Santo (New Orleans), 87; as tourist destinations, 54, 77; Touro Cemetery (Newport, RI), 84–85, **85**, 86, **86**, 237n76; Valley Cemetery (Manchester, NH), 87, **88**; West Laurel Hill Cemetery (Philadelphia), 156, 211; Westminster Cemetery (Baltimore), 60, 237n76; West Point Cemetery (NY), 211, **212**, 246n1; Woodland Cemetery (Philadelphia), 88, 237n82; Woodlawn Cemetery (NY), 156, 211, 247n28

INDEX   267

cemetery gateways, 10, 59–60, 211: biblical inscriptions, 70, 81–82, 237n76; in colonial burying grounds, 70, 83, **83**, 84, **84**, 86, 88, 90; debates over style, 73–76; Egyptian Revival, 3, 9, 13–14, 60, 65–66, **66**, 68, **69**, 70–71, 74–75, **82**, **85**, 86–87, **88**, **89**, 169; Gothic Revival, 75, 75, 82, 87; iconography on, 83–84; for Jewish cemeteries, 84–85, **85**. See also Bigelow, Jacob; cemeteries; Dearborn, General Henry A.S.

cemetery guidebooks, 11, 50–51, 53, 59, 67, 71–72, 75–77, 81, 88–89, 235n33, 236n45, 236n52, 236n54, 237n65, 237nn71–72, 237n82, 243n74

cemetery monuments, 26, 54, 216: ancient, 25, 55, 67; colonial, 51, 59, 234n4; eclecticism, 9–10, 59, 72, 143; gravestones, 51, 59, 166, 230n25, 234n4, 235n20; iconography, 51, 60, 72, 166, 244n6; mausoleums, 26, 54, 59, 62, 72, 124, 143, 156, **157**, 158, **159**, 200, 211, **212**, **213**, 236n50, 238n3; obelisks, 59, 60, 70–73, 77, 86, **86**, 92, 215, 226; portals, 70, 128, 211, **214**; presidential, 124, 200 238n3; quarrying and carving technology, 59, 195–96, 235n35; sculpture, 10, 59, 72; side-hill tombs, 26, 58–59, 70, 77, **78–80**, 81, 211, 236n50, 237n70; sphinxes, 156–58, **157**, **159**, **160**, 211, **212**, 226, 240n2, 243n75

Chalmette Battle Monument (New Orleans), 95, **95**, 219. See also War of 1812

Champollion, François. See Hieroglyphics

Channing, Walter, 42

Christopher Columbus Monument (Baltimore), 60, **61**

Church, Reverend Pharcellus, 54–56, 234n16, 234n19

civilizations, ancient: Greece, 2, 6–9, 24–27, 40, 47, 54, 65, 73, 122, 145, 148, 154–55, 197, 206, 231n32; Mesopotamia, 24, 29, 209, 234n88; North American, 21–23, 198; Rome, 4, 6–10, 24–27, 39–40, 47, 54, 62, 65, 73, 148, 206, 217, 231n32

Civil Rights Movement. See Broken Obelisk

Civil War commemoration, 14, 136, 142, 240n5, 240n8; citizen-soldier statue, 135, 137, 161, 188; Confederate monuments, 124, 130, 134–35, **136**, 137, 188, 220–21, 247n39; early impulses, 127, 129; emancipation, 130–33, 137, 145, 160, 242n49; "The First Civil War Monument," 137; Hollywood Memorial Association, 134–35; ladies' memorial associations, 129, 134, 137, 241n8; northern versus southern, 129–30, 188, 240n8; obelisks, 137; preservation of the Union; reconciliation, 188; Soldiers' and Sailors' Monuments, 129–37, **138**, 241n11, 241n19. See also Jefferson Davis Monument; Lincoln, Abraham; Shaw Memorial (Boston); Sphinx (Mount Auburn); United Daughters of the Confederacy; Washington National Monument

Cleopatra: in film, 209–10

Cleopatra's Needle, 4, 31, **203**, 246n17; negotiations for, 200–1; re-erection in Central Park, 202. See also obelisks

Cleveland, Grover, 208

Columbian Exposition (World's Fair) of 1893, 4, 31–32, 206–8; Luxor Temple reproduction, 4, 208; obelisks, 207–8

Conan Doyle, Sir Arthur, 46, 233n92

Cook, Clarence, 197, 246n4

Cook, Eliza, 28, 31

culture, American, 2, 13, 16, 47, 87, 162, 164–65, 234nn12–13, 234n20, 244n15; civic, 25–27; commemorative, 13, 50, 57, 164, 207, 222; consumer, 32–33, 48, 59, 125; defense of, 17, 20–21, 25; foreign criticisms of, 2, 18–20; popular, xi, 4–5, 7–8, 16, 32–33, 209, 237n81; print, 48, 76, 190; visual, 165–66, 238n6

Dallas, George, 170

Davis, A.J., 120

Davis, Jefferson, 135, 220. See also Jefferson Davis Monument

Dearborn, General Henry A.S., 57, 74, 90, 104

Dearborn, Nathaniel, 72, 77, 81, 236n54, 237n71

Death and the Sculptor. See French, Daniel Chester

Denon, Baron Dominique Vivant, 8; Déscription de l'Égypte, 2, 33, 65

268 INDEX

Dickens, Charles, 2, 19–20, 230n6
Dimmock, Charles H., 134. See also Civil War commemoration
Downing, Andrew Jackson, 6, 229n15. See also architectural revivalism
Drake-Cardeza, Charlotte, 156, 211

Edwards, Amelia B., 229n10, 246n18: and the Egypt Exploration Fund, 4–5
Egypt: biblical associations, 1, 24, 85–86; Cairo, x, 2, 201, 204, 239n42, 246n20, 247n21; care for the dead, 3–4, 14, 25, 50, 55, 66, 70, 89; climate, 31; Colossi at Memnon, 114, 173; Giza, 28, 88, 110, 114, 129, 144–45, 150, 167, 204, 205, 215; Great Pyramid, 88, 110, 114–15, 164, 169, **205**, 246n18, 246n55; Great Sphinx, 28–29, 114, 128, 143–45, 150, 204, **205**, 215, **215**; Karnak, 27, 65, **67**, 87, 183, 204, 208; Luxor, 4, 8, 27, 183, 208; modern, 4, 31, 43, 204; the Nile River, x-xi, 2–3, 24, 27–31, 42–43, 47, 66, 142, 191, 197, 205–6, 217; as parent of civilization, 6, 8, 24, 27, 40, 149; pharaohs, x-xi, 2–5, 7, 17, 25, 27, 32, 35–36, 39–40, 48, 91, 114–15, 149, 155, 158, 206, 208, 229n10, 231n23, 246nn18–19; Philae, 208, 211; pyramids, xii, 2, 5, 7, 25, 28–30, 43, 50, 55, 65, 74, 88, 110, 114–15, 133, 152, 167, 188, 197, 204, 211, 232n56; religion, 73–74, 191, 205; temples, x, xii, 7, 29, 35, 46, 65, 67, 91, 188, 197, 211, 219, 232n56; tombs, x, xii, 7, 45, 67, 232n56; travel narratives, 3, 27–32, 47, 114, 150, 188, 204–6, 229n6, 246n20. See also Cleopatra's Needle; Egyptian architecture; hieroglyphics; mummies; obelisks
Egypt Exploration Fund, 4–5, 206
Egyptian architecture, **67**; elements of, x, 62, 65, 77, 83, 87, 128, 183, 208; as earliest, 67, 186; qualities associated with, 5, 7, 17, 29, 55, 64–67, 71, 74, 76, 89, 92, 107, 122, 133, 218. See also Egypt; obelisks; Sphinx (Great); sphinxes; symbolism
Egyptian Revival; archaeological verisimilitude, 45, 65, 68, 81, 140, 158; and architectural eclecticism, xi, 8, 10–11, 15, 72, 76, 87, 89; Christianizing elements, 68, 70, 81–83; chronology of, 12; criticisms of, 9, 51, 71–74, 160–61, 164, 179; French, xi, 8; geographic extent, xi, 12–13; Jewish use of, 84–86, 230n25, 237n76, 237n78; movie palaces, 210, **210**; associations with paganism, 71, 74–75; as part of Neoclassical aesthetic, 60; popularity in cemeteries, 72–73, 76; twentieth century, xi, 12, 68, 237n81; variety of expressions, 9, 26, 68. See also architectural revivalism; cemetery gateways; cemetery monuments; Columbian Exposition (World's Fair) of 1893; memorials; Midwinter Fair (1894); museums
Egyptology, 5, 45, 47, 195, 229n2, 232n58
Egyptomania, xi, 2, 230n20, 230n25, 233n84; and cinema, 33, 48, 195, 209–11; European, xi, 7–8, 33, 232n54; middle class culture, 13, 17–18, 33; and Mummymania, 33, 211, 232n54; twentieth century, 5, 33, 48, 87, 195, 211. See also Bonaparte, Napoleon; Egyptology; Ethnology; mummies; museums
Eiffel Tower, 185. See also Washington National Monument
England, xi, 7–8, 18, 20, 33, 201, 208, 246n18. See also Dickens, Charles; Egyptology; Egyptomania; Europe; European; Moore, Thomas; mummies; museums; popular literature; Trollope, Frances
Ethnology, 4, 18, 32–33, 38–41, 43–45, 47, 149, 151, 232n52, 233nn82–83. See also Gliddon, George; Morton, Samuel George; Nott, Josiah; Types of Mankind
Europe: comparisons to American society, 20–21, 231n8, 231n15, 231n20; Dark Ages, 151; influence of America on, 172; influence of antiquity on, 24, 27; landscape, 9, 30
European: acquisition of Egyptian obelisks, 201; burial traditions, 51, 98, 235n31; colonization of the Americas, 23; criticisms of America, 8, 13, 17, 23; Egyptian Revival, 8, 230n20; Egyptology, 5, 47; Egyptomania, 7–8, 33–36, 232n54; garden architecture, 60; immigrants, 21; memorial traditions, 103–5; Rococo, 156; travelers to the United States, 18–20, 54, 167. See also Dickinson, Charles; Moore, Thomas; Trollope, Frances

Evarts, William M. See Cleopatra's Needle
Everett, Edward, 57–58, 90, 104, 110, **111**, 115, 118, 124, 235n27, 239n35, 239n46

Floyd Memorial (Sioux City), 217–18, 247n32
Fort Griswold, 92, 94, 105, 115–19, 121, 123, 240n59. See also Griswold, Charles; Groton Monument; Revolution, American
Fosdick, L., 117. See also Groton Monument
Foster, Lafayette S., 121–22, 124, 240n66. See also Groton Monument
France, xi, 7–8, 201, 208, 246n18. See also Bonaparte, Napoleon; Egyptian Revival; Egyptomania; hieroglyphics; museums; popular literature
fraternal organizations: Freemasons, 1, 68, 106, 135, 170, 172, 229n1; Odd Fellows, 68, 237n76, 237n82
French, Daniel Chester, 128, 158, 160, **160**, 161 243n76
Fuller, Stephen P., 77, **80**
funerary practices: caskets, 4, 51; embalming, 4, 35, 50–51; interment, 50, 54, 58, 77, 134

Gallier, James, 72–74, 76, 236n57
Garfield, James, 200
Gates, Major General Horatio, 96. See also Saratoga Battle Monument
Gliddon, George, 37–39, 41, 44, 48, 149–50, 233nn82–83; Otia Aegyptiaca, 38–39, 41, 68, 85, 149–50, 230n21, 233n68, 233n71, 236n49, 237n77, 242n54, 243n56; Tremont affair, 41–43, 48, 150, 233n77, 233nn79–80. See also Ethnology; Types of Mankind
Godefroy, Maximilian, 60, 62–63, 221, 235n38; Baltimore Battle Monument, 62, **62**, 221, 230n25, 238n15; Westminster Cemetery carriage gate, 60, 237n76
Gorringe, Lt. Commander Henry H., 202, 246nn15–17. See also Cleopatra's Needle
Gothic Revival. See architectural revivalism
Grant Memorial, 15, **201**, 246n1, 246nn10–12: and architectural eclecticism, 197–99, 246nn2–7; calls for, 191, 195; comparisons to the Washington Monument, 200;

design for, 200; Monument Association, 196
Graveyards, 59: ancient, 54–55; colonial, 51, 88, 90; poor conditions of, 49, 52–53; Egyptian Revival entrances, **82**, **83**, **84**, **85**, **89**, 237n76; revitalization efforts, 50, 70–71, 83–84, 86
Greece. See civilizations, ancient
Greek Revival. See architectural revivalism
Greenough, Horatio, 103, 238n13
Griswold, Charles, 103, 118–21, 124, 238n12, 239nn52–57, 240n58. See also Groton Monument
Groton Monument: Association, 98, 104–5, 117, 122–23, 239n20, 239n51; centennial celebration, 121–22, 240n66; cornerstone ceremony, 103, 117, 121, 123; dedication, 120; fear of collapse, 121; Fort Griswold Massacre, 105, 115, 119, 240n59, 240n70; national identity, 120, 122–23. See also Arnold, Benedict; Bulkeley, Charles; Fort Griswold; Fosdick, L.; Foster, Lafayette S.; Griswold, Charles; Ledyard, Colonel William; monuments; New London County Historical Society; obelisks; Potter, Nathaniel F.

Hayes, Rutherford B., 178
headstones. See gravestones
Hieroglyphics, 5, 74, 232n61; Champollion's work on, 2, 4, 8, 24, 34–35; Gliddon's translations of, 37–38, 41, 43, 230n21, 233n68; Rosetta Stone, 2; Young's work on, 24, 34
Holmes, Oliver Wendell, Sr., 42, 192–93, 235n22, 245n66
Howells, William Dean, 137, 139, 143, 145, 161, 241n20

iconography. See allegorical figures; symbolism

Jackson, Andrew, 168, 177; grave of, 238n3
Jackson, Stonewall, 135
Jacksonian Era, 58
Jefferson Davis Monument, 16, 124, 219, 222, 238n14, 247nn38–42; Association, 220;

Jefferson Davis Monument *(cont.)*
comparisons to Washington Monument, 200; dedication, 221; United Daughters of the Confederacy, role of, 220
Jefferson, Thomas: design for Monticello, 6; grave of, 238n3; ideas concerning Native American mounds, 21–22, 231n16; interest in Egypt, 1–2
Johnson, Andrew: appeal to complete the Washington National Monument, 177; grave of, 238n3
Joy, Nabby, 77, **79**, 237n69

King, Clarence, 198–99, 246nn5–6
King, Martin Luther, Jr., 12, 225–26. See also Broken Obelisk

Lafayette, General, 106
Ledyard, John: in Egypt, 1–2, 229n2
Ledyard, Colonel William, 116, 121, 238n12. See also Fort Griswold; Groton Monument
Lewis and Clark Expedition. See Floyd Memorial (Sioux City)
Lexington Battle Monument, 100, **101**
Lincoln, Abraham, 152, 191, 196: comparison to Washington, 177; Emancipation Proclamation, 137; Gettysburg Address, 137; Lincoln Memorial, 222; monument, calls for, 176, 244n35; tomb at Springfield, 124, 238n3, 238n14
Lincoln, Solomon, 132–33, 241n11
lions, 140, 143, **144**, 147, 152–53, 155, 207, 211, 218–19, **219**. See also McKinley Monument; symbolism; Thorwaldsen's Lion of Lucerne
Lowell, Francis Cabot, 77, **79**, 237n70
Long, Robert Cary, Jr.: gateway design for Green Mount Cemetery (Baltimore), 87
Longfellow, Henry Wadsworth, 42

MacDonough Monument, 95, 97. See also War of 1812
Manifest Destiny, 6; connection to monumental obelisks, 102–3
Massachusetts Charitable Mechanic Association, 110. See also Bunker Hill Monument

Massachusetts Horticultural Society, 57, 77, 235n24
mausoleums. See cemetery monuments; Garfield, James; Grant Memorial; Lincoln, Abraham; Zaghloul, Saad
McDonald, Wilson, 196–97, 246n3
McKinley Memorial (Buffalo), 16, 124, 218, **219**, 222, 238n14, 247n33; use of lions, 219
McKinley, William, 218
Medical College of Virginia, 68, **69**
Melville, Herman, 28, 114, 231n38, 231n40
memorials. See Bennington Battle Monument; Broken Obelisk; Bunker Hill Monument; cemetery monuments; Chalmette Monument; Christopher Columbus Monument (Baltimore); Civil War commemoration; Floyd Memorial (Sioux City); Grant Memorial; Groton Monument; Jefferson Davis Monument; Lexington Battle Monument; Lincoln, Abraham; MacDonough Monument; McKinley Memorial (Buffalo); Richard Montgomery Monument (NYC); New Jersey Veterans' Monument; San Jacinto Battle Monument; Saratoga Battle Monument; Shaw Memorial (Boston); Washington National Monument
middle class, 13–14, 38; attitudes toward death, 56; femininity, 149; hegemony over taste, 10, 50, 59; involvement in Rural Cemetery Movement, 50, 53–54
Midwinter Fair (1894), Fine Arts Building, 208, **209**
Mills, Robert, 172, 244n14; design for Washington Monument (Baltimore), 166–68. See also Washington National Monument
Milmore, Martin: death, 158; execution of Boston Soldiers' and Sailors' Monument, 134; and the Sphinx at Mount Auburn, 128, 139–40, 142–43, 158, 160–61, 241n26. See also French, Daniel Chester; Sphinx (Mount Auburn)
Milmore Memorial. See French, Daniel Chester
Mississippi River, 3, 23, 102, 231n44, 232n46, 232n48: cities with Egyptian names along its banks, 30, 232n47; comparisons with the Nile, 3, 30
monument companies, 215, **215**, 247n29

monuments. See cemetery monuments; Civil War commemoration; memorials

Montgomery, Major General Richard, 166; See also Richard Montgomery Monument (NYC)

Moore, Thomas, 18–19

Morgan, General Daniel, 96

Morton, Dr. Samuel George, 39–41, 44, 149–50, 233nn72–74, 233n82, 242n53, 242n55. See also Ethnology; Gliddon, George; Nott, Josiah; Types of Mankind

Mount Auburn Cemetery: Association, 57, 247n29; Board of Trustees, 76, 127, 129, 134, 139–40, 143, 145, 240n7, 241n14, 241n21–22; gateway, 57, 60, 63–66, **66**, 68, 70–74, 81, 84, 87, 144; as model for other cemeteries, 9, 50, 57. See also Bigelow, Jacob; cemeteries; cemetery gateways; Rural Cemetery Movement; Sphinx (Mount Auburn)

Mummies, xi, 13, 32, 47, 232n54, 232nn56–57, 233n66, 233n75, 245n47: in cinema, 33, 210–11; in literature, 5, 35–38, 46, 232n62, 232n64, 233n67, 233nn90–92; in museums, 32–34, 45–46, 232nn59–60; and mummification, 3; parts of, 34; and race theory, 33, 39, 43–45, 242n52; unwrapping of, 4, 18, 33–37, 41–43, 48, 150, 233nn76–81. See also Egyptomania; Gliddon, George; popular literature; race theory; Types of Mankind

Museums: Barnum's Museum, 33; Boston Museum of Fine Arts, 45–46, 206; British Museum, 8, 36; Bullock's Egyptian Hall (London Museum), 7, 33; Louvre, 8; Metropolitan Museum of Art, 45, 206, 230n22, 246n17; Niagara Falls Museum, 34, 232n59; Peale's Museum of Natural History, 33–34; Western Museum of Cincinnati, 34; Woods Museum, 34

Nast, Thomas, **207**. See also Theatrical productions

Native Americans: as allegorical figures, 166; mounds, 21–23, 39, 49, 198, 231n16; and the Washington National Monument, 172

national identity, xi, 2, 5–7, 10, 12, 14, 18, 27, 59, 98, 106, 122–25, 190, 196

Neill, Reverend Henry, 56, 235n22

Neoclassicism, 5, 7, 9, 11–12, 26, 63, 200; French, 60; in mourning iconography, 51, 60, 166, 234n4. See also architectural revivalism

New Jersey Veterans' Monument, 220

New London County Historical Society, 126. See also Groton Monument

Newman, Barnett. See Broken Obelisk

Nile River. See Egypt; Mississippi River

Nott, Josiah C., 39, 43–44, 149–50, 233nn82–83. See also Ethnology; Gliddon, George; Morton, Samuel George; Types of Mankind

obelisks: ancient, 25, 65, 91, 101, 114, 186, 192, 215, 217, 230n20, 246nn14–17; collective ownership of, 125–26; connections to Manifest Destiny, 102–3, 230n25, 238n9; and modern technology, 110–11, 167, 182–83; modifications for American use, 102, 104, 114, 189, 230n25; qualities associated with, 102–3, 108, 114–15, 120, 123–24, 126, 133, 164, 168, 170, 193, 218; souvenirs, 125, **125**, 126; as symbols of national identity, 7, 12, 14, 98, 106, 120, 122–25, 188–90, 193, 196, 217, 226; transformation into an American monumental form, 12, 16, 115, 164, 194, 196, 222, 226; use in modern cemeteries, 9, 59–60, 65, 70–73, 76–77, 81, 84, 86, **86**, 87, 92, 126–27, 169, 195, 215–16, 238n3. See also architectural revivalism; Bennington Monument; Broken Obelisk; Bunker Hill Monument; Chalmette Battle Monument; Christopher Columbus Monument; Cleopatra's Needle; Columbian Exposition of 1893 (World's Fair); Egyptian Revival; Floyd Memorial; Groton Monument; Jefferson Davis Monument; MacDonough Monument; McKinley Memorial (Buffalo); New Jersey Veterans' Monument; San Jacinto Battle Monument; Saratoga Battle Monument; Washington National Monument

Odd Fellows. See fraternal organizations

Olmstead, Denison, 82, 237n75

Orientalism, Cairo Street as orientalist fantasy, 4, 208; Egyptian Revival and, 11, 230n24; and modern Egypt, 204

Pan American Exposition, 218. See also McKinley, William
Peery's Egyptian Theater, 210, **210**. See also Egyptian Revival; Egyptomania
Penfield, Frederic Courtland, 205, 246n18, 247n21
Perkins, Colonel Thomas Handasyd, 104
Piranesi, Giovanni Battista, 8. See also Egyptian Revival
Poe, Edgar Allan, 36–38, 46, 233n67. See also popular literature
Polk, James K., 170
popular literature: "After Three Thousand Years," 46, 233n90; Dracula, 46; Frankenstein, 35, 37; "Lost in a Pyramid, or The Mummy's Curse," 46, 233n91; "Lot No. 249," 46, 233n92; "Mr. Grubbe's Night With Memnon," 36, 233n65; The Mummy! A Tale of the Twenty-Second Century, 35, 232n62; "The Mummy's Foot," 35–36, 232n64; "Some Words With A Mummy," 36–38, 233n67
Potter, Nathaniel F., 120. See also Groton Monument
Prince, Frederick O., 133, 241n12. See also Civil War commemoration
Putnam, Reverend George, 58, 235n29. See also Rural Cemetery Movement
pyramid of Caius Cestius, 62
pyramids. See cemetery monuments; Egypt

Reconstruction era, 15, 45, 177–78, 222, 227, 242n41
Revolution, American, 14, 112, 118, 129, 133; and American martyrdom, 100, 105, 119, 121, 124, 170, 226; in American memory, 98, 103, 123–24, 129, 165; memorialization efforts, 92–95, 98, 104, 106, 115, 129, 199, 238n3, 238n6, 239n47; and national identity, 102, 106, 130. See also Arnold, Benedict; Bennington Battle Monument; Bunker Hill Monument; Fort Griswold; Groton Monument; Lexington Battle Monument; Richard Montgomery Monument; Saratoga Battle Monument; Washington, George; Washington National Monument
Revolution, French, 118

Revolution, Haitian, 118, 152
religion: attitudes toward death, 56–57; Christianity, 24, 50, 68, 70, 74–75, 81, 83–84, 115, 123, 149, 217–18, 236n55, 236n64; Judaism, 85–86, 230n25, 236n55, 237n78. See also Egypt; Egyptian Revival
Richard Montgomery Monument (NYC), 98–99, **99**, 100, 238nn5–6
rivers: see Egypt; Mississippi River
Rogers, Isaiah, 83, **83**, 84, **85**
Rogers, Randolph, 136
romanticism, 11, 28, 54, 229n15: Gothic literature, 35, 112, 114; the picturesque, 31, 50, 56, 67, 71, 89, 204, 235n24, 236n52, 236n64; the sublime, 28–29, 66, 73–74, 114, 121, 169, 193, 204, 206, 225
Rome. See civilizations, ancient
Roosevelt, Franklin, 221
Rosetta Stone. See hieroglyphics
Rothko Chapel, 225–26. See also Broken Obelisk
Rural Cemetery Movement: consecration addresses, 13, 49–50, 52, 54–57, 234n2, 234n7, 235n29; egalitarian ideals, 57–59; inspiration for, 49, 53. See also Bigelow, Jacob; cemeteries; cemetery gateways; cemetery guidebooks; Dearborn, Henry A.S.; Mount Auburn Cemetery; Story, Joseph

San Jacinto Battle Monument, 12, 16, 220–22, **223**, 224, 247nn43–44
Saratoga Battle Monument, 14, 94, 96, **96**, 183
Schuyler, General Philip, 96. See also Saratoga Battle Monument
Searle, Henry R., 180, **181**. See also Washington National Monument
Shaw Memorial (Boston), 135, 241n18
side-hill tombs. See cemetery monuments
slavery, 151, 173; Civil War, role in, 145, 150–52; emancipation, mention of on war memorials, 130–33, 137, 141, 152–53, 160–61, 240n8, 242n49, 243n84; freedmen, postwar status of, 33, 44–45, 152–53; in poetry, 146; pro-slavery ideology, 39–40, 44, 149–50; and race, 149–50
Spanish-American War, 222
Sparks, Jared, 42

INDEX   273

Sphinx (Great), 128, 143–45, 148, 204, 205, 207, 215, 215; and race theory, 149–50; travelers' observations of, 28–29, 114, 150. See also Twain, Mark; Volney, M.C.F.

Sphinx (Mount Auburn), 14–15, 57, 141, 142, 180, 219, 240n1, 242n37; Bigelow's choice of a sphinx, 145; Bigelow's donation, 139–40, 241nn21–22, 241nn24–27; design, 140–42, 148, 241n29; gender, 148–49, 152; inscriptions, 140–41; intended meaning, 128, 152–54, 162; location in Mount Auburn Cemetery, 128, 142; misinterpretations, 140, 154–56, 160–62, 191; in poetry, 154–55, 242nn44–46; proposal for, 127, 241n14; race, 148–50, 153; reviews of, 142–43, 145, 153, 242nn38–39; unveiling ceremony, 142–43. See also Bigelow, Jacob; Civil War commemoration; French, Daniel Chester; Milmore, Martin; Thorwaldsen's Lion of Lucerne

sphinxes, 180, **180**, 243n75: in American cemeteries, 156–58, **157**, **159**, 211, 226, 240n2; Egyptian, 145, 148, 156, 158; Greek, 145–46, 154–55; in poetry, 146–48, 154–55. See also Bruff, Joseph Goldsborough; Milmore Memorial; Sphinx (Great); Sphinx (Mount Auburn)

Statue of Liberty, 149

Story, Joseph, 49–50, 52, 54–55, 57–58, 76–77, 90, 165, 234n2, 237n68, 244n4; obelisk at Mount Auburn, 77

Story, William Wetmore, 180, 182, 245n48

Strickland, William, 85, 87

Suez Canal, 4

Symbolism, xii, 6, 10–11, 25–26, 58–59, 70, 90, 92, 126, 129, 133, 140, 145, 160–62, 180, 183, 191, 201, 216, 225–26: colonial, 51, 81, 83, **83**, 234n4; Confederate, 135, 220; Egyptian, x, 68, 74–75, 85, **85**, 108, 140–41, 152–53, 156, 191–92; feminine, 149, 152; lions, 143, 152, 219; masonic, 1; mourning figure, 165–66; of national identity, 97, 106, 110, 115, 120, 122, 124–26, 129, 154, 164, 168, 170, 175, 188–90, 193, 226; urn and willow, 51, 60, 166, 234n4. see also allegorical figures; cemetery gateways; Civil War commemoration; Sphinx (Mount Auburn)

synagogues, 9, 26, 68, 85; Mikveh Israel (Philadelphia), 85. See also Egyptian Revival

technology, 5, 17, 19, 29, 35, 37–38, 41, 63–65, 70, 144, 169, 229n17, 236nn40–41, 238n8; ancient vs. modern, 24, 30, 47, 68, 110, 184, 190, 231n29; electricity, 25, 37, 182–83; elevators, 182–83, **185**; steam power, 25, 110, 231nn27–28; stone quarrying and carving, 59, 102, 110, 167, 189, 195–96, 235n35. See also Bigelow, Jacob; Washington National Monument

theatrical productions: Egypt, a Daughter of the Nile, 206; The Little Corporal, 206, **207**

Thorwaldsen's Lion of Lucerne, 143, **144**. See also Sphinx (Mount Auburn)

Ticknor, George, 108. See also Bunker Hill Monument

Tocqueville, Alexis de, 231n12

tombs. See cemetery monuments; Egypt

tourism: to American monuments, 125–26, 174–75, 190; to cemeteries, 54, 77, 156, 234n13; to Egypt, 3, 27–28, 30, 32, 114, 204–5, **205**, 211, 229n6, 229n11, 247n26; to museums, 45; to the United States, 17–20, 31, 230nn1–2, 230nn4–6, 231n7

Town, Ithiel, 120. See also Groton Monument

travel literature, 27, 32, 47, 188, 204, 206, 246n20. See also Cook, Eliza; Dickens, Charles; Ledyard, John; Melville, Herman; Moore, Thomas; Trollope, Frances; Twain, Mark; Volney, M.C.F.; Woolson, Constance Fenimore

Trollope, Frances, 2, 19–20, 230n5

Tudor, William, 104

Tutankhamen, Carter's discovery of, 5, 87, 195, 210. See also Egypt; Egyptomania

Twain, Mark, 28–29, 114, 174, 230n21, 231n39, 245n26

Tyler, President John, 112

Types of Mankind, 43–44, 149, 233n82. See also Gliddon, George; Morton, Samuel George; mummies; Nott, Josiah

Van Brunt, Henry, 163, 179, 196, 199, 243n1, 245nn44–45, 246n2, 246n7. See also Washington National Monument

Volney, M.C.F., 3, 150

Walter, Cornelia, 53, 56, 74–75, 234n10, 235n21. See also cemetery guidebooks; Rural Cemetery Movement

Walter, Thomas Ustick, 87

War of 1812, 92–93, 95, 167, 219. See also Chalmette Battle Monument (New Orleans); MacDonough Monument

war memorials. See Civil War commemoration; memorials; Revolution, American

Warren, Joseph, 166

Washington, George: apotheosis, 165–66, 183, 244n7; death, 165; descriptions of his character, 163–65, 172, 176, 182, 239n22; Mount Vernon, 166, 238n3; Story's eulogy, 165, 244n4

Washington National Monument, 187: capstone setting, 183, 184; Casey's completion of, 178, 182–84; during the Civil War, 174–76; cornerstone ceremony, 170, 172–73; criticism of, 178–79, 191–93; dedication, 164, 186–89; early efforts, 163–68; elevator, 182–83, 185; Force's design, 168, 169; Know-Nothing Party take-over, 173–74; Mills's final design, 170, 171, 178–79; Mills's first design, 168–69; and national identity, 188–90, 193; new designs, 179–80, 180, 181, 182; during Reconstruction, 177; reviews of, 164, 184–88; Society, 168, 177, 179; as tallest manmade structure in the world, 185–86; transformative influence, 194, 196, 222; unfinished state, controversy over, 174, 176–78. See also Arthur, Chester; Bruff, Joseph Goldsborough; Casey, Thomas Lincoln; Holmes, Oliver Wendell, Sr.; Johnson, Andrew; Mills, Robert; Searle, Henry R.; Story, William Wetmore; Van Brunt, Henry; Winthrop, Robert C.

Webster, Daniel, 104, 106, 107, 116, 118, 124, 238n10, 238n16, 239n18, 239n21, 239n22; Bunker Hill cornerstone oration, 102–3, 106–8, 120; Bunker Hill dedication oration, 112, 114–15, 133, 173. See also Bunker Hill Monument

Wilkinson, Frederick, 86–87

Willard, Solomon, 108–9, 114, 238n11, 239n21, 239nn26–27. See also Bunker Hill Monument

Winthrop, Robert C.: Washington National Monument cornerstone oration, 172–73, 244n16, 244nn18–23; Washington National Monument dedication oration, 188–89, 192–93, 245n60. See also Washington National Monument

Woolson, Constance Fenimore, 114, 204, 239n42, 246n20

Young, Thomas. See hieroglyphics

Zaghloul, Saad, x–xi

www.ingramcontent.com/pod-product-compliance
Lightning Source LLC
Chambersburg PA
CBHW030512080526
44586CB00011B/156